JUNIOR
Picture
Dictionary

Miles
Kelly

First published in 2016 by Miles Kelly Publishing Ltd
Harding's Barn, Bardfield End Green, Thaxted, Essex, CM6 3PX, UK

Copyright © Miles Kelly Publishing Ltd 2016

This edition printed 2017

2 4 6 8 10 9 7 5 3 1

Publishing Director Belinda Gallagher
Creative Director Jo Cowan
Editorial Director Rosie Neave
Editors Fran Bromage, Claire Philip, Sarah Parkin
Cover Designer Simon Lee
Designers Simon Lee, Joe Jones, Kayleigh Allen
Production Elizabeth Collins, Caroline Kelly
Reprographics Stephan Davis, Jennifer Cozens, Thom Allaway
Assets Lorraine King

ISBN 978-1-78617-346-1

Printed in China

British Library Cataloging-in-Publication Data
A catalog record for this book is available from the British Library

ACKNOWLEDGMENTS
All artwork from the Miles Kelly Artwork Bank

Made with paper from a sustainable forest

www.mileskelly.net

CONTENTS

CONTENTS

CONTENTS

CONTENTS

CONTENTS

The Big Bang

The vast explosion that caused the beginning of the Universe

1 At the beginning of the Universe, a huge explosion blasted out vast amounts of energy

2 Millions of years later, gases clustered into clouds

3 The clouds clumped together to form galaxies

4 The Universe is getting bigger all the time as galaxies rush outward

Galaxies

Giant groups of stars are called galaxies,
and there are many different types

Barred spiral

Elliptical

Irregular

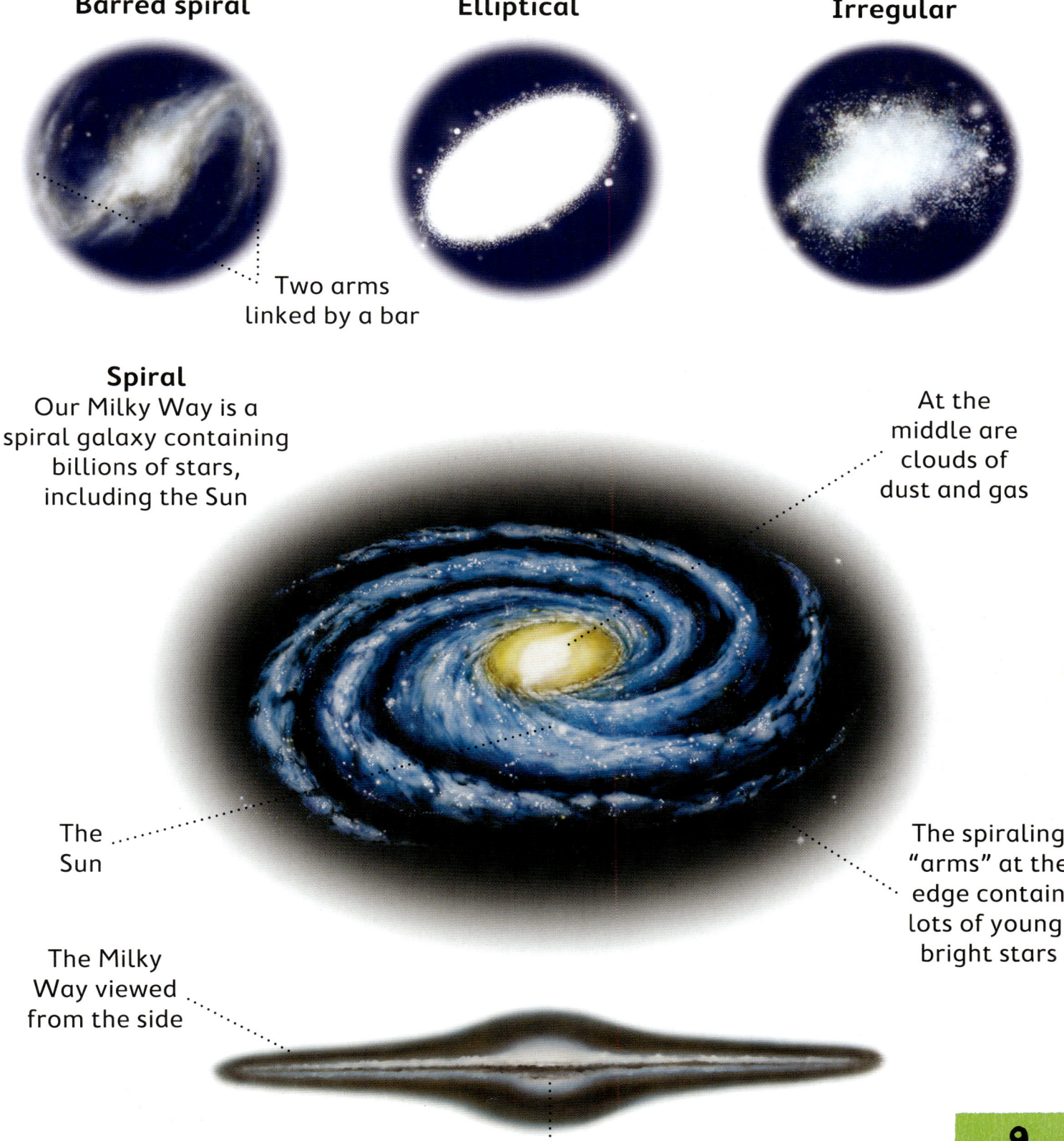

Two arms
linked by a bar

Spiral
Our Milky Way is a
spiral galaxy containing
billions of stars,
including the Sun

At the
middle are
clouds of
dust and gas

The
Sun

The spiraling
"arms" at the
edge contain
lots of young,
bright stars

The Milky
Way viewed
from the side

Central bulge

The Solar System

Our Solar System includes the Sun and all
of the planets traveling around it

Orbiting planets

The planets orbit (travel around) the
Sun. Each moves at a different speed

Jupiter

Mars

Venus

Earth

Mercury

Sun

Formation of Earth

Earth formed approximately
4.6 billion years ago

① Cloud starts
to spin

② Dust gathers
into balls of rock,
which form a
small planet

10

Neptune

Saturn

Uranus

Pluto
Dwarf planet

(4) Volcanoes erupt, releasing gases, which help to form the first atmosphere

(3) The Earth begins to cool and a hard shell forms

(5) At first, the land above sea level was made up of one large piece of land. It is now split into seven continents

Life of a star

Stars are different sizes depending
on how old they are — they live
for millions of years

3 Once the gas
and dust have
blown away, the
star can be seen

2 Gas and dust spin
together, growing hotter
and hotter until a new
star starts to shine

1 Gas and dust
collect in a big
cloud called
a nebula

4 Toward the
end of its life, a
star may become
a red giant

The Sun

This is our nearest star, which is a giant ball of extremely hot gases

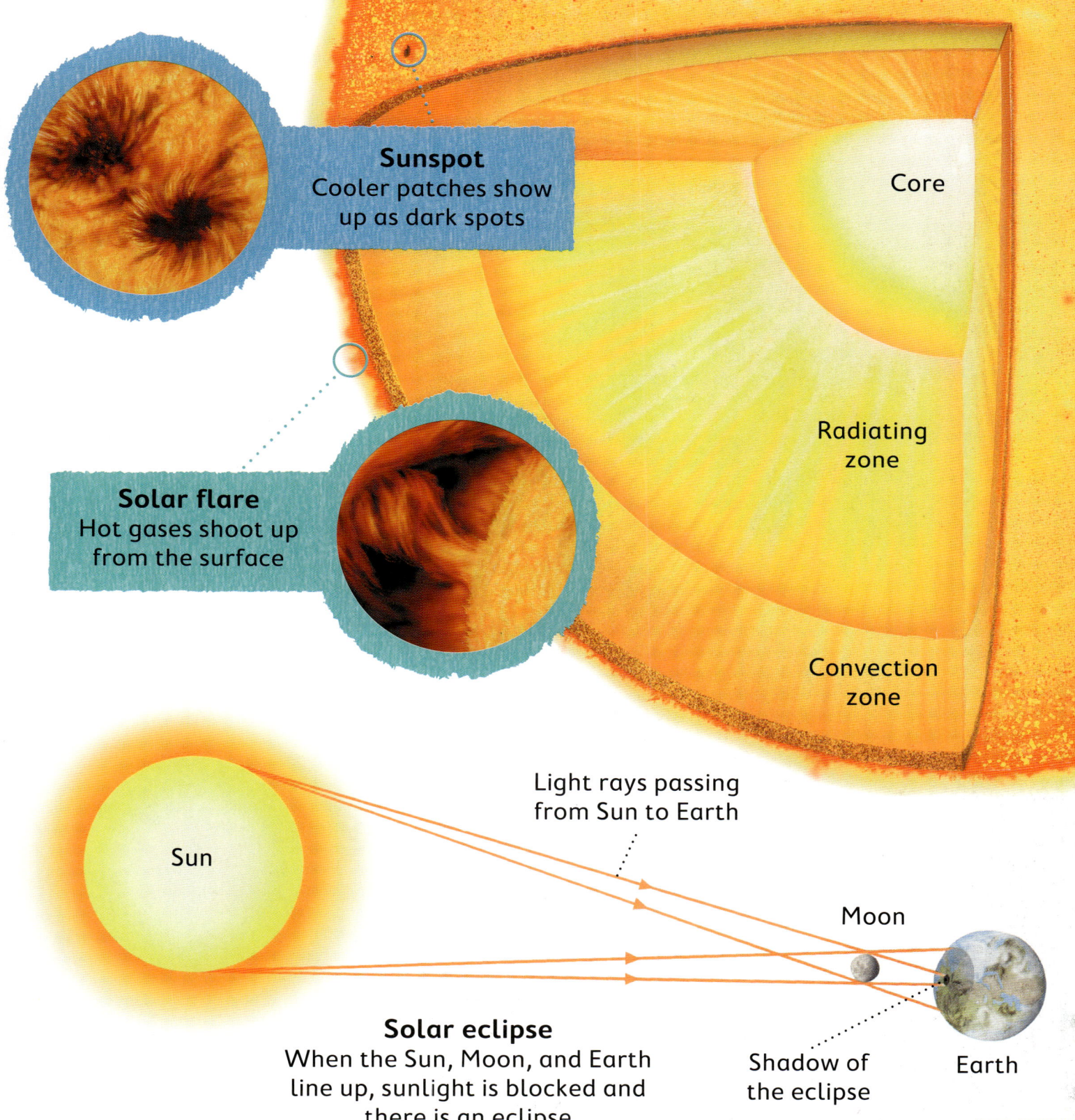

Sunspot
Cooler patches show up as dark spots

Solar flare
Hot gases shoot up from the surface

Core

Radiating zone

Convection zone

Sun

Light rays passing from Sun to Earth

Moon

Earth

Shadow of the eclipse

Solar eclipse
When the Sun, Moon, and Earth line up, sunlight is blocked and there is an eclipse

13

The Moon

Earth has one moon, which is made of rock.
Some planets have several moons, or none at all

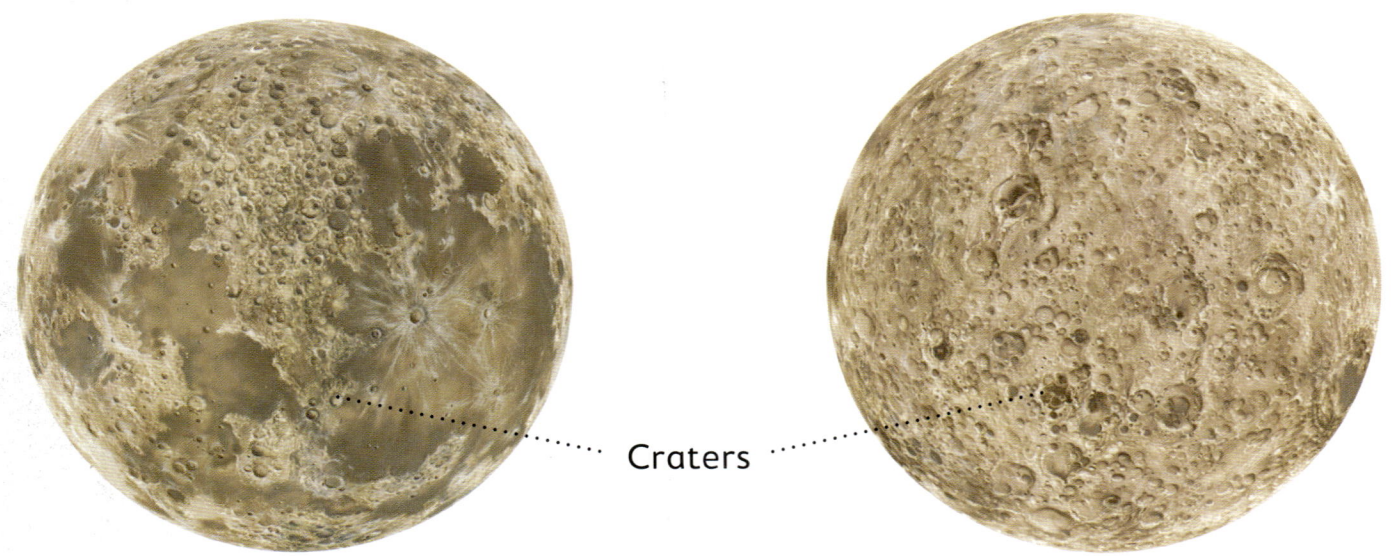

Craters

Near side
The side we can always
see from Earth

Far side
The opposite side, which
never faces our planet

Phases

The Moon appears to change from New to Full Moon and back
again as it travels around Earth. This takes one month

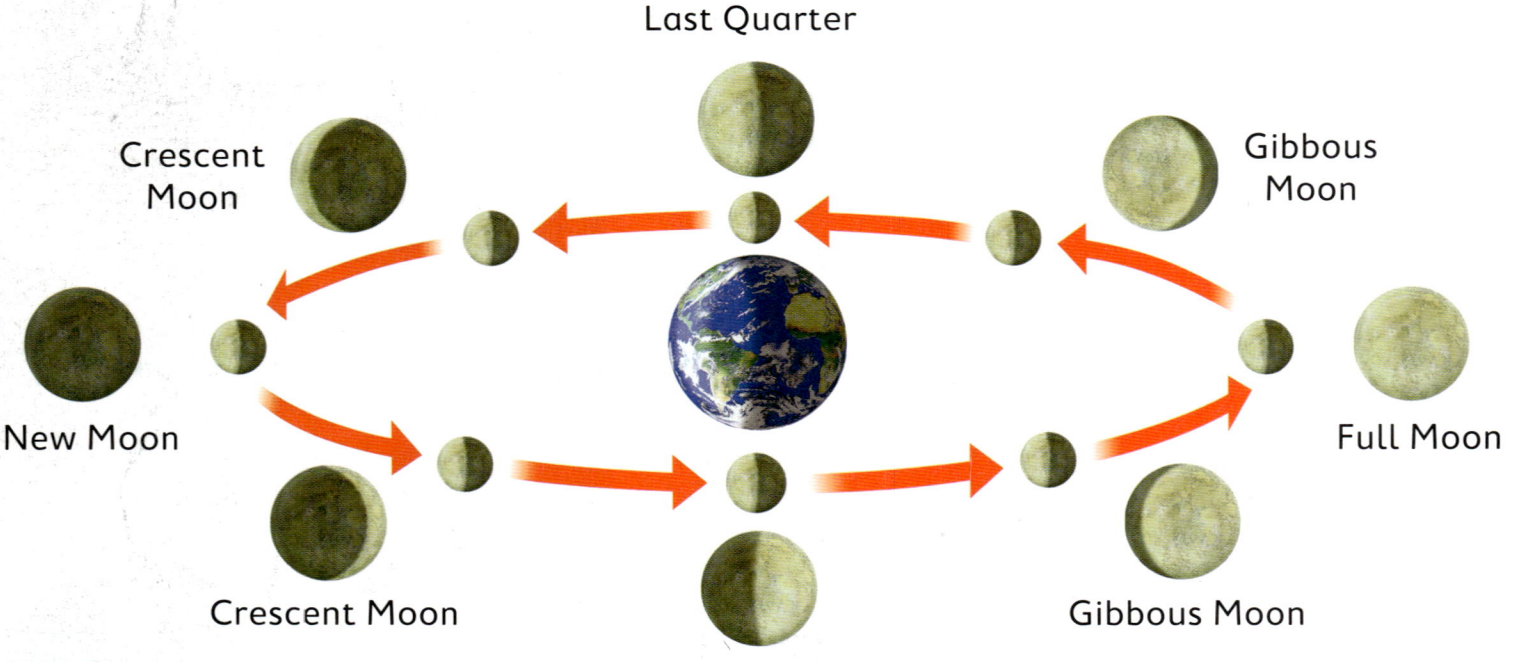

Last Quarter

Crescent
Moon

Gibbous
Moon

New Moon

Full Moon

Crescent Moon

Gibbous Moon

First Quarter

Comets, asteroids, and meteors

There are lots of clumps of dust, rock, and ice in space

Jupiter

Mars

Asteroids
Large chunks of rock

Halley's Comet
This comet passes Earth roughly every 75 years and is shown here on the Bayeux Tapestry during the Battle of Hastings in 1066

Most asteroids circle the Sun between Mars and Jupiter in the Asteroid Belt

Comet
Formed of dust and ice, these bright objects have long tails, which streak across the night sky

Meteors
Clumps of small rock sometimes called shooting stars

Star charts

Different constellations (star patterns) can
be seen depending on your position on the planet

Ophiuchus (*Serpent Bearer*)
Aquila (*Eagle*)
Hercules (*Strongman*)
Serpens (*Serpent*)
Lyra (*Lyre*)
Sagitta (*Arrow*)
Equuleus (*Foal*)
Corona Borealis (*Northern Crown*)
Delphinus (*Dolphin*)
Boötes (*Herdsman*)
Cygnus (*Swan*)
Draco (*Dragon*)
Pegasus (*Winged Horse*)
Coma Berenices (*Berenice's Hair*)
Lacerta (*Lizard*)
Virgo (*Virgin*)
Andromeda (*Chained Princess*)
Canes Venatici (*Hunting Dogs*)
Cepheus (*King*)
Leo (*Lion*)
Ursa Minor (*Little Bear*)
Cassiopeia (*Queen*)
Pisces (*Fishes*)
Ursa Major (*Great Bear*)
Camelopardalis (*Giraffe*)
Triangulum (*Triangle*)
Leo Minor (*Little Lion*)
Lynx (*Lynx*)
Perseus (*Hero*)
Aries (*Ram*)
Cancer (*Crab*)
Hydra (*Sea Serpent*)
Auriga (*Charioteer*)
Cetus (*Whale*)
Gemini (*Twins*)
Taurus (*Bull*)
Canis Minor (*Little Dog*)
Orion (*Hunter*)

Constellations visible from the Northern Hemisphere
The half of the Earth that is
north of the Equator

Constellations visible from the Southern Hemisphere
The half of the Earth that is south of the Equator

Orion (*Hunter*)

Lepus (*Hare*)

Canis Major (*Great Dog*)

Columba (*Dove*)

Eridanus (*River Eridanus*)

Puppis (*Stern*), Carina (*Keel*), and Vela (*Sail*)

Caelum (*Chisel*)

Pictor (*Painter's Easel*)

Fornax (*Furnace*)

Sextans (*Sextant*)

Hydra (*Sea Serpent*)

Dorado (*Goldfish*)

Recticulum (*Net*)

Phoenix (*Phoenix*)

Cetus (*Whale*)

Volans (*Flying Fish*)

Crater (*Cup*)

Crux (*Southern Cross*)

Chamaeleon (*Chameleon*)

Grus (*Crane*), Tucana (*Toucan*), and Pavo (*Peacock*)

Musca (*Fly*)

Apus (*Bird of Paradise*)

Centaurus (*Centaur*)

Corvus (*Crow*)

Triangulum Australe (*Southern Triangle*)

Indus (*Indian*)

Aquarius (*Water Carrier*)

Virgo (*Virgin*)

Piscis Austrinus (*Southern Fish*)

Ara (*Altar*)

Corona Australis (*Southern Crown*)

Scorpius (*Scorpion*)

Capricornus (*Sea Goat*)

Libra (*Scales*)

Serpens (*Serpent*) and Ophiuchus (*Serpent Bearer*)

Sagittarius (*Archer*)

Earth

Our planet is the the third planet from the Sun and the only one known to have water and the ability to support life

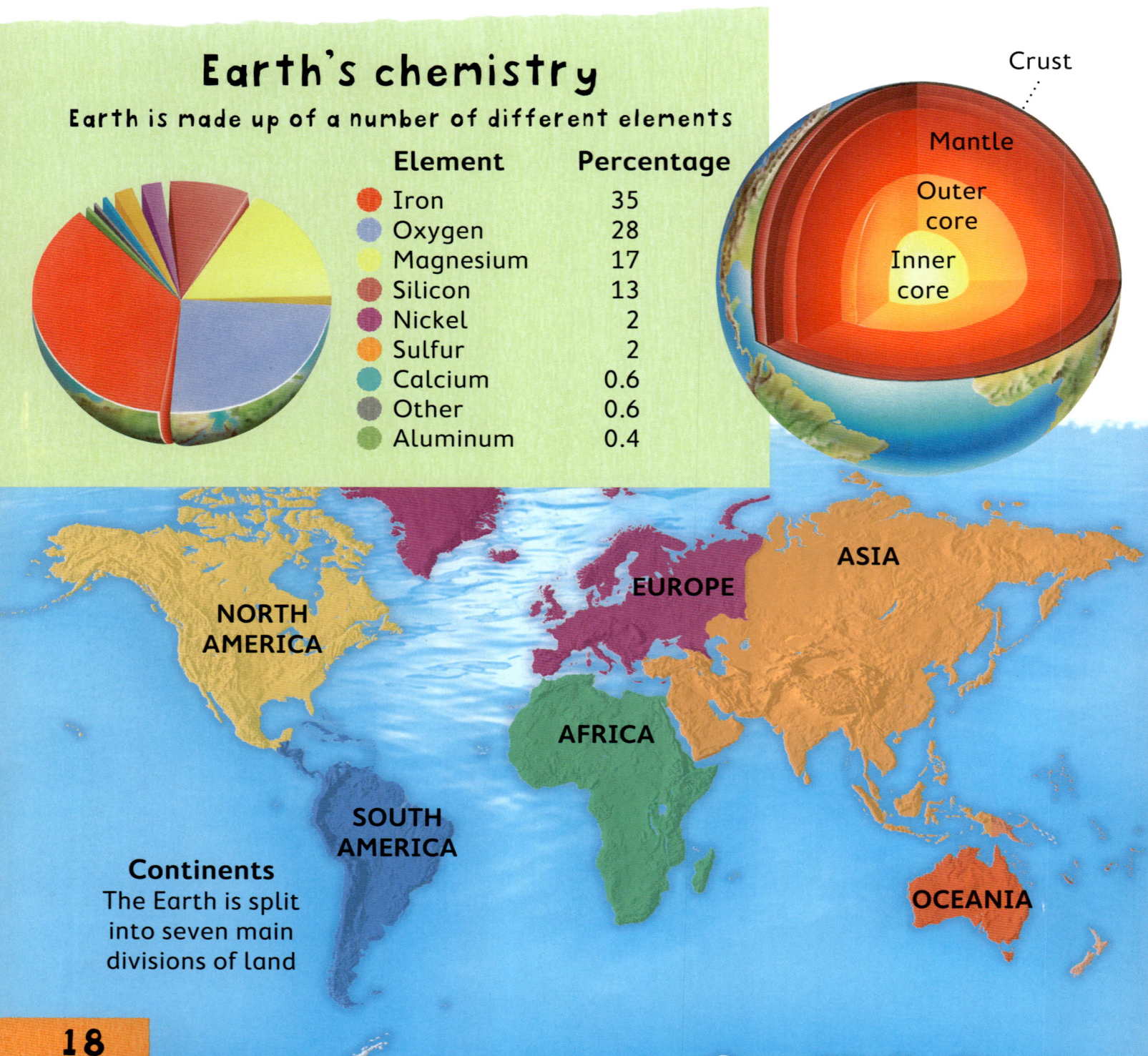

Earth's chemistry

Earth is made up of a number of different elements

Element	Percentage
Iron	35
Oxygen	28
Magnesium	17
Silicon	13
Nickel	2
Sulfur	2
Calcium	0.6
Other	0.6
Aluminum	0.4

Crust

Mantle

Outer core

Inner core

ASIA

EUROPE

NORTH AMERICA

AFRICA

SOUTH AMERICA

OCEANIA

Continents
The Earth is split into seven main divisions of land

ANTARCTICA

Spinning Earth

Our planet spins constantly on a tilt as it orbits the Sun. Different parts of the Earth's surface face the Sun—giving us yearly seasons

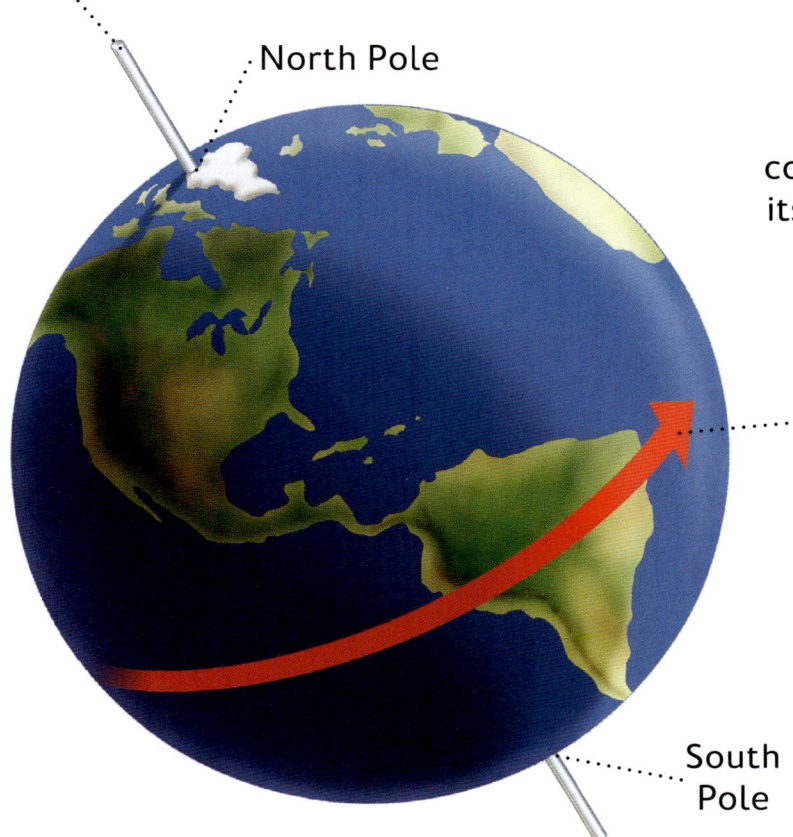

Axis

North Pole

Axis
In one day, the Earth completes one full rotation on its axis, a tilted imaginary line which joins the North and South Poles

Direction of spin

South Pole

Magnetic poles
Liquid iron is at the very center of the Earth. As our planet spins, it makes the iron behave like a magnet

Lines show direction of magnetic force

Seasons in the Northern Hemisphere
It takes 365 days (one year) for the Earth to travel around the Sun

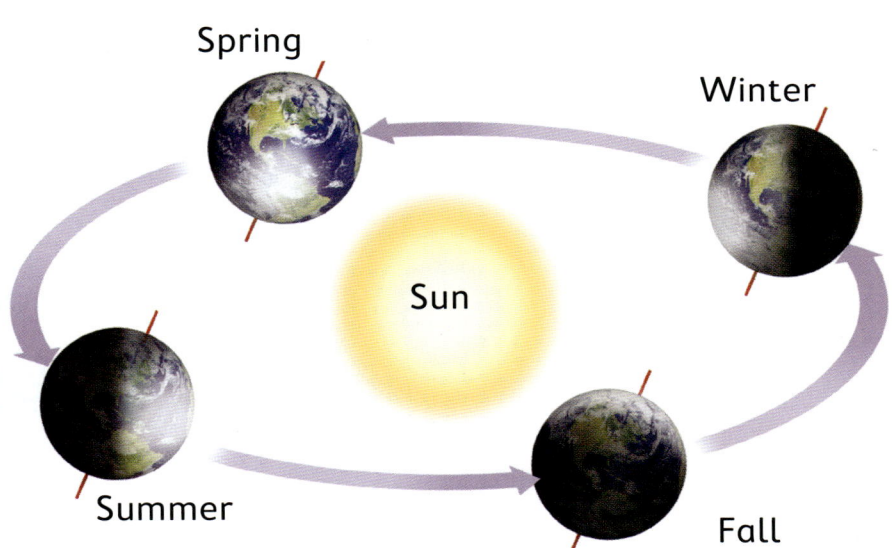

Spring

Winter

Sun

Summer

Fall

19

Continental drift

The slow movement of Earth's continents over millions of years

220 million years ago (mya)
When Earth first formed, it was made up of just one large piece of land, known as Pangea

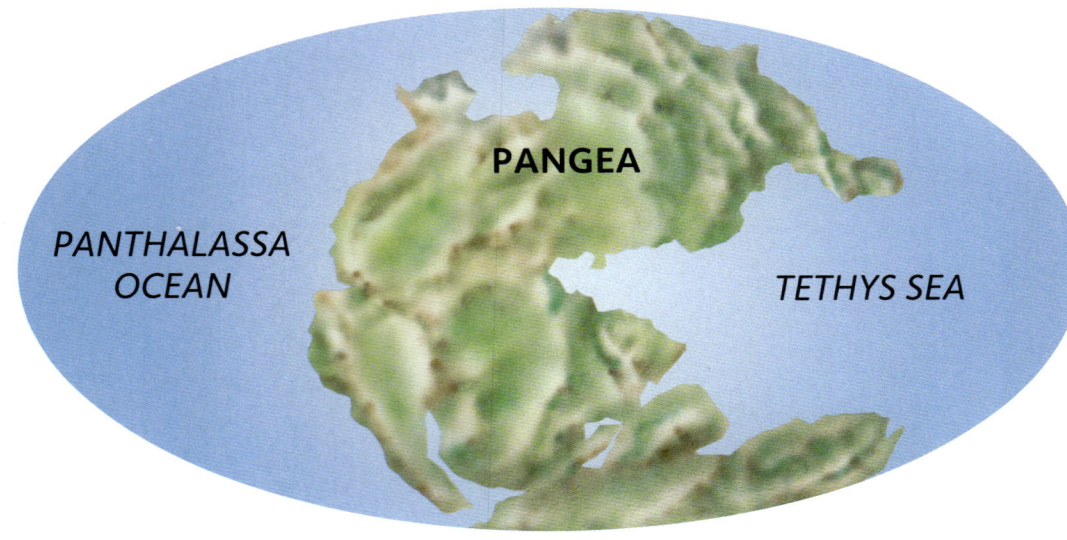

PANGEA

PANTHALASSA OCEAN

TETHYS SEA

200 mya
Tectonic plates (pieces of Earth's crust) moved slowly over the Earth's surface, causing Pangea to separate

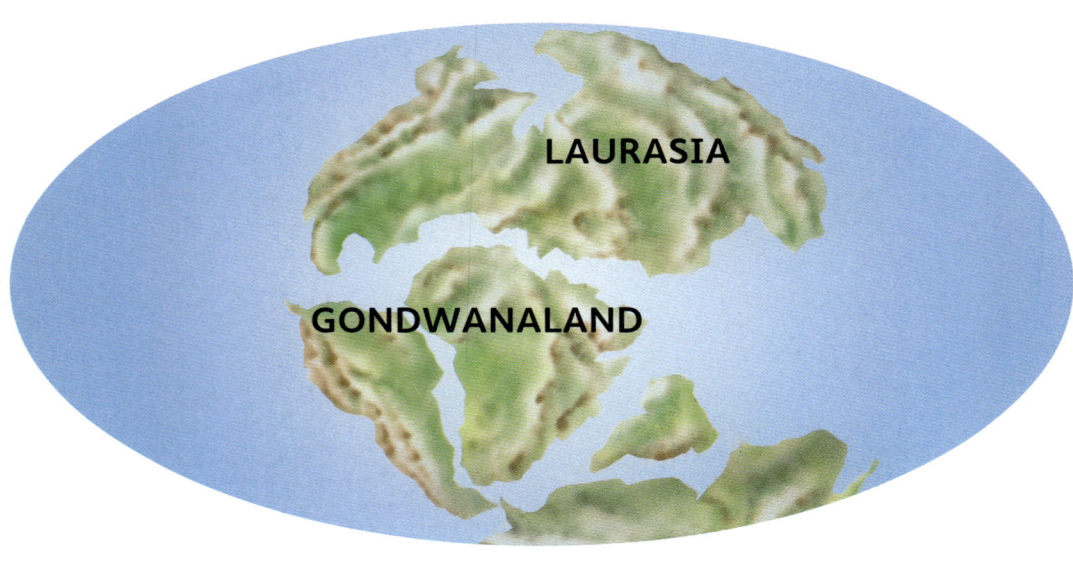

LAURASIA

GONDWANALAND

135 mya
India breaks off from Africa and the South Atlantic Ocean opens up

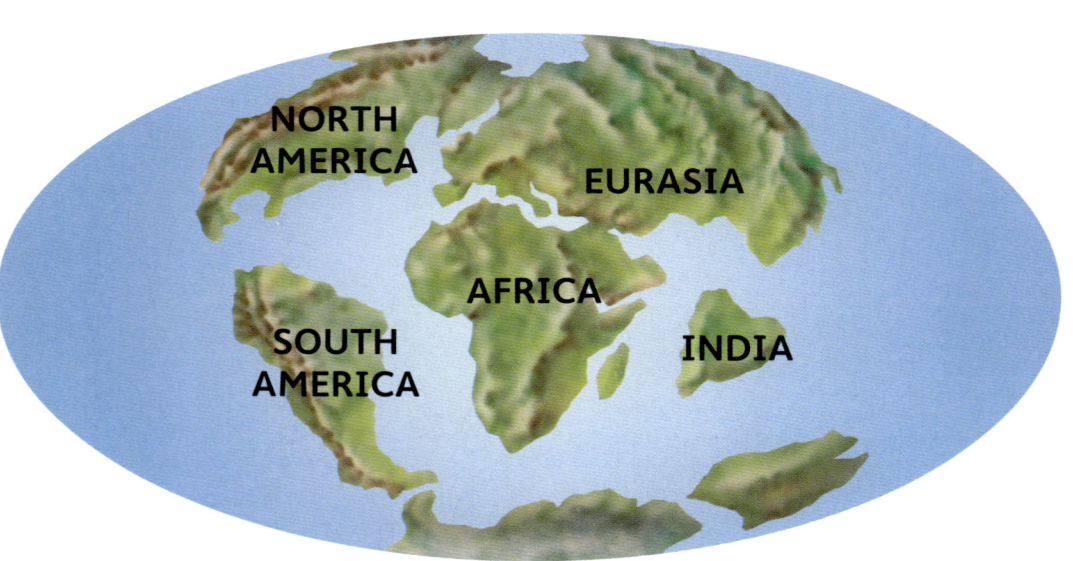

NORTH AMERICA

EURASIA

AFRICA

SOUTH AMERICA

INDIA

Today
There are seven continents but Earth's tectonic plates are still shifting

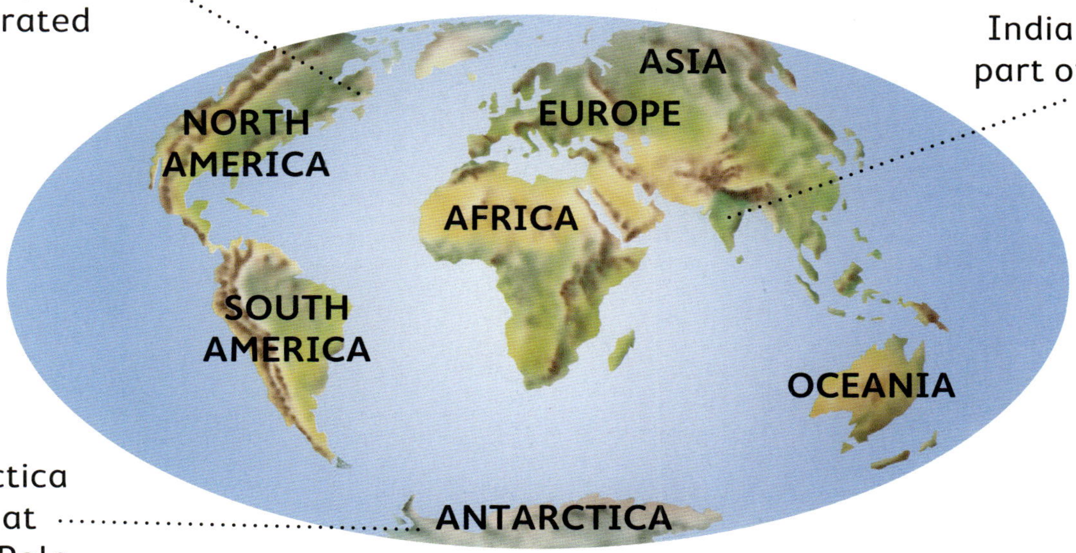

North America and Europe now separated

India now part of Asia

NORTH AMERICA

ASIA
EUROPE

AFRICA

SOUTH AMERICA

OCEANIA

Antarctica now at South Pole

ANTARCTICA

Tectonic plates
Earth's surface is broken into sections that are always shifting. The seven largest are shown here

1 Pacific plate
2 North American plate
3 South American plate
4 African plate
5 Eurasian plate
6 Indian-Australian plate
7 Antarctic plate

Rock cycle

Rocks form deep inside the Earth, move, and sometimes change. They can move up to the surface and eventually return below the ground

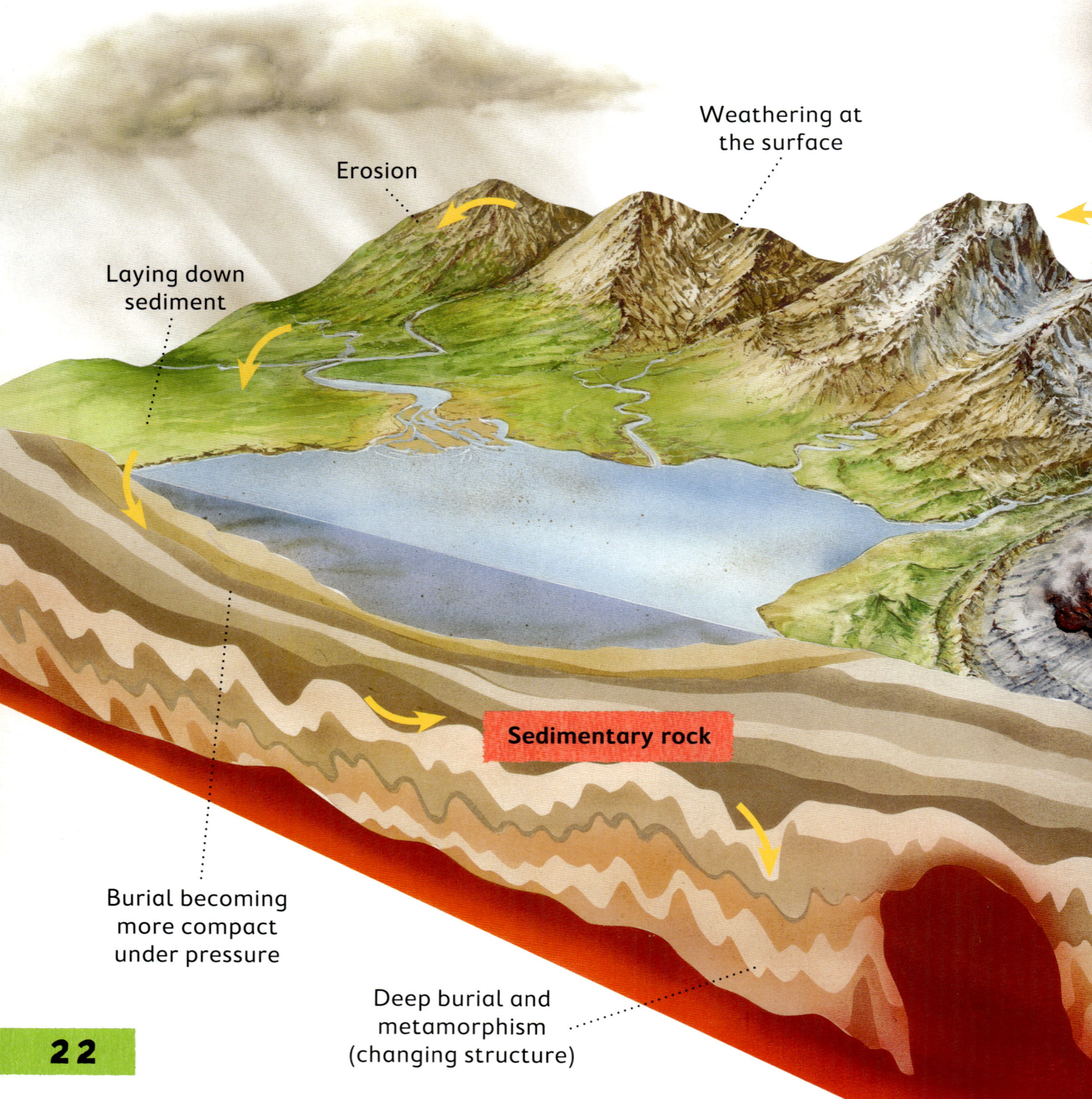

Weathering at the surface

Erosion

Laying down sediment

Sedimentary rock

Burial becoming more compact under pressure

Deep burial and metamorphism (changing structure)

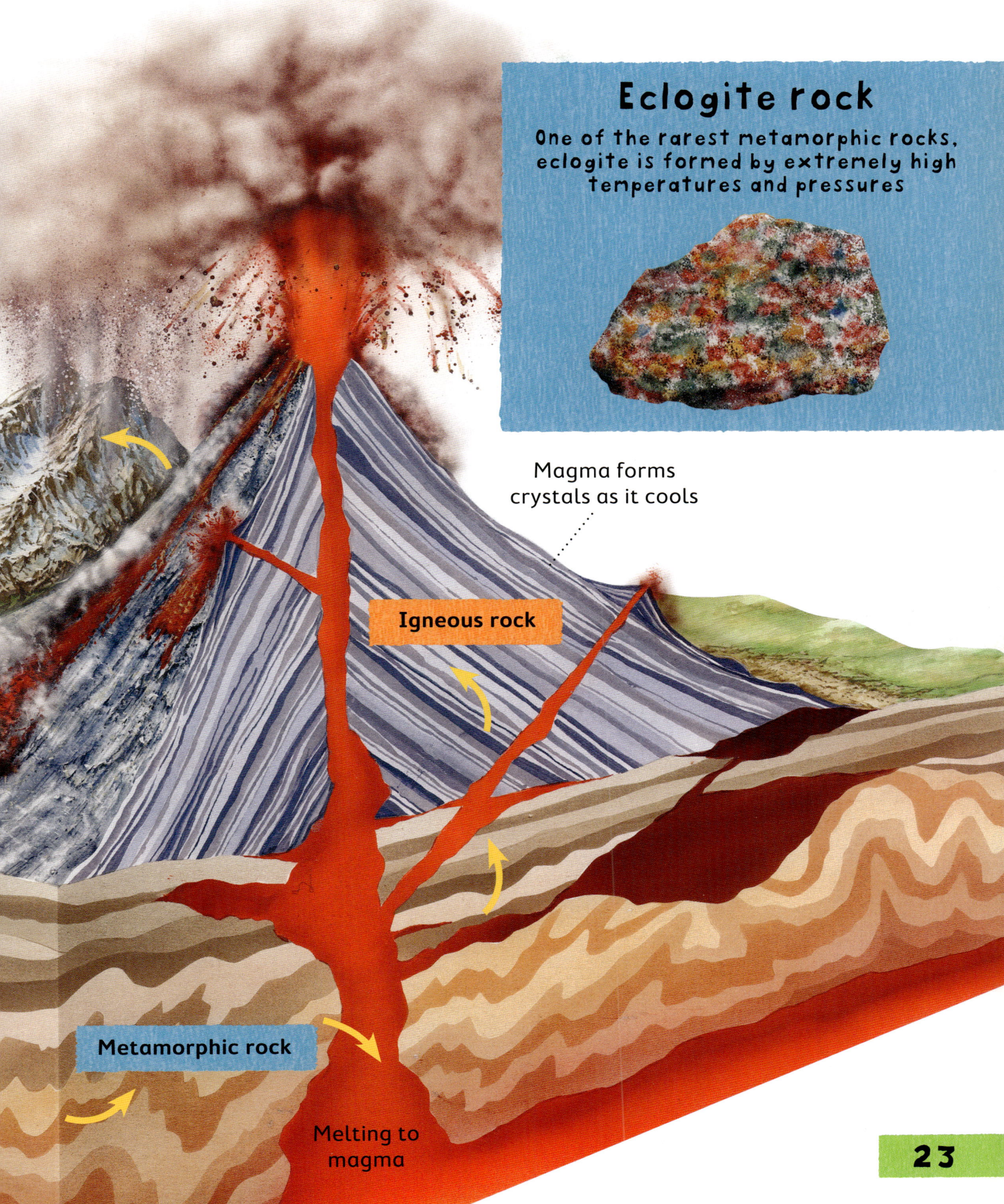

Eclogite rock

One of the rarest metamorphic rocks, eclogite is formed by extremely high temperatures and pressures

Magma forms crystals as it cools

Igneous rock

Metamorphic rock

Melting to magma

Erosion

Many different forces can break down rock

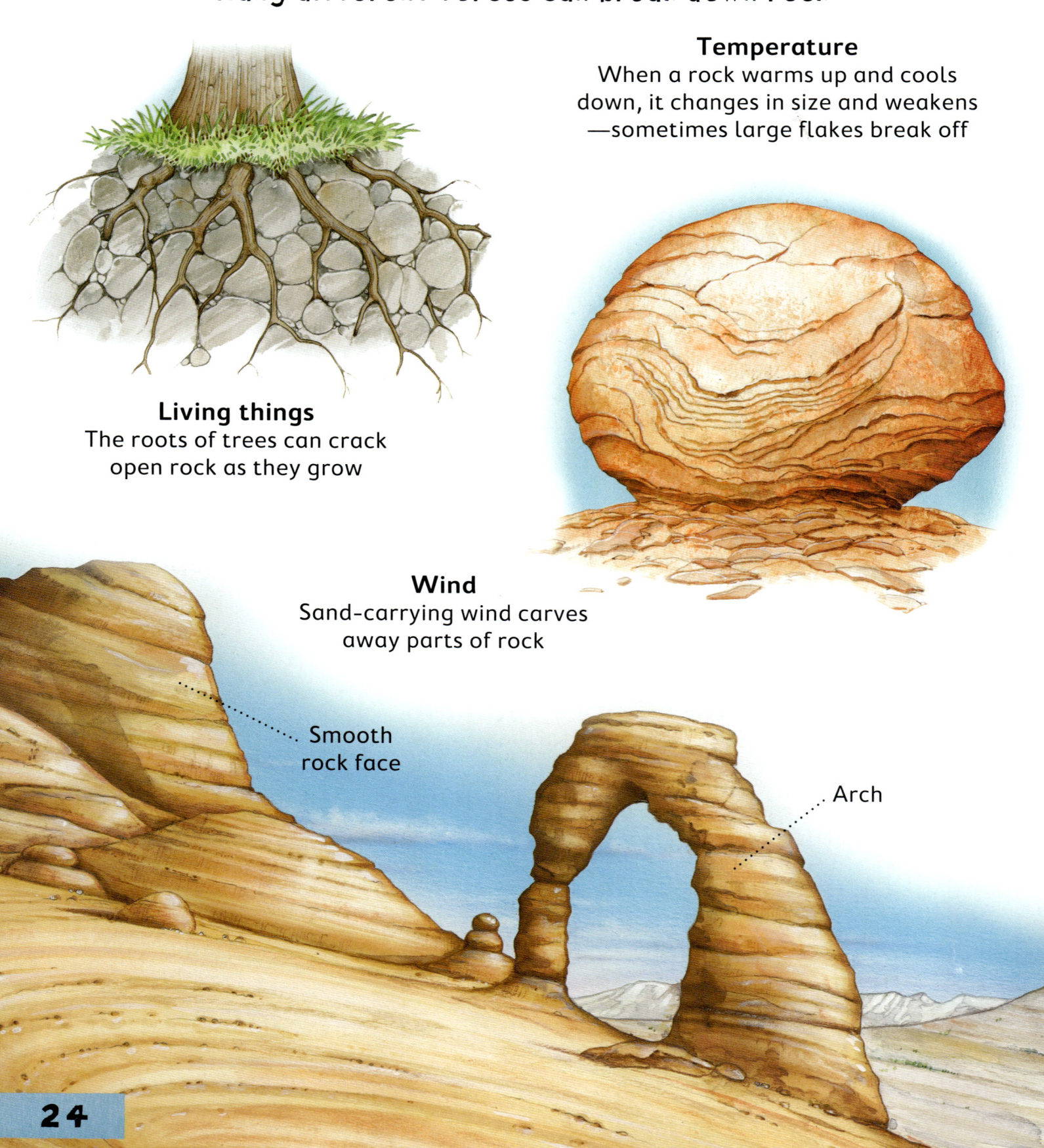

Temperature
When a rock warms up and cools down, it changes in size and weakens —sometimes large flakes break off

Living things
The roots of trees can crack open rock as they grow

Wind
Sand-carrying wind carves away parts of rock

Smooth rock face

Arch

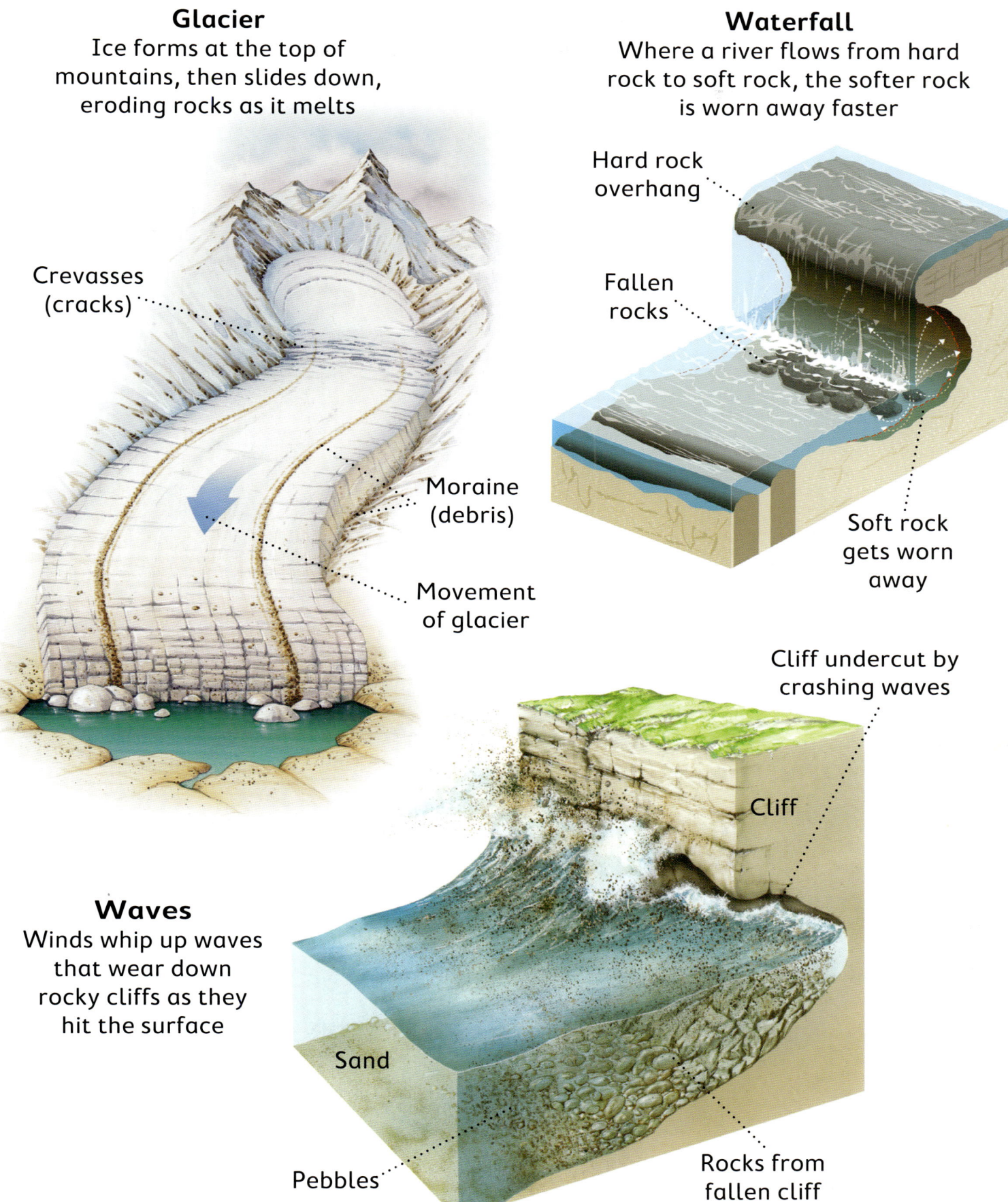

Glacier
Ice forms at the top of mountains, then slides down, eroding rocks as it melts

Crevasses (cracks)

Moraine (debris)

Movement of glacier

Waterfall
Where a river flows from hard rock to soft rock, the softer rock is worn away faster

Hard rock overhang

Fallen rocks

Soft rock gets worn away

Cliff undercut by crashing waves

Cliff

Waves
Winds whip up waves that wear down rocky cliffs as they hit the surface

Sand

Pebbles

Rocks from fallen cliff

Rocks

Combinations of particles from one or more minerals

Breccia

Mudstone

Gabbro

Sandstone

Syenite

Chalk

Eclogite

Slate

Serpentinite

Minerals

The natural chemicals from which rocks are made

Quartz

Pyrite

Gypsum

Galena

Flint

Calcite

Barite

Bauxite

Gold

Wulfenite

Silver

Stibnite

Gneiss

Zircon

Gemstones

Crystals of natural minerals that are often used in jewelry. Everybody has a birthstone, depending on which month they were born in

Garnet
January

Amethyst
February

Aquamarine
March

Diamond
April

Emerald
May

Pearl
June

Ruby
July

Peridot
August

Sapphire
September

Opal
October

Topaz
November

Turquoise
December

Volcanoes

Places where magma (red-hot liquid rock) emerges through the Earth's crust and onto the surface

1	Main vent
2	Clouds of ash, steam, and smoke
3	Lava flowing away from vent
4	Branch pipe
5	Magma chamber
6	Layers of rock from previous eruptions

Volcano types

Volcanoes erupt in different ways and have different shapes

Shield volcano
This has a low, wide shape with gently sloping sides

Crater volcano
Made when the top of a cone-shaped volcano explodes and sinks into the magma chamber

Cone-shaped volcano
This has steep sides built up of layers of lava and ash

Earthquakes

Sudden, often violent, shaking of the ground caused by the movement of the Earth's crust

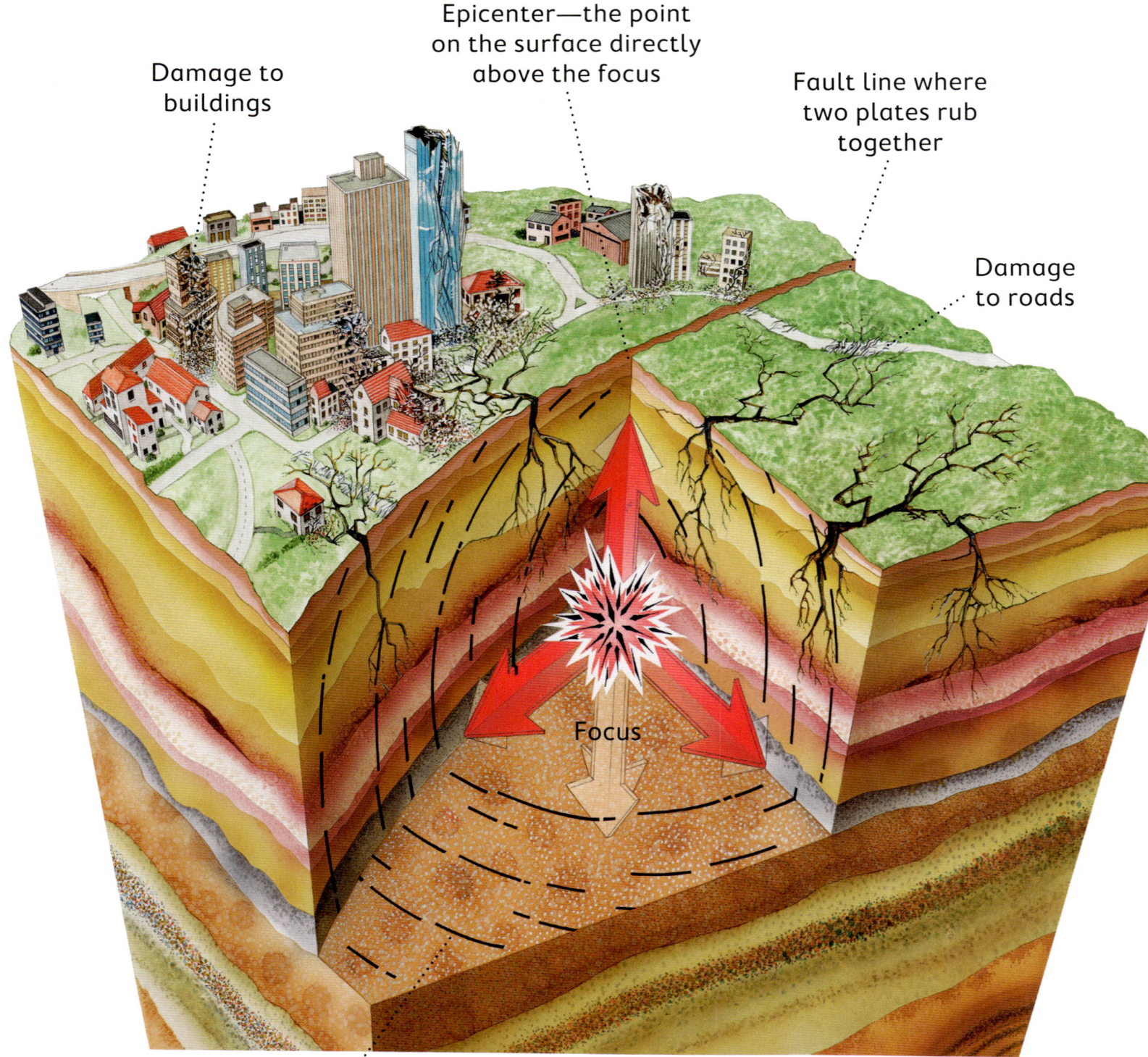

Damage to buildings

Epicenter—the point on the surface directly above the focus

Fault line where two plates rub together

Damage to roads

Focus

Shock waves from the focus

Tsunamis

Enormous waves produced by an earthquake
or volcanic eruption under the sea

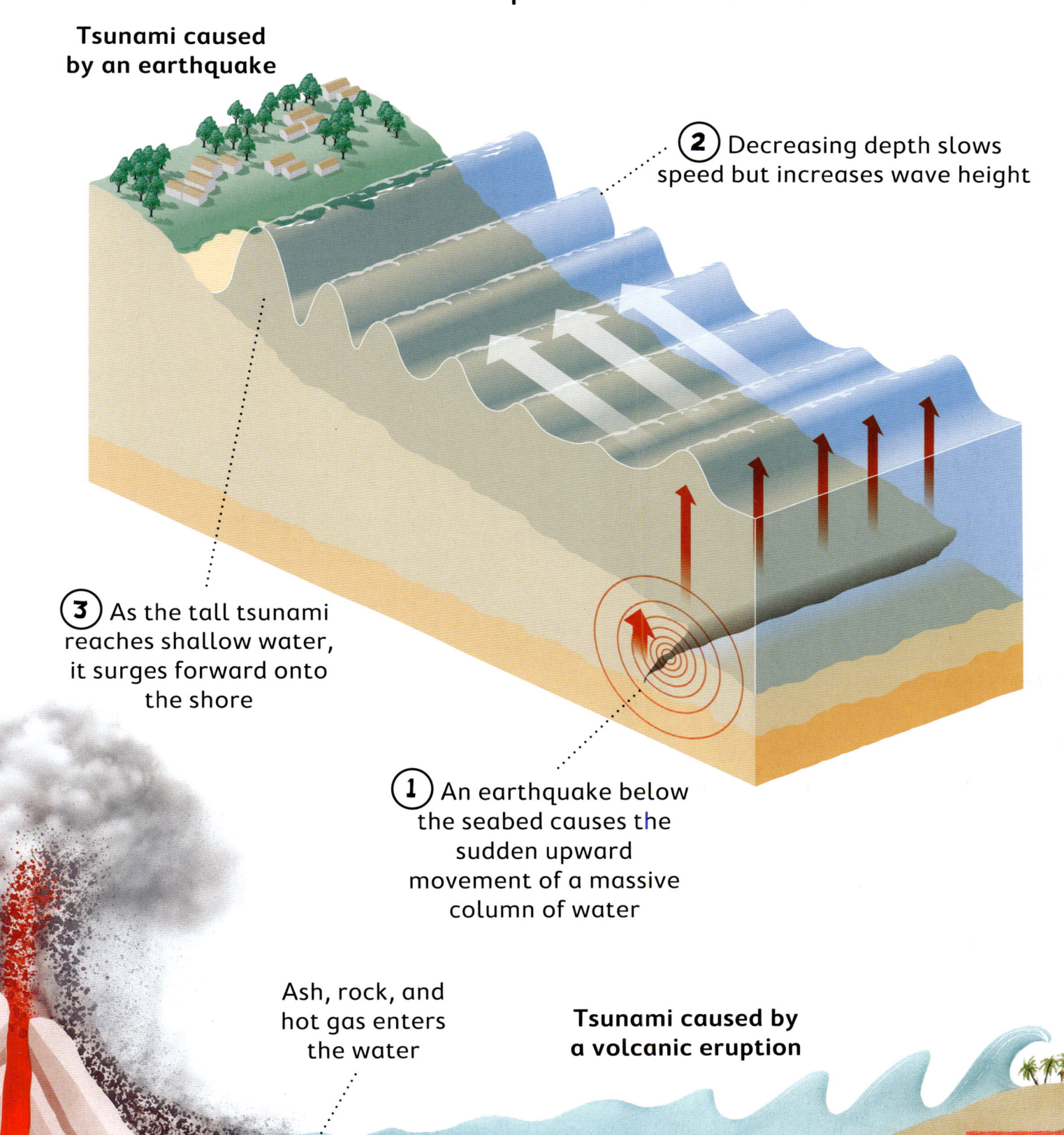

**Tsunami caused
by an earthquake**

2 Decreasing depth slows
speed but increases wave height

3 As the tall tsunami
reaches shallow water,
it surges forward onto
the shore

1 An earthquake below
the seabed causes the
sudden upward
movement of a massive
column of water

Ash, rock, and
hot gas enters
the water

**Tsunami caused by
a volcanic eruption**

31

Mountains

It takes millions of years for mountains to form.
Here are three ways they can take shape

Volcanic mountain
These mountains are
formed when lava cools
after an eruption

Ash and lava
form volcanic
mountains

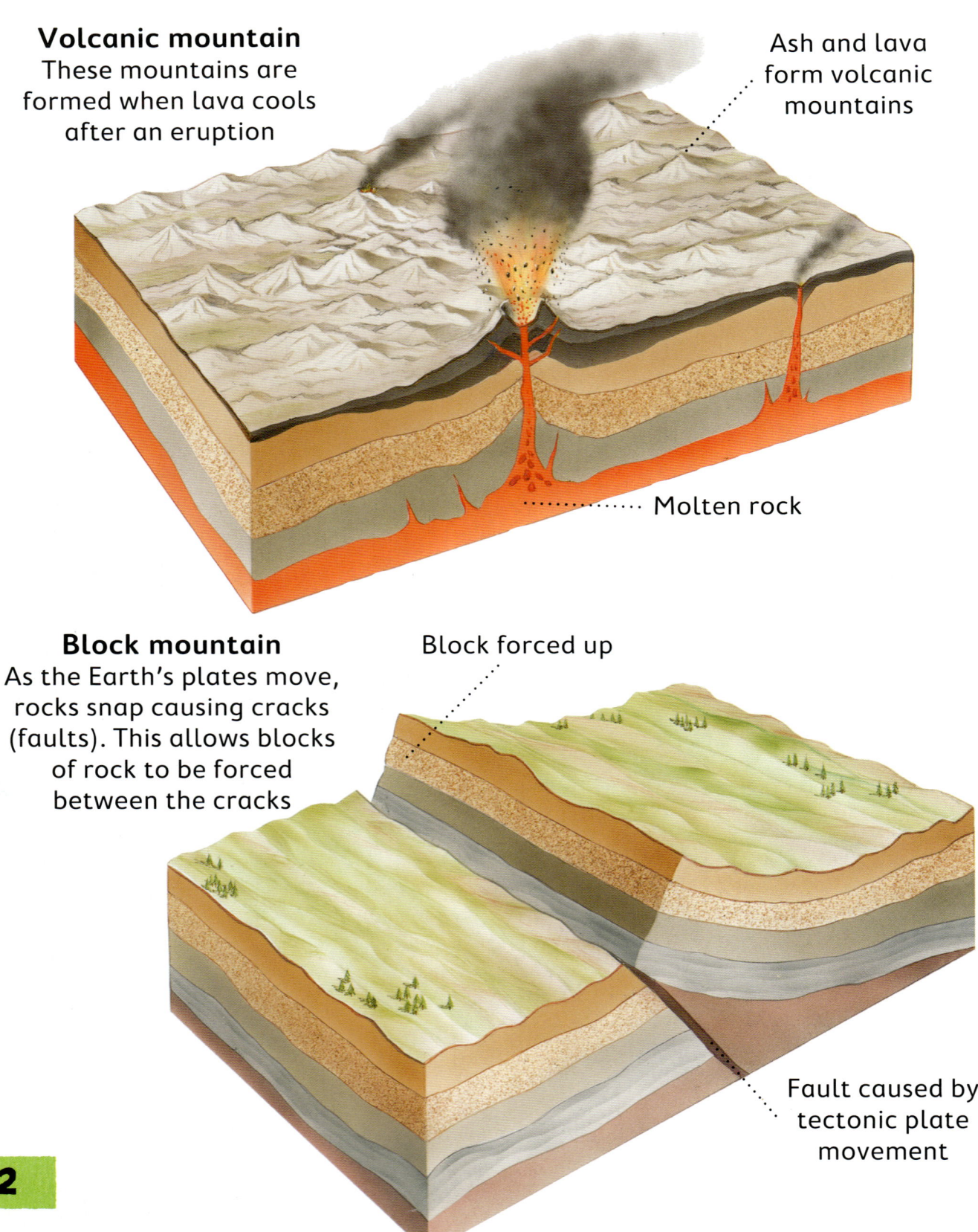

Molten rock

Block mountain
As the Earth's plates move,
rocks snap causing cracks
(faults). This allows blocks
of rock to be forced
between the cracks

Block forced up

Fault caused by
tectonic plate
movement

Fold mountain
The Himalayas are a range of fold mountains in Asia, created as tectonic plates crashed together

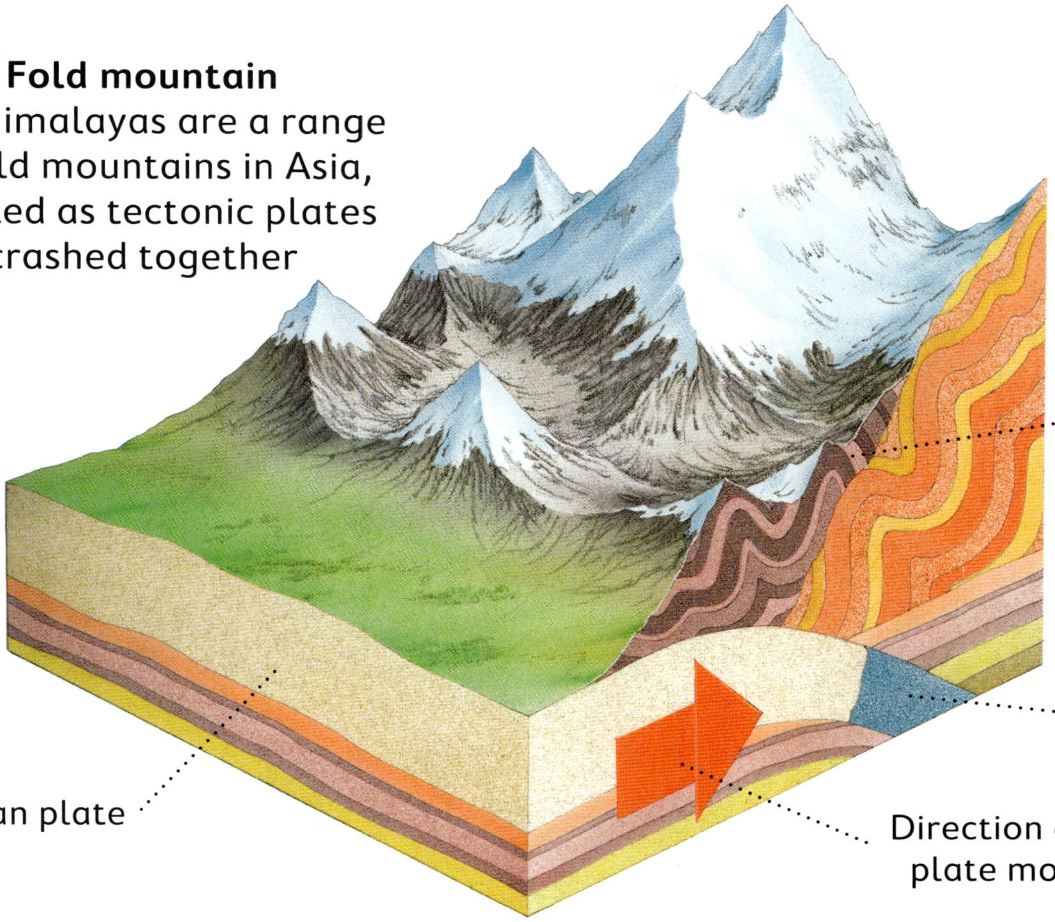

Folded rock layers

Asian plate

Direction of Indian plate movement

Indian plate

Highest mountains

The tallest peaks on six of the seven continents, shown to scale

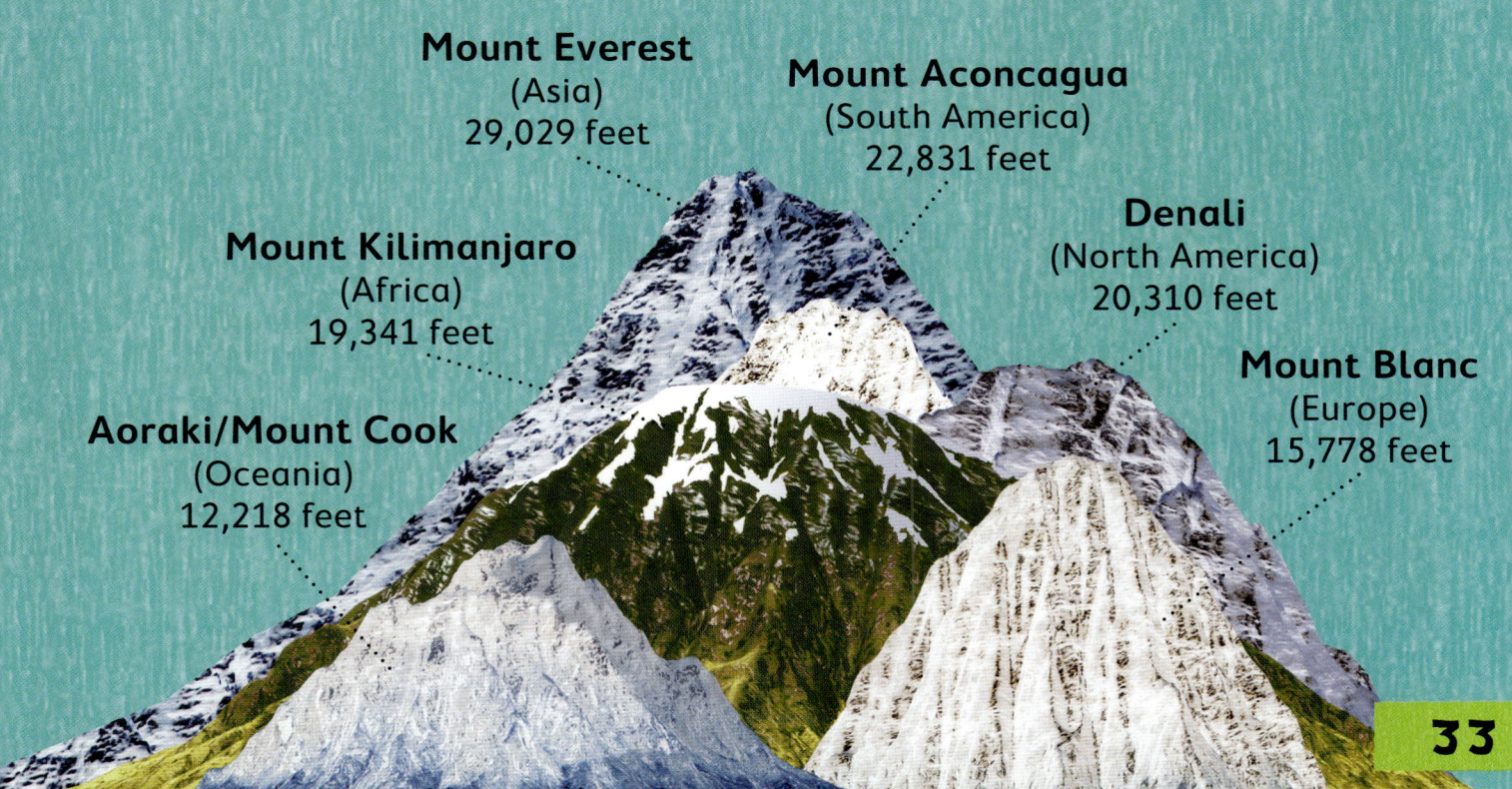

Mount Everest
(Asia)
29,029 feet

Mount Aconcagua
(South America)
22,831 feet

Denali
(North America)
20,310 feet

Mount Kilimanjaro
(Africa)
19,341 feet

Mount Blanc
(Europe)
15,778 feet

Aoraki/Mount Cook
(Oceania)
12,218 feet

33

Oceans

Huge areas of water, which cover approximately two thirds of our planet

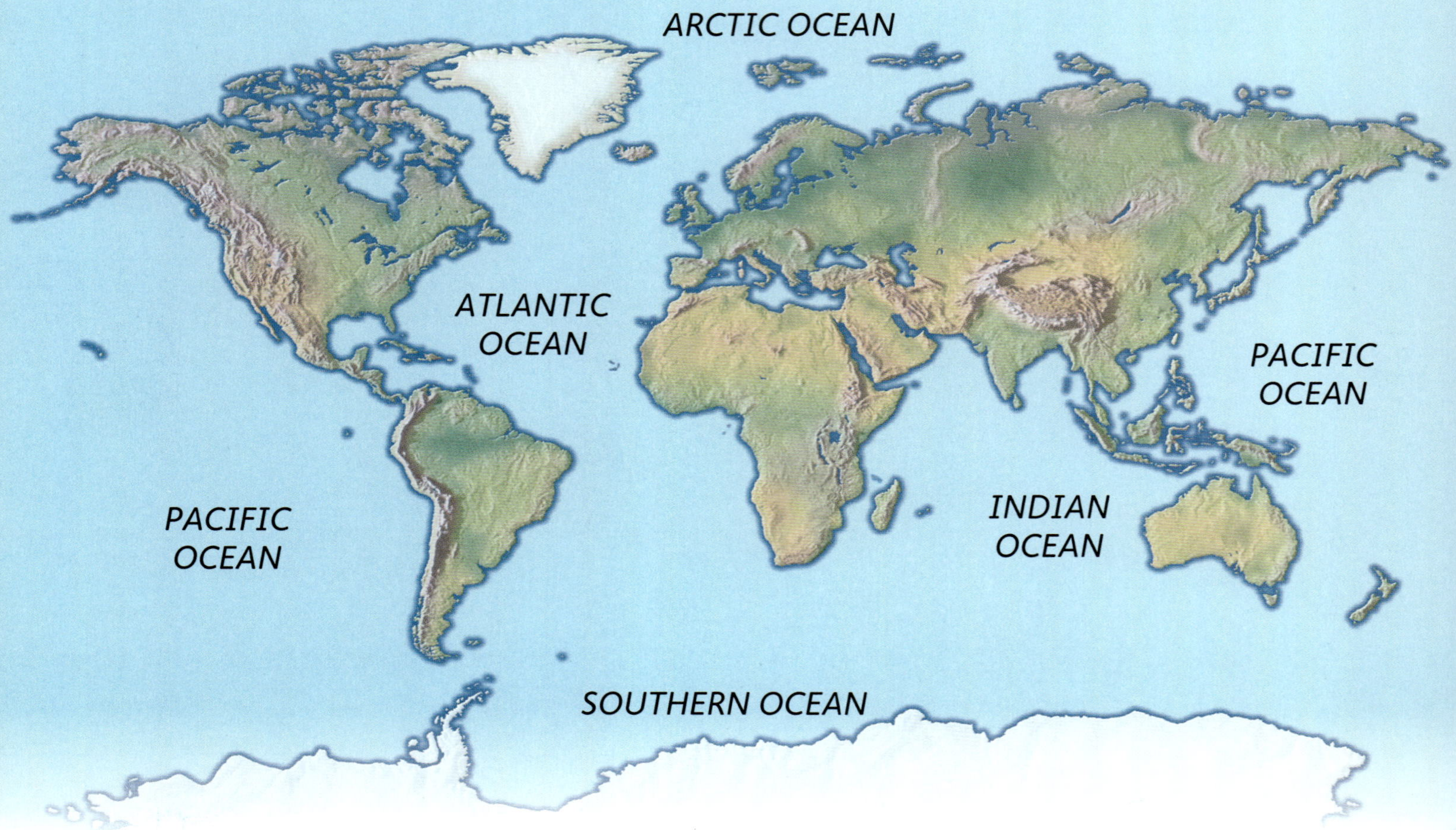

ARCTIC OCEAN

ATLANTIC OCEAN

PACIFIC OCEAN

PACIFIC OCEAN

INDIAN OCEAN

SOUTHERN OCEAN

High tide
The sea moves upward and inland as the tide rises

Intertidal zone

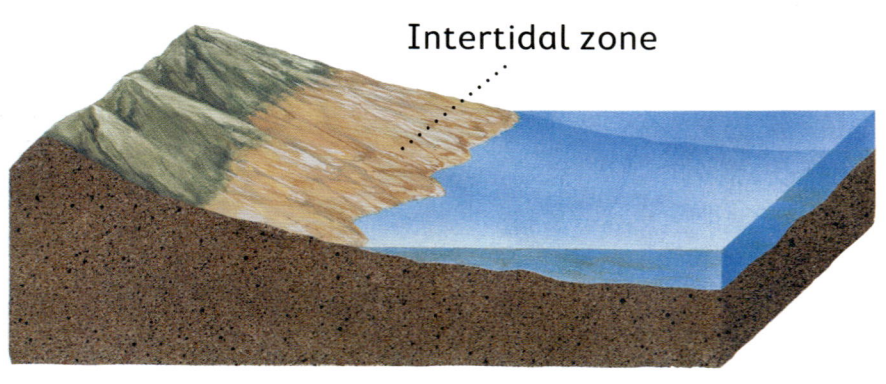

Low tide
The sea ebbs, retreating as the tide drops

Ocean currents

In the ocean, water is continually moving, passing around the globe in giant streams called currents

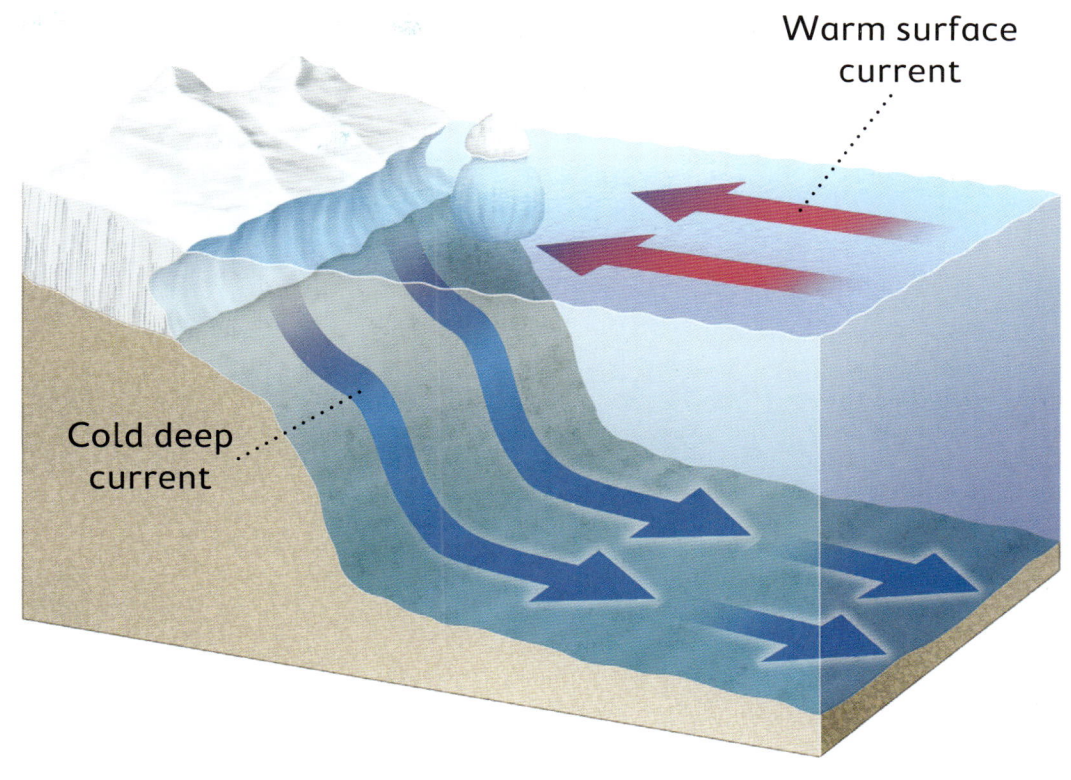

Warm surface current

Cold deep current

Ocean floor

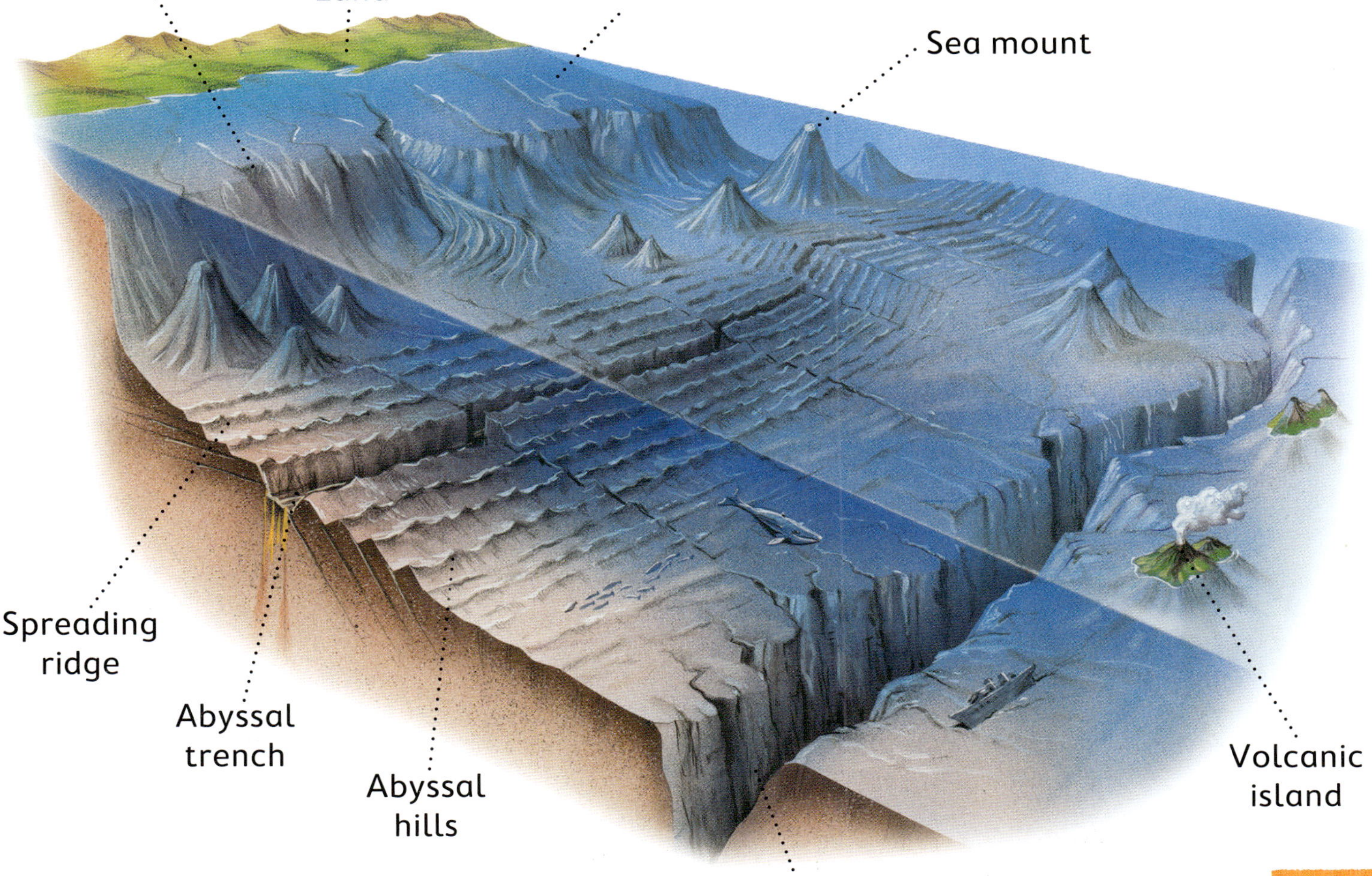

Continental slope

Land

Continental shelf

Sea mount

Spreading ridge

Abyssal trench

Abyssal hills

Ocean trench

Volcanic island

Rivers

High in the mountains, streams join to form the headwater of a river

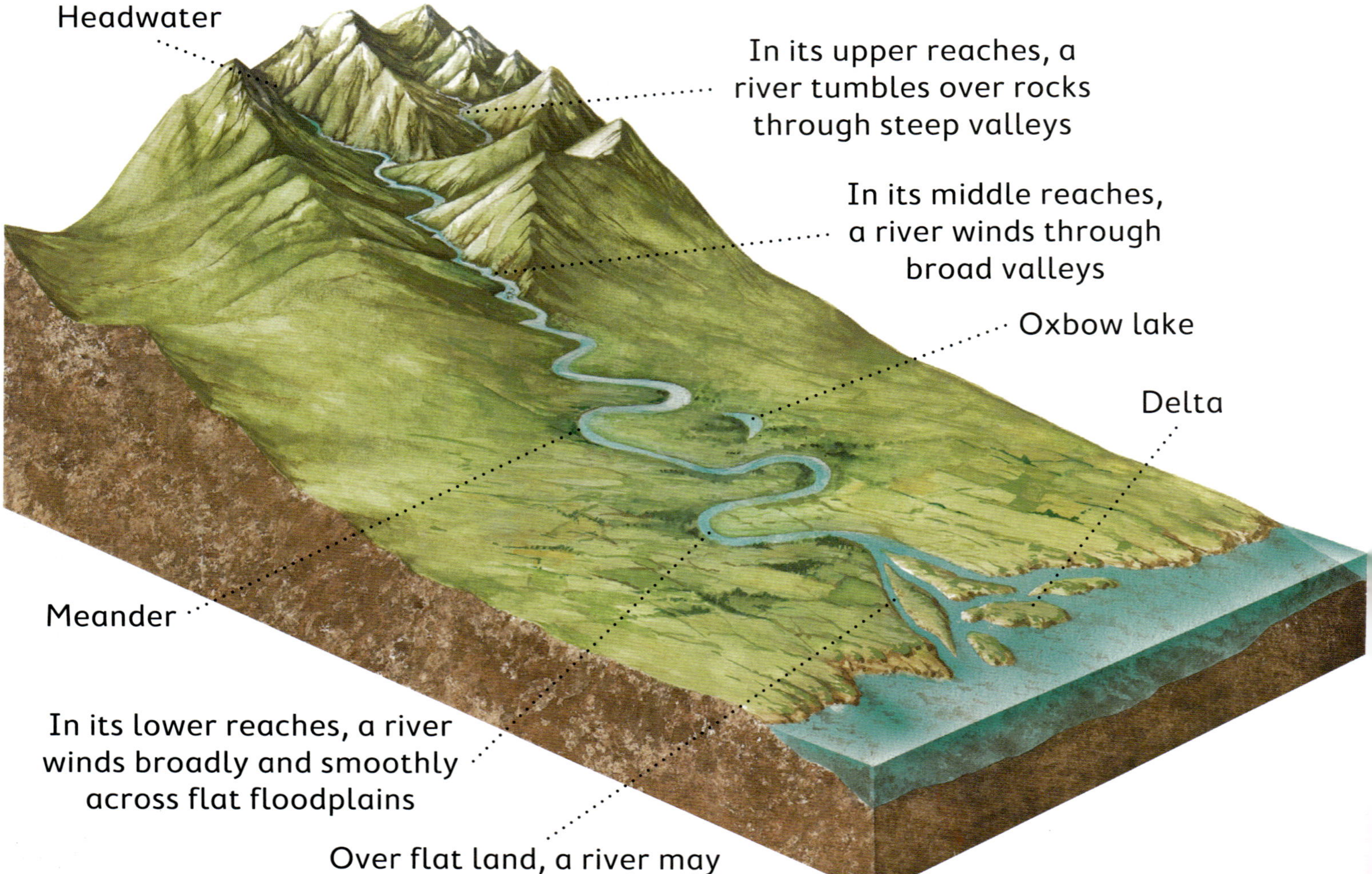

Headwater

In its upper reaches, a river tumbles over rocks through steep valleys

In its middle reaches, a river winds through broad valleys

Oxbow lake

Delta

Meander

In its lower reaches, a river winds broadly and smoothly across flat floodplains

Over flat land, a river may split into branches

Delta

Rivers slow down as they flow into the sea and often dump mud and sand in a fan-shape, or delta

Outlets

River

Mud and sand deposits build up land

Lakes

Lakes form in hollows in the ground sometimes left when glaciers melt or plates in the Earth's crust split open

Landslide lake
If a landslide falls into a river and blocks the flow of water, a lake will form

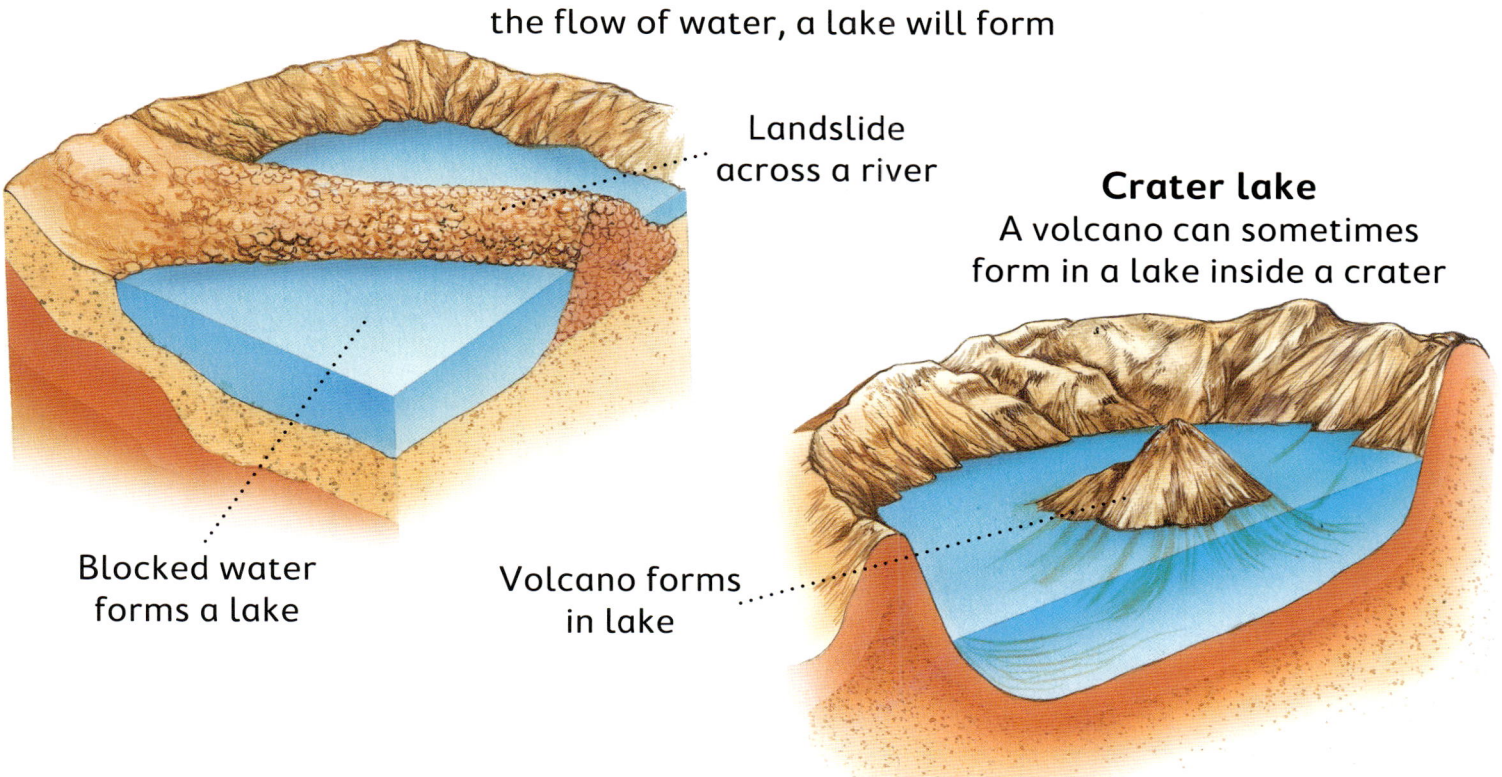

Landslide across a river

Crater lake
A volcano can sometimes form in a lake inside a crater

Blocked water forms a lake

Volcano forms in lake

The Great Lakes

The largest group of freshwater lakes are located on the border of the United States and Canada

Lake Superior

Lake Huron

Lake Ontario

Lake Michigan

Lake Erie

Seashore

A place where the sea meets the land

1. Shingle beach
2. Shingle spit
3. Stump
4. Needle
5. Stack
6. Arch
7. Headland
8. Cave
9. Circular bay
10. Waves
11. Cliffs
12. River
13. Delta
14. Mudflats
15. Salt marsh
16. Sandy beach

Rock pool

As the tide retreats, pools of water are often trapped on rocky beaches, creating homes for many seashore species

Rain forests

These are warm, steamy environments where a lot of rain falls every year

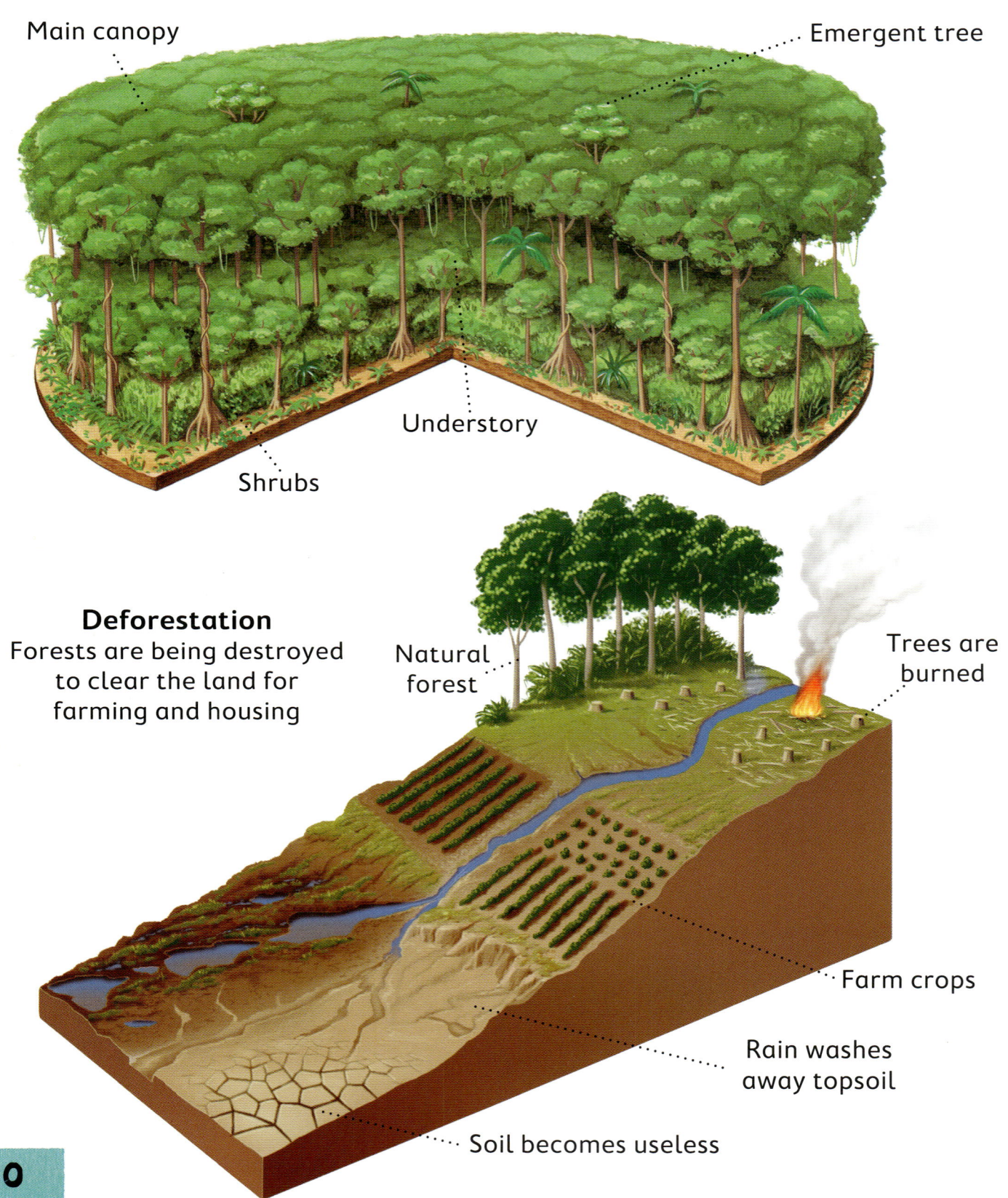

Main canopy

Emergent tree

Understory

Shrubs

Deforestation
Forests are being destroyed to clear the land for farming and housing

Natural forest

Trees are burned

Farm crops

Rain washes away topsoil

Soil becomes useless

Deserts

The driest places on Earth are deserts. Some deserts do not have any rain for many years

Oasis

Rock beneath the desert

Ridges of sand being blown into dunes

Sand dunes

Depending on the type of wind and sand, dunes form in different shapes and patterns

Transverse dune

Seif dune

Barchan dune

Parabolic dune

Star dune

Atmosphere

Layers of gases surround Earth in a "blanket"

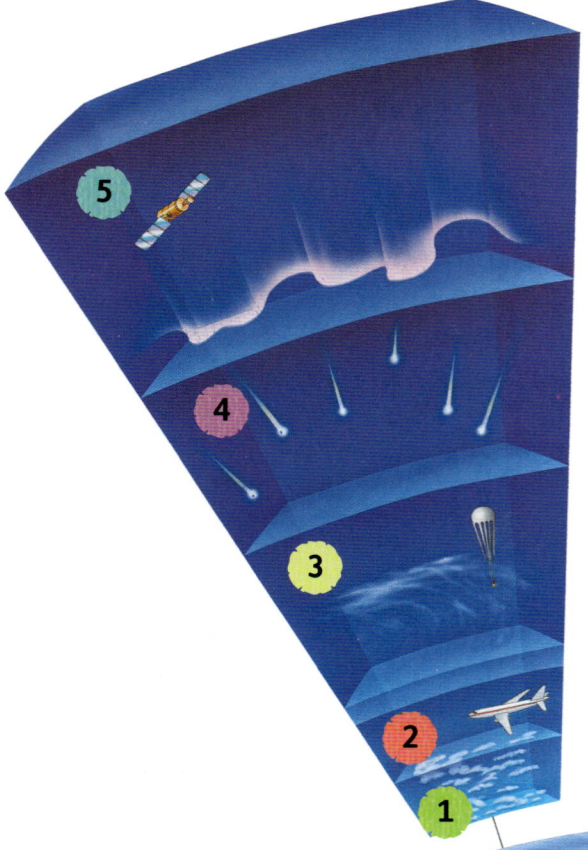

5 Exosphere
Low level satellites orbit within the outer layer. Auroras appear above the Poles in the upper atmosphere

4 Thermosphere
The atmosphere protects us from meteorites

3 Mesosphere
The ozone layer protects us from the Sun's UV rays

2 Stratosphere
Most long-distance aircraft travel in this section

1 Troposphere
Clouds form and most weather takes place in the lowest level

Global warming

Pollution in the atmosphere causes carbon dioxide to trap heat, raising the temperature of the Earth

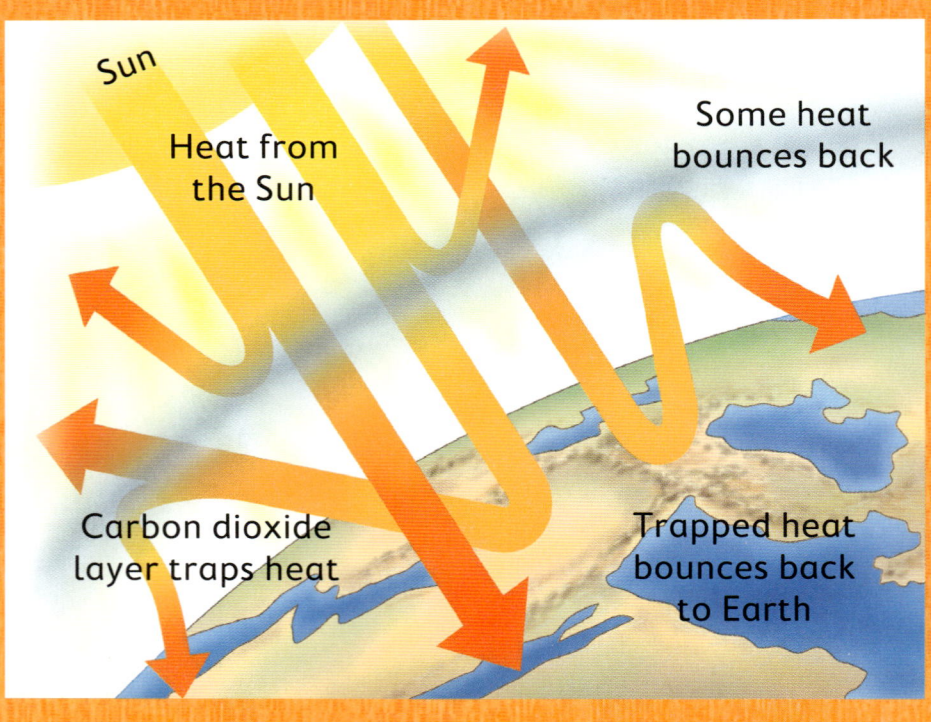

Sun

Heat from the Sun

Some heat bounces back

Carbon dioxide layer traps heat

Trapped heat bounces back to Earth

Climate

The weather conditions of a specific area or region

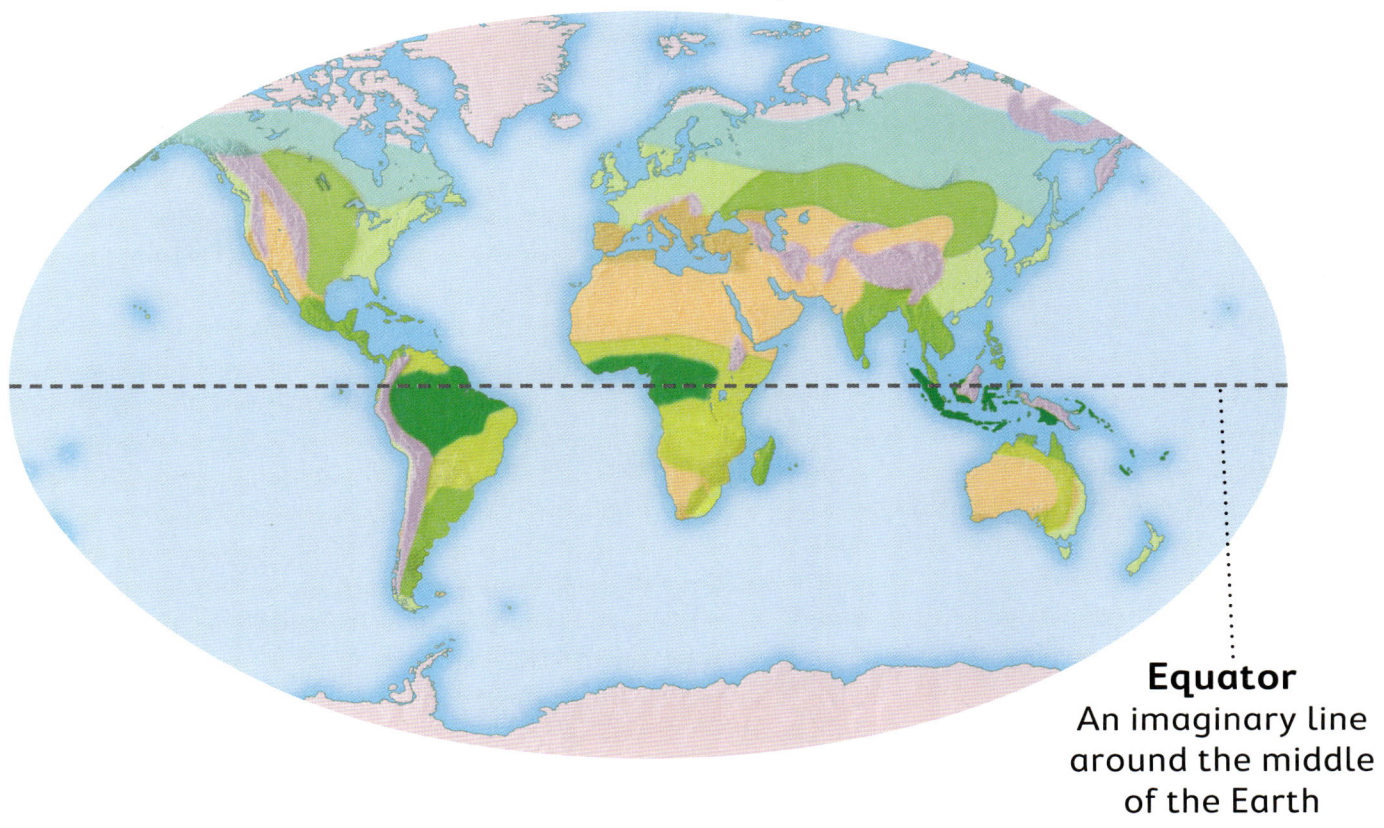

Equator
An imaginary line around the middle of the Earth

Types of climates

Around the world there are different climates.
The warmest are found close to the Equator

Tropical forest

Tropical grassland

Mountainous

Dry temperate

Wet temperate

Desert

Polar

Temperate grassland

Cold temperate

43

Water cycle

On Earth, water is continually rising and falling in a cycle

1. Water evaporates from the sea
2. Water vapor condenses to form clouds
3. Clouds rise
4. Water vapor is given off by forests
5. Clouds become larger and heavier as more water vapor sticks together
6. Clouds become too heavy —the water falls to land as rain
7. Rain falls into rivers, which run back to the sea

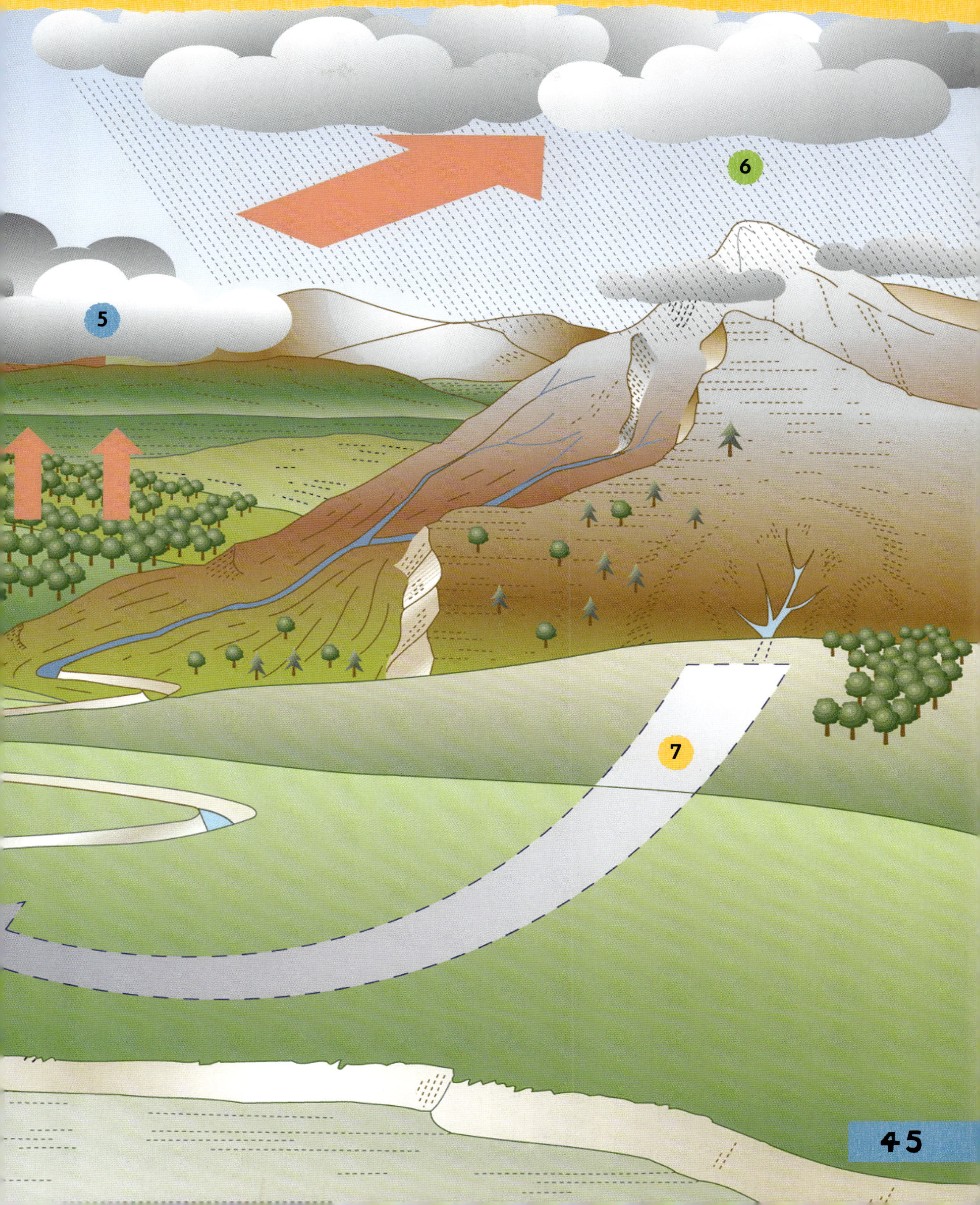
5
6
7

Clouds

Billions of water droplets form clouds in the sky. There are many different shapes and sizes

1. Virga
2. Cumulonimbus
3. Cumulus
4. Cirrostratus
5. Stratus
6. Cirrus
7. Contrails
8. Stratocumulus

Formation

Clouds form when warm, rising air meets lower temperatures, such as at mountaintops

Wind

Winds blow because air is constantly moving from areas of high pressure to areas of low pressure

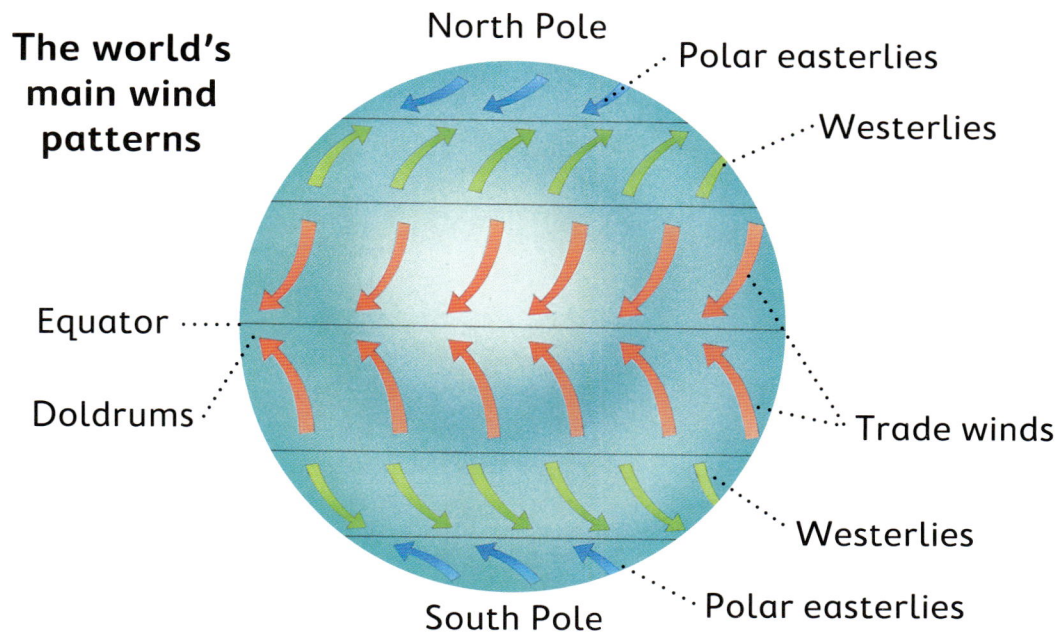

The world's main wind patterns

North Pole

Polar easterlies

Westerlies

Equator

Doldrums

Trade winds

Westerlies

Polar easterlies

South Pole

Beaufort Scale

The numbered scale that measures wind force

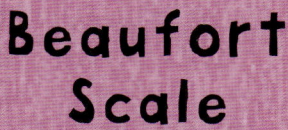 0: Calm

 1: Light air

 2: Light breeze

 3: Gentle breeze

 4: Moderate breeze

 5: Fresh breeze

 6: Strong breeze

 7: Near gale

 8: Gale

 9: Strong gale

 10: Storm

 11: Violent storm

 12: Hurricane

47

Plants

About 800 million years ago plants began to grow on land

Lichen

Monkey puzzle tree

Archaefructus

Cycad

Ginkgo leaf

Cooksonia

Classification

The scientist Carl Linnaeus (1707–1778) classified organisms in a clear, scientific way. This is how the magnolia plant is classified

KINGDOM—Plantae
PHYLUM—Angiosperms
CLASS—Magnoliids
ORDER—Magnoliales
FAMILY—Magnoliaceae
GENUS—*Magnolia*
SPECIES—*Magnolia virginiana*

Magnolia
There are about 210 species

Sea life

The first animals on Earth lived in the sea

Trilobite

Pterygotus

Ammonite

Ottoia

Anomalocaris

Charnia

Fish

The first fish appeared in the sea about 500 million years ago

Panderichthys

Hemicyclaspis

Climatius

Pikaia

Dunkleosteus

Cephalaspis

Pleuracanthus

Eusthenopteron

Hybodus

Amphibians

The first animals to live on land
still had to return to water to breed

Acanthostega

Ichthyostega

Triadobatrachus

Eogyrinus

Diplocaulus

Gerrothorax

Mastodonsaurus

51

Reptiles

The first reptiles' waterproof skin and tough eggs helped them to survive

Land reptiles

Varanosaurus

Cynognathus

Dimetrodon

Diictodon

Hylonomus

Chasmatosaurus

Lystrosaurus

Coelurosauravus

Protosuchus

Moschops

Marine reptiles

Archelon

Proganochelys

Mosasaurus

Elasmosaurus

Dinosaur anatomy

Dinosaurs are divided into two groups—saurischians (lizard-hipped) and ornithischians (bird-hipped)

Ilium

Ischium

Pubis

Lizard-hipped dinosaur

Ilium

Pubis

Bird-hipped dinosaur

Tyrannosaurus rex (lizard-hipped)

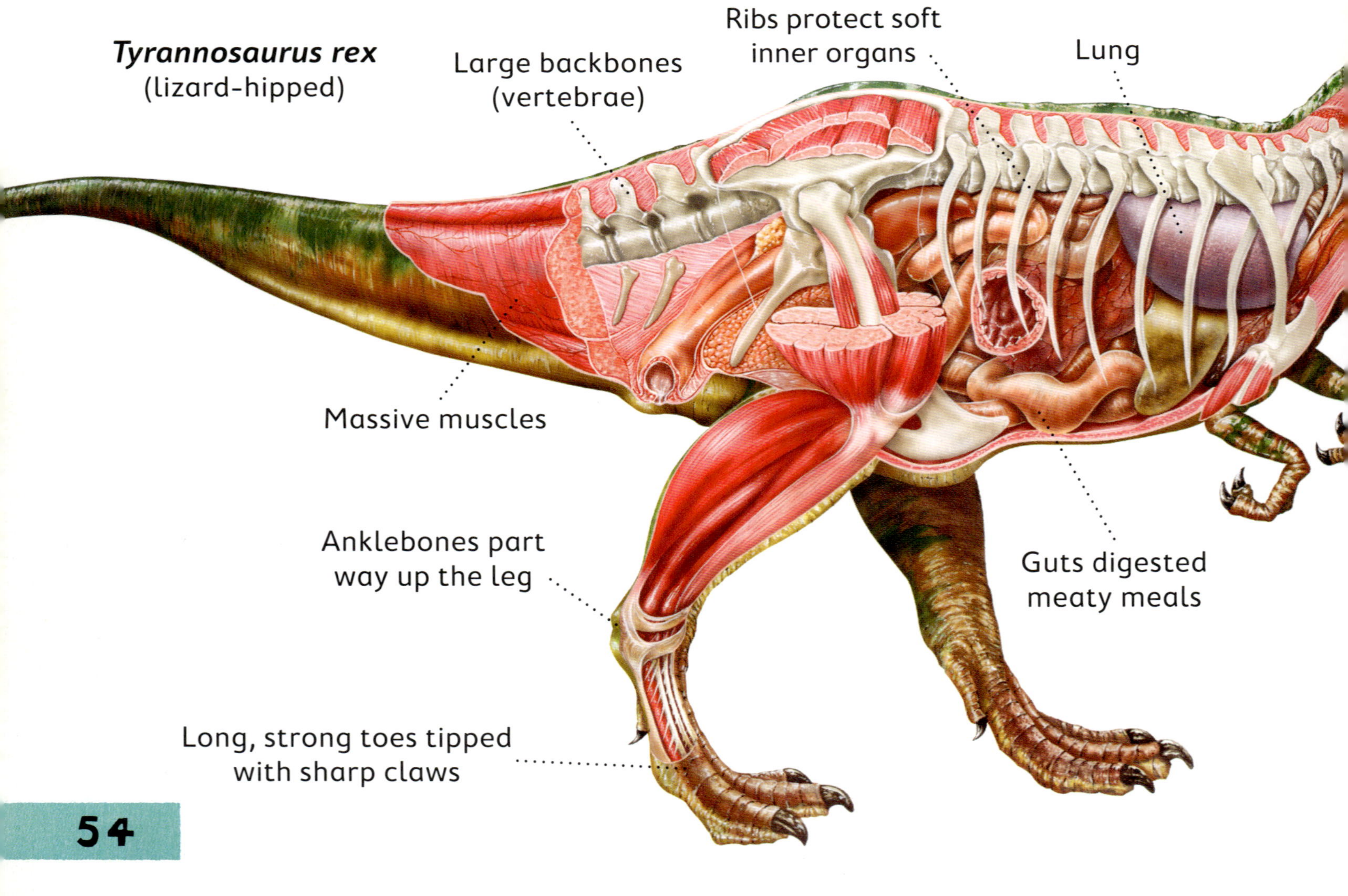

Large backbones (vertebrae)

Ribs protect soft inner organs

Lung

Massive muscles

Anklebones part way up the leg

Guts digested meaty meals

Long, strong toes tipped with sharp claws

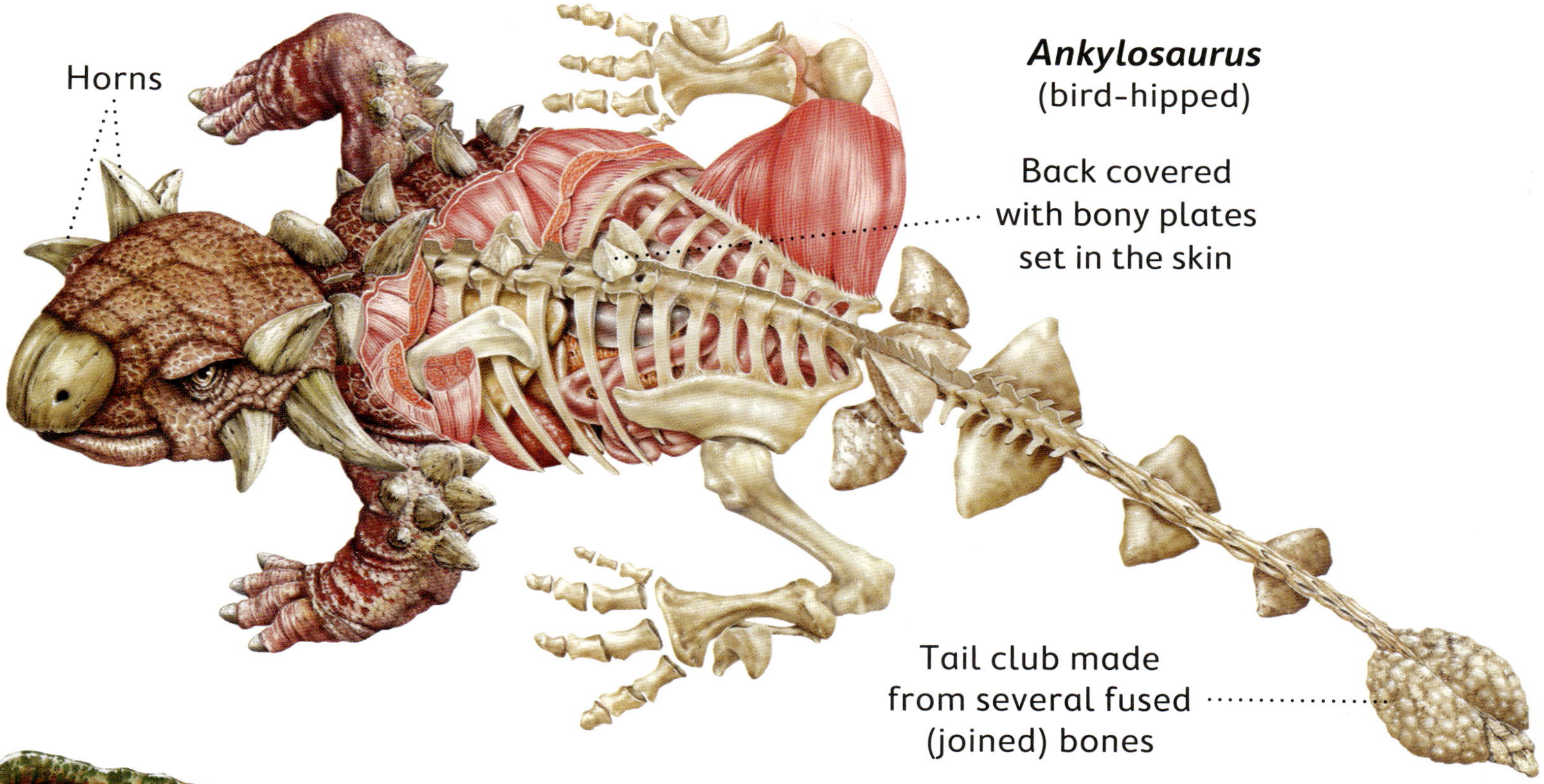

Horns

Ankylosaurus
(bird-hipped)

Back covered
with bony plates
set in the skin

Tail club made
from several fused
(joined) bones

Large
snout

Dinosaur teeth

By examining the teeth of different dinosaurs,
we can discover what dinosaurs ate

Baryonyx
Meat eater

Edmontosaurus
Plant eater

Long, thin teeth
for tearing up fish

Flat, blunt teeth for
crushing plants

Attack

Some dinosaurs were equipped with speed and weapons to make them expert predators

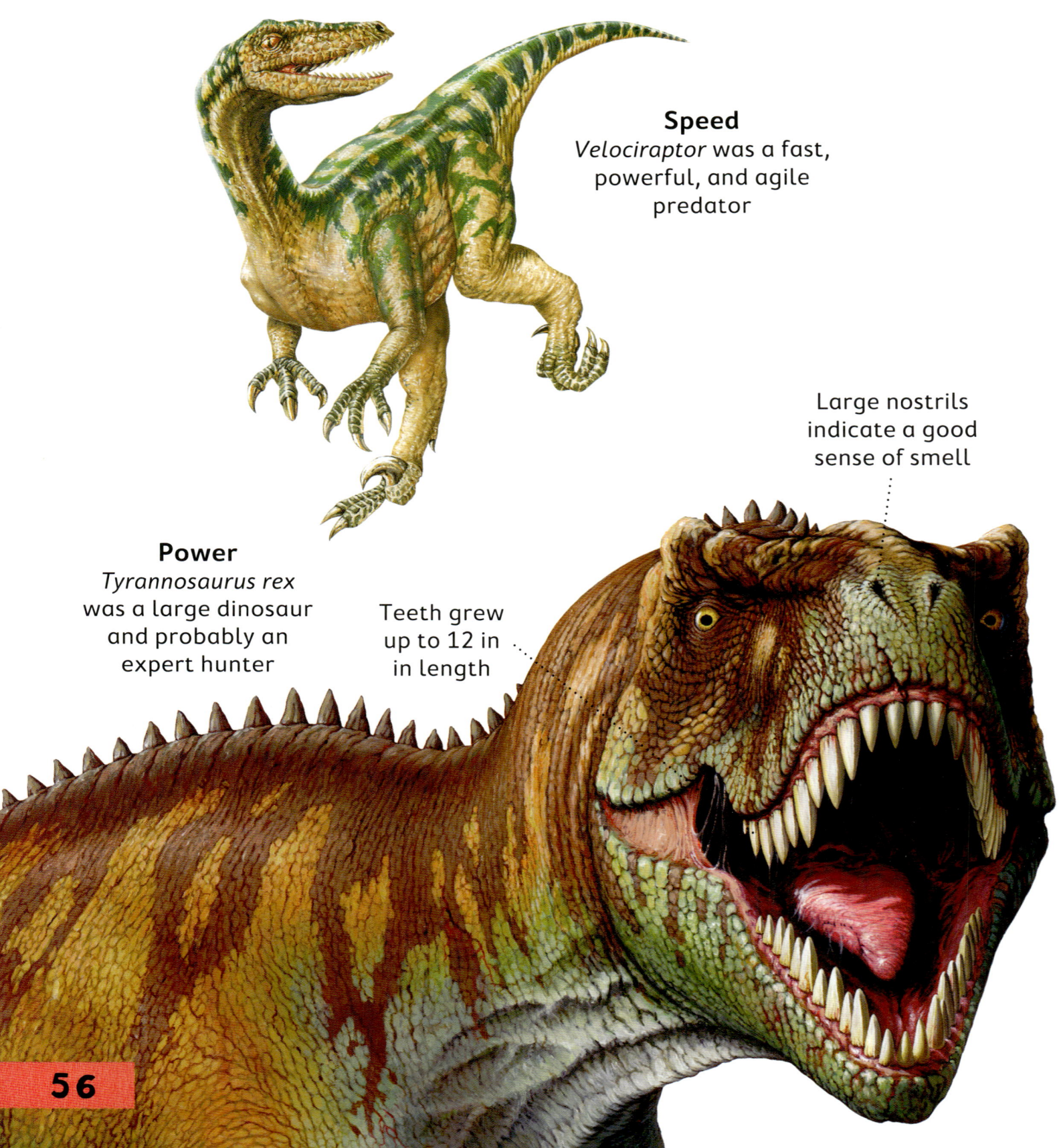

Speed
Velociraptor was a fast, powerful, and agile predator

Large nostrils indicate a good sense of smell

Power
Tyrannosaurus rex was a large dinosaur and probably an expert hunter

Teeth grew up to 12 in in length

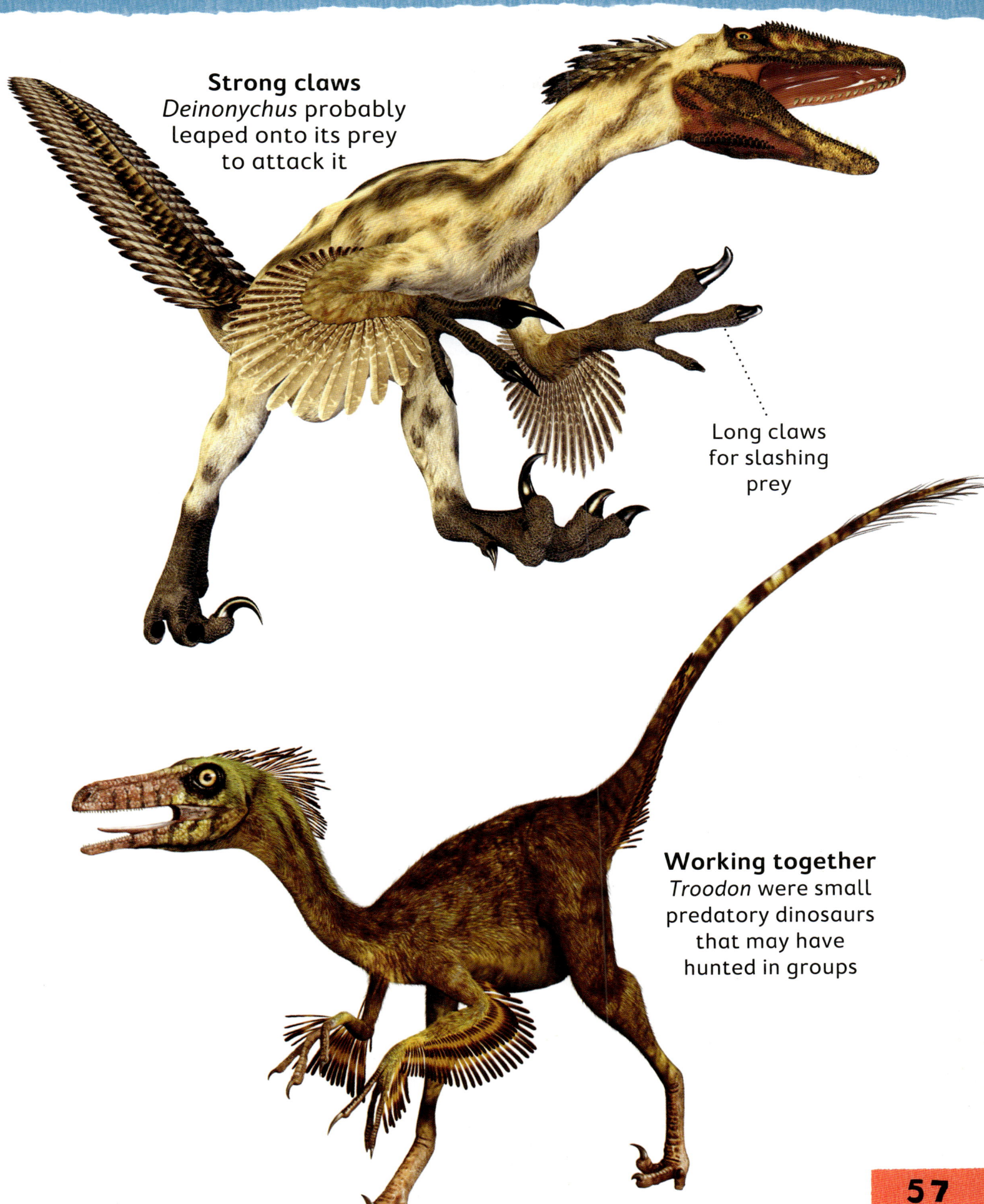

Strong claws
Deinonychus probably leaped onto its prey to attack it

Long claws for slashing prey

Working together
Troodon were small predatory dinosaurs that may have hunted in groups

Defense

The bodies of some dinosaurs were adapted to provide them with protection from attack

Ceratopsia

A group of dinosaurs with distinctive neck frills, horned faces, and parrotlike beaks

Styracosaurus   **Chasmosaurus**   **Triceratops**

Horns
Triceratops used its horns to defend against *Tyrannosaurus rex*

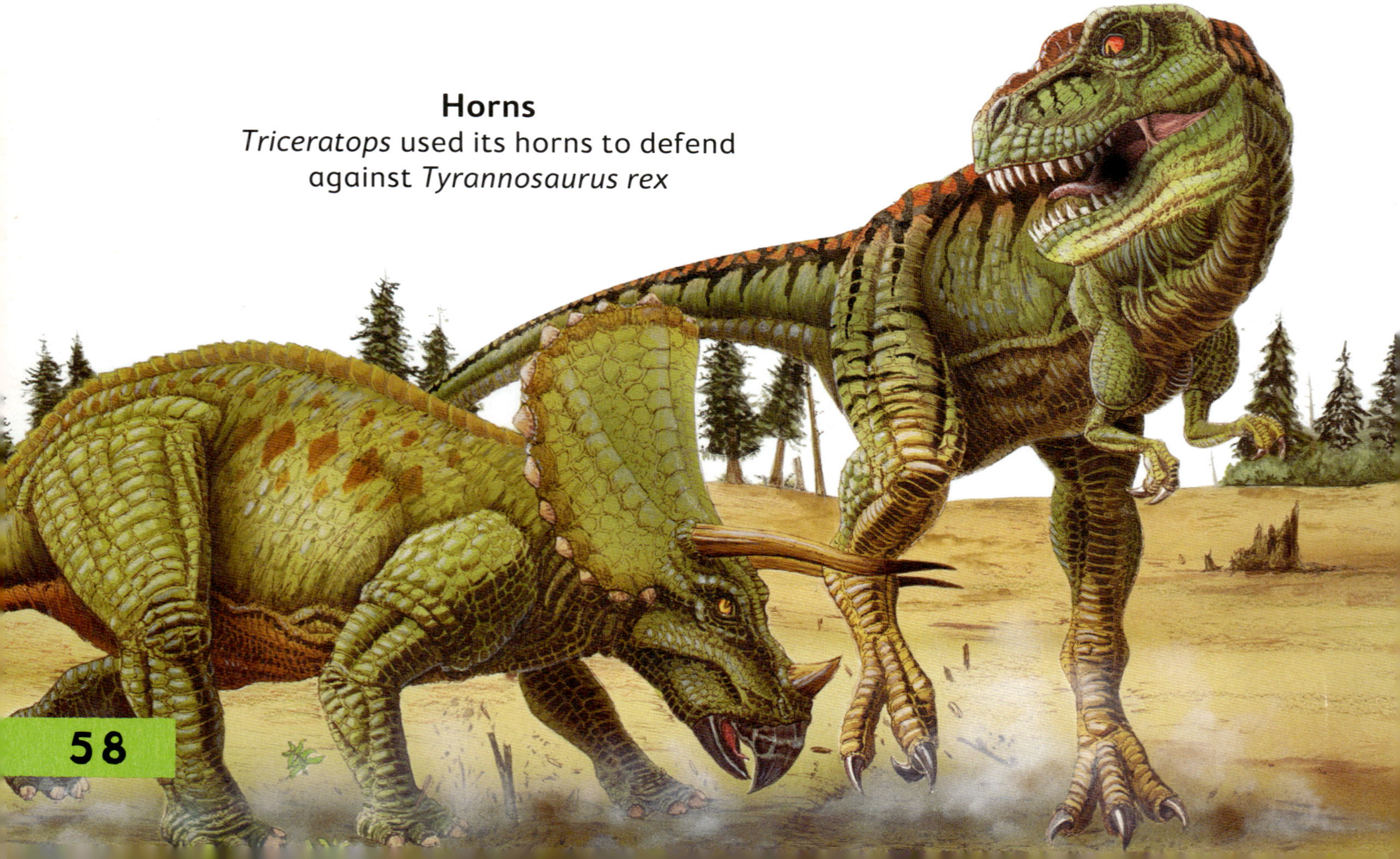

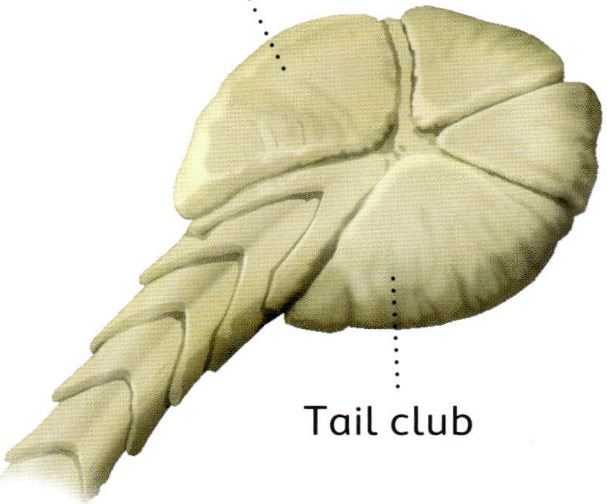

Tail club

A group of dinosaurs called ankylosaurs used their strong tail clubs to fight off attackers

Fused plates of bone

Tail club

Euoplocephalus

Dinosaur skin

Certain groups of dinosaur had armored skins

Saltasaurus

Large bony plates

Scutes (bony plates in the skin) and nodules

Scelidosaurus

Cone-shaped plates

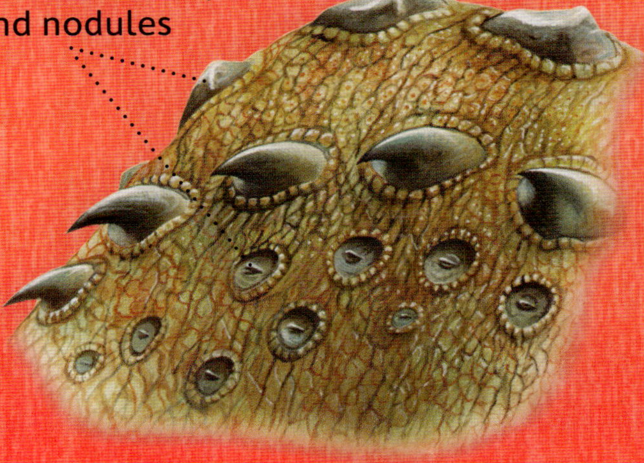

Sauropelta

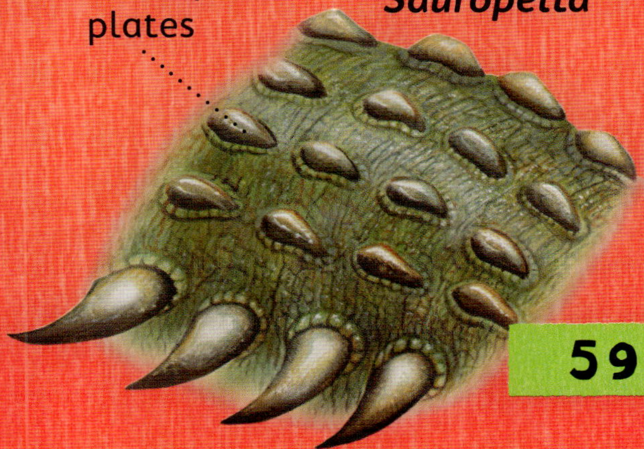

Triassic dinosaurs

252–201 million years ago these dinosaurs roamed Earth

Plateosaurus

Thecodontosaurus

Coelophysis

Herrerasaurus

Procompsognathus

Staurikosaurus

Massospondylus

Riojasaurus

Saltopus

Jurassic dinosaurs

Many different dinosaurs lived during
this period, 201–145 million years ago

Dilophosaurus

Barosaurus

Brachiosaurus

Ornitholestes

Eustreptospondylus

Coelurus

Tuojiangosaurus

Compsognathus

Allosaurus

Anchisaurus

Cretaceous dinosaurs

These dinosaurs lived during the last part of the Age of Dinosaurs, 145–66 million years ago

Tyrannosaurus rex

Troodon

Parasaurolophus

Spinosaurus

Stegosaurus

Protoceratops

Giganotosaurus

Gallimimus

Edmontonia

Baryonyx

Triceratops

Birds

Fossils of the first birds, which appeared about 155 million years ago, were mistaken for dinosaurs

Argentavis
magnificens

Archaeopteryx

Confuciusornis

Gastornis

Titanis

Hesperornis

Ichthyornis

Waimanu

Mammals

After the mass extinction of the dinosaurs, a different group of animals, the mammals, became successful

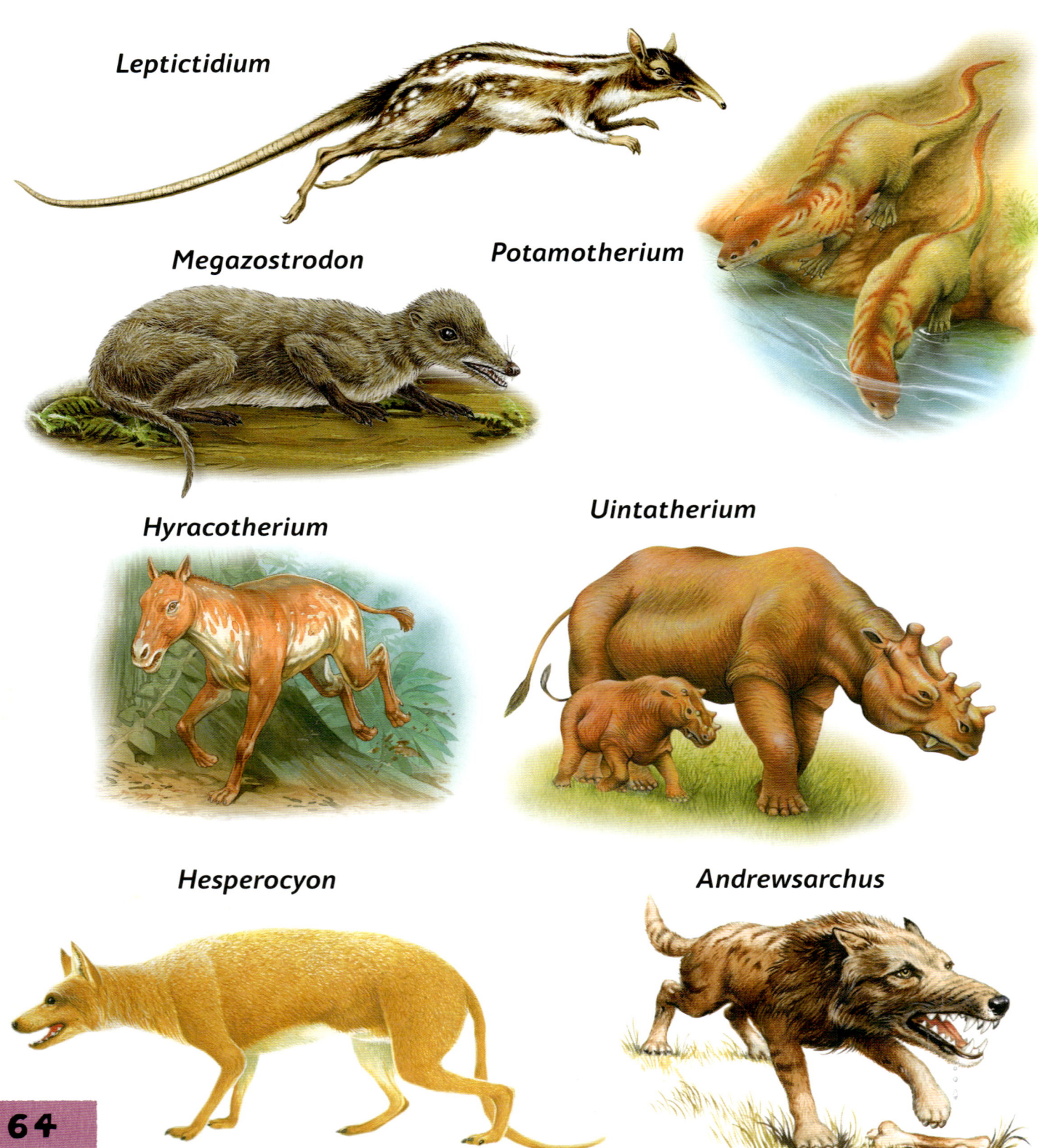

Leptictidium

Megazostrodon

Potamotherium

Hyracotherium

Uintatherium

Hesperocyon

Andrewsarchus

Woolly mammoths

Smilodon

Early humans

Over the last four million years there have probably been more than 20 different species of humans

Homo erectus
Lived almost two million years ago

Australopithecus afarensis
Lived over three million years ago

Homo neanderthalensis
Lived about 250,000 years ago

Fossil formation

Fossils are the remains of animals and plants that died a very long time ago and became preserved in rocks

Ichthyosaur

(1) After death, the ichthyosaur sinks to the seabed. Worms, crabs, and other scavengers eat its soft body parts

(3) Millions of years later the upper rock layers wear away and the fossil remains are exposed

(2) Sediments cover the hard body parts, such as bones and teeth, which gradually turn into solid rock

PREHISTORIC LIFE

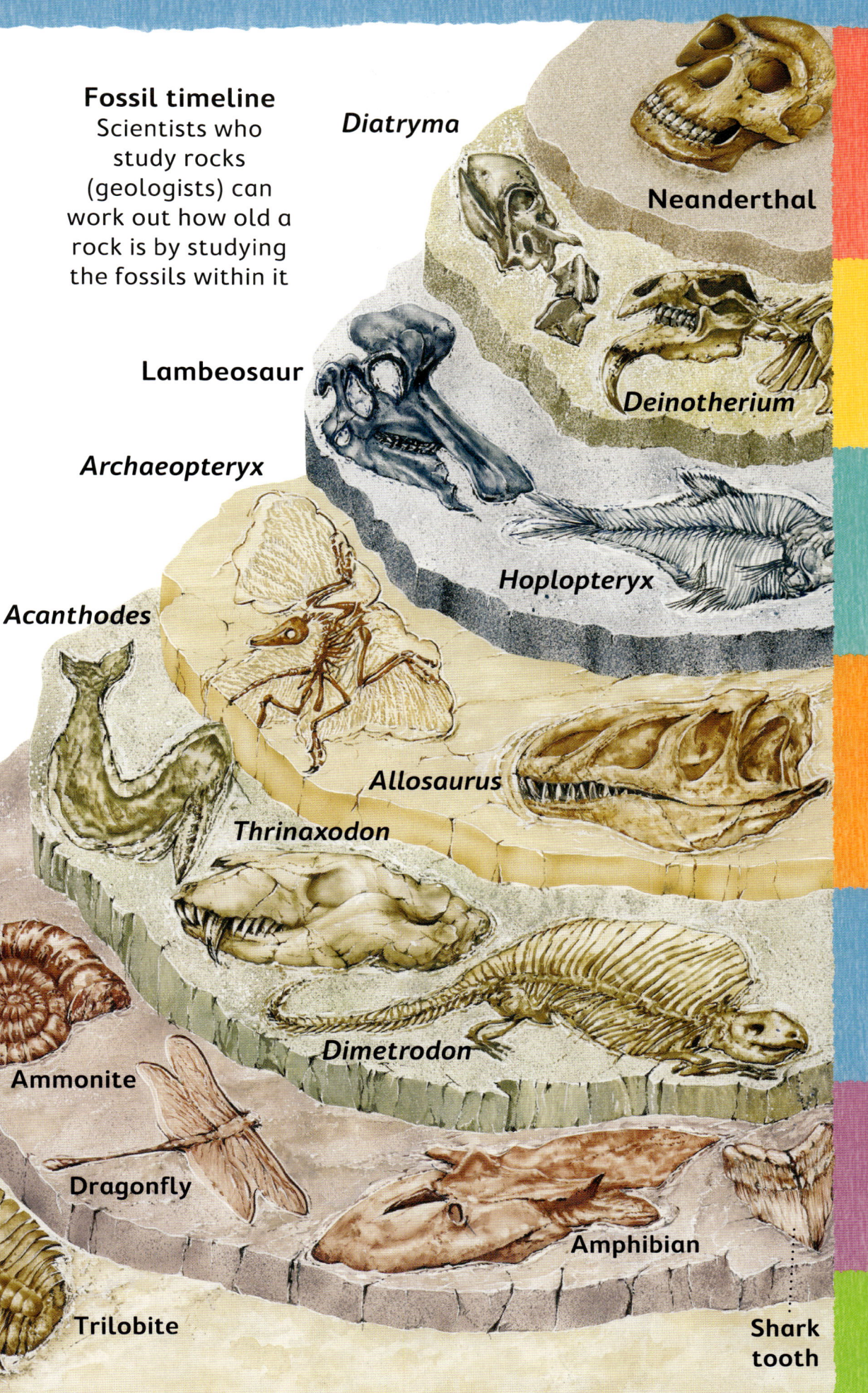

Fossil timeline
Scientists who study rocks (geologists) can work out how old a rock is by studying the fossils within it

Diatryma

Neanderthal

Lambeosaur

Archaeopteryx

Deinotherium

Acanthodes

Hoplopteryx

Allosaurus

Thrinaxodon

Ammonite

Dimetrodon

Dragonfly

Amphibian

Trilobite

Shark tooth

NEOGENE
23 million years ago (mya) onward

PALEOGENE
66–23 mya

CRETACEOUS
145–66 mya

JURASSIC
201–145 mya

PERMIAN-TRIASSIC
299–201 mya

DEVONIAN-CARBONIFEROUS
416–299 mya

CAMBRIAN-ORDOVICIAN
542–416 mya

Plant groups

There are more than 400,000 different kinds of plant. Similar plant types are put together in different groups

Mosses grow in shady, damp places and do not make seeds

Algae vary from tiny, single-celled organisms to huge fronds of seaweed

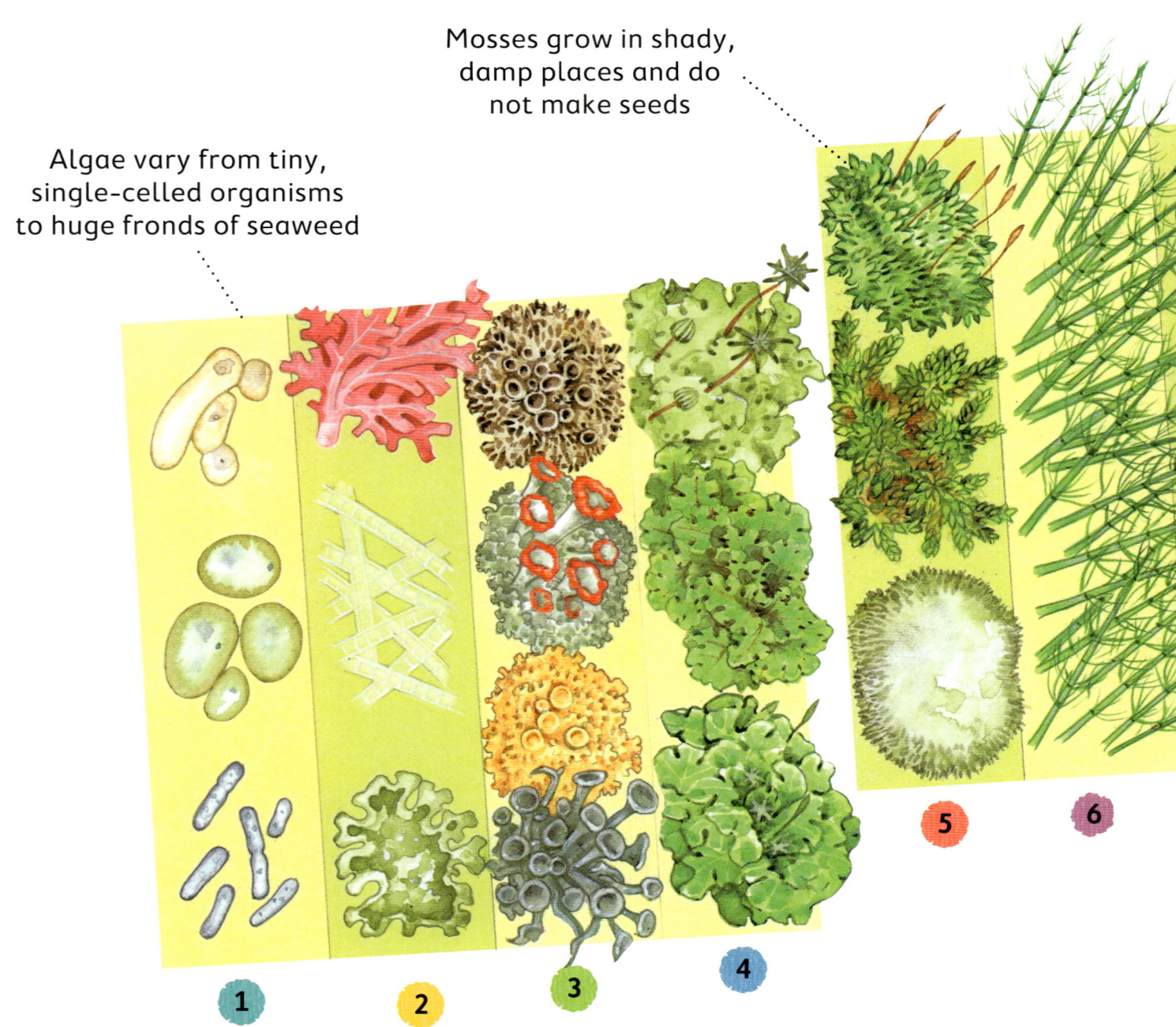

1 2 3 4 5 6

Cycads are mostly short, stubby palmlike trees

There are more than 250,000 species of flowering plants

1	Microscopic plants		8	Ferns
2	Algae and seaweeds		9	Cycads
3	Lichens		10	Conifers
4	Liverworts		11	Ginkgos
5	Mosses		12	Flowering plants
6	Horsetails		13	Broad-leaved trees and bushes, flowers, and herbs
7	Club mosses			

Parts of a plant

Most plants have the same basic form, with roots, stems, and leaves. Some plants, known as angiosperms, also grow flowers

Chrysanthemum

Flower head

Bud

Leaf

Stem

Roots

Anther

Filament

Stamen

Flowers

These colorful blooms attract insects and other pollinating animals

Hibiscus

Petal

Style

Ovary

Ovule

Sepal

70

Leaves

Plants have developed many different shapes of leaf in order to survive in different conditions

Cordate

Lanceolate

Palmate

Pinnate

Lobed

Needle

Pedate

Inside a leaf

The leaves of a plant are essential for its survival. It is where photosynthesis occurs

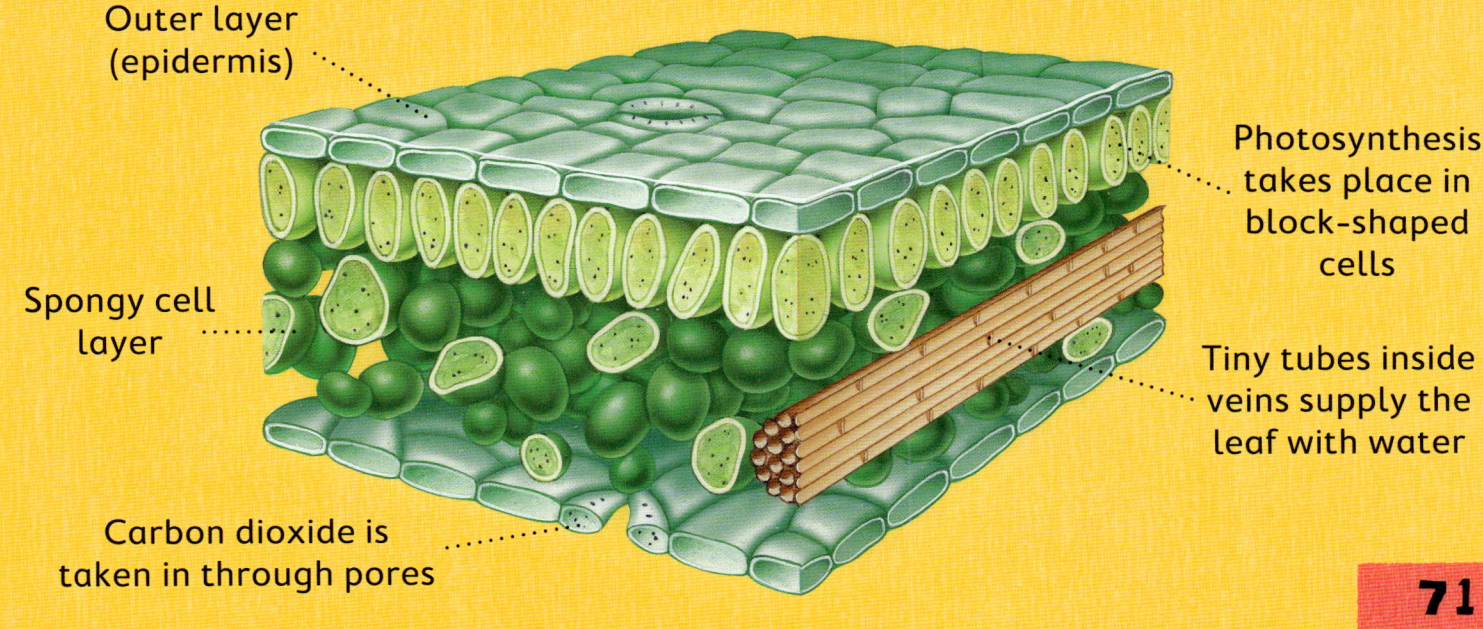

Outer layer (epidermis)

Photosynthesis takes place in block-shaped cells

Spongy cell layer

Tiny tubes inside veins supply the leaf with water

Carbon dioxide is taken in through pores

Photosynthesis

This is the process by which most plants use the energy from sunlight to turn carbon dioxide and water into sugar for food

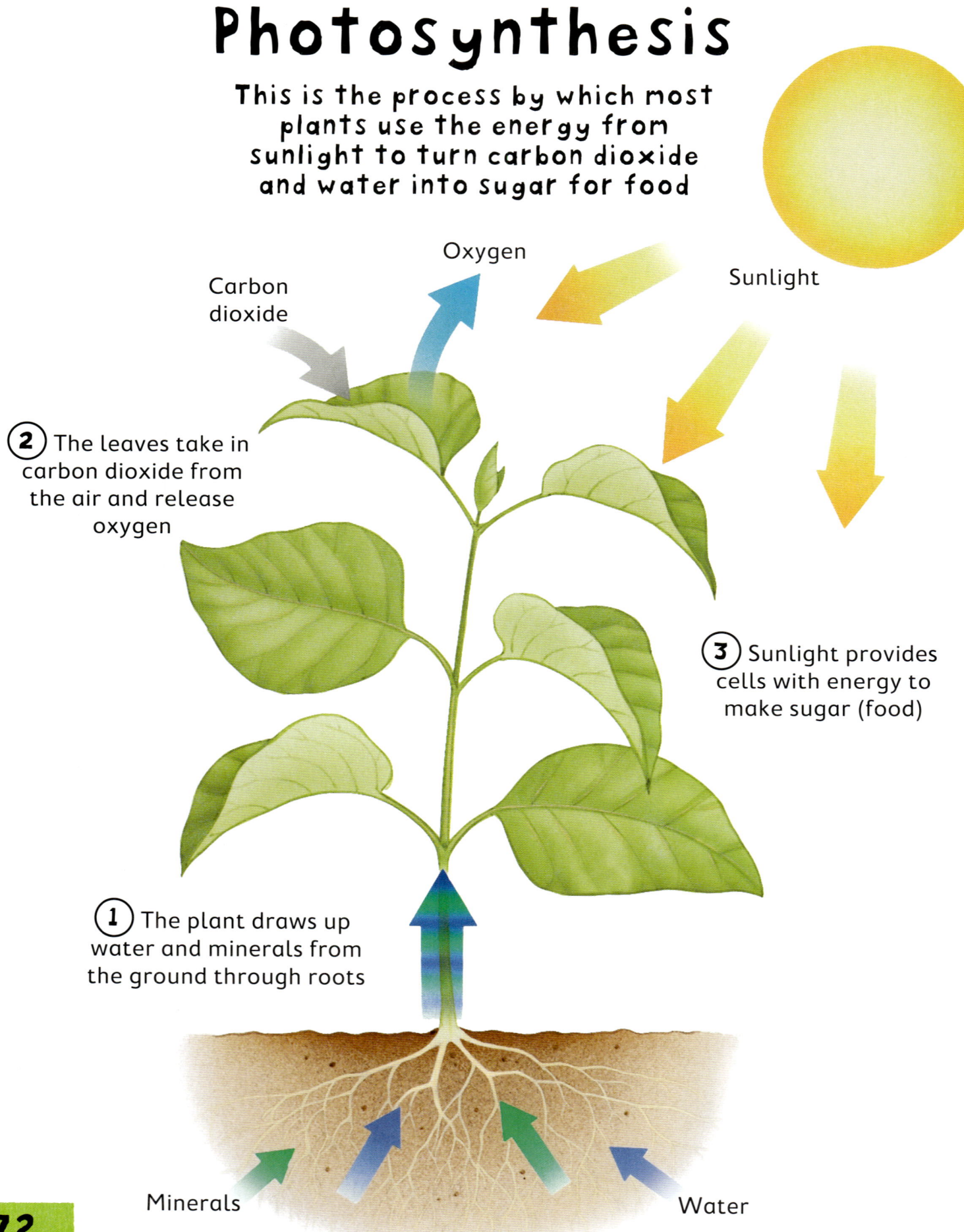

Oxygen

Carbon dioxide

Sunlight

(2) The leaves take in carbon dioxide from the air and release oxygen

(3) Sunlight provides cells with energy to make sugar (food)

(1) The plant draws up water and minerals from the ground through roots

Minerals

Water

Germination

When a seed settles in the soil, it takes in water, swells up, and opens so that the new plant can grow. This process is called germination

1 When a seed germinates, a root grows down from it and a green shoot grows up

2 The shoot grows cotyledons (seed leaves)

3 The stem and roots grow longer, and the plant begins to grow new leaves

Plant reproduction

For flowers to reproduce, insects and other animals, as well as wind and water, carry pollen from flower to flower

Insect pollination
Bees collect pollen on their back legs. As they land on flowers, the collected pollen is transferred to flowers of the same species

Wind pollination
Catkins are groups of flowers that hang down from a twig. Wind rocks the catkins and stamens, making the plant release its pollen

Fertilization
Pollen cell travels down the style toward the ovule

1. Stigma
2. Style
3. Filament
4. Anther
5. Ovule
6. Pollen

Self pollination
Some plants, such as this bee orchid, can pollinate themselves

Seeds and fruit
After pollination, the fertilized ovule develops into a seed

Mature cherry fruit contains the seed

Mosses

These are simple plants that have no flowers, true roots, or leaves. They reproduce from minute spores

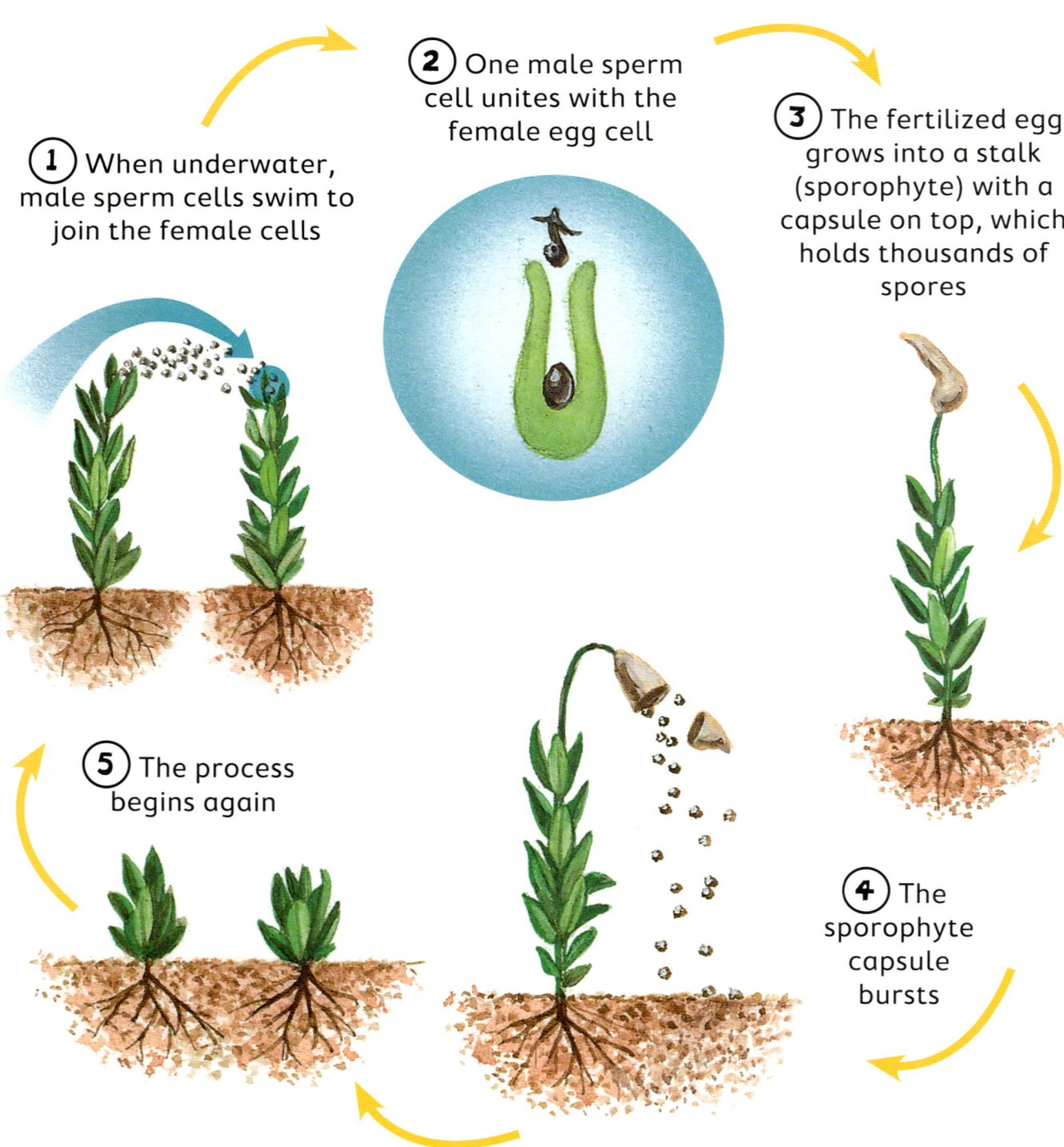

(1) When underwater, male sperm cells swim to join the female cells

(2) One male sperm cell unites with the female egg cell

(3) The fertilized egg grows into a stalk (sporophyte) with a capsule on top, which holds thousands of spores

(5) The process begins again

(4) The sporophyte capsule bursts

Carnivorous plants

Plants that trap insects and other
small organisms for food

Sundew

Digestive juices dissolve
insects that land on the
sticky tentacles

Pitcher plant

Slippery
surface

Venus flytrap

Nectar lures
the insect in

Jawlike
leaves

Trigger
hairs

Once the insect
lands, the "jaws"
clamp shut on
the victim

Insects caught
in thick liquid

Insect being
digested

Seaweeds

Types of plants, called algae, which grow in the sea

Knotted wrack

Sea lettuce

Bladder wrack

Oarweed

Dulse

Polysiphonia, a type of red seaweed, often grows on knotted wrack

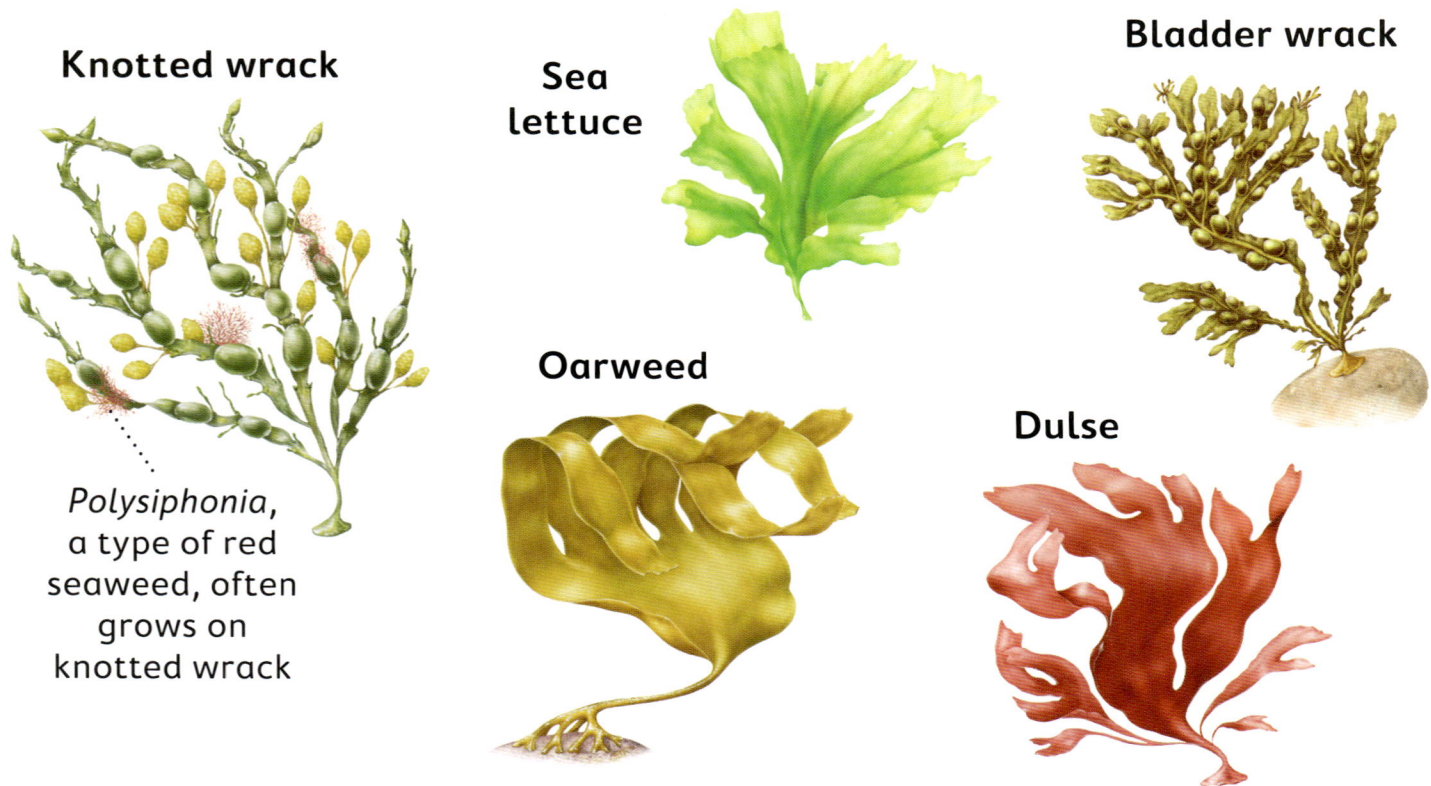

Zones
Different seaweeds grow in the different zones of a rocky seashore

Upper intertidal zone

Intertidal zone
The area above water at low tide and under the water at high tide

Mid intertidal zone

Lower intertidal zone

Grasses

Plants with long, narrow leaves and small, fibrous roots that often grow wild

Bamboo

Marram grass

Blue gramma grass

Red oat grass

Spinifex

Common cordgrass

Dallisgrass

Crested wheat grass

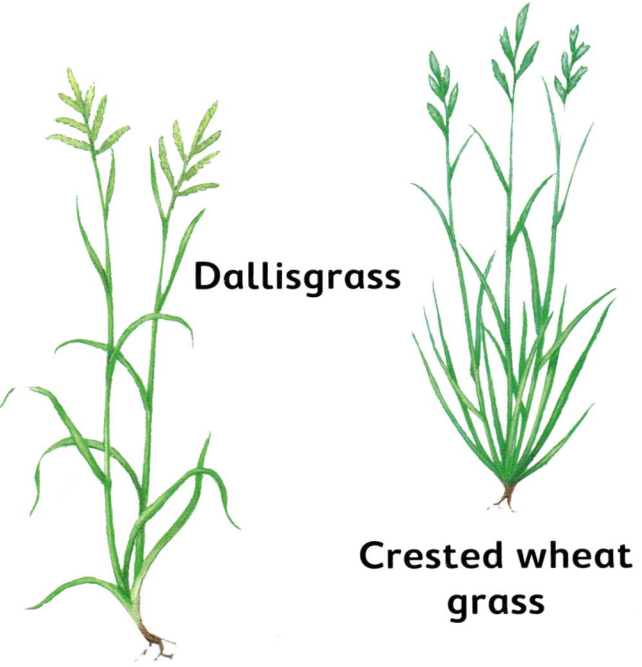

American prairie

The enormous prairies (grasslands) of North America cover over one million square miles

Herbs

These plants are often used in cooking and as medicines

Thyme

Mint

Dill

Rosemary

Sage

Chives

Basil

Parsley

Bay

Fennel

Shrubs

Small, treelike plants with woody stems and several branches, spreading out near to the ground

Buddleia

Cone-shaped flower head made up of tiny flowers

Hazel

Round, hairy leaves have pointed tips and green husks protect the nut

Bramble

Pink or white flowers with thorny stems. Blackberries are the shrub's fruit

Blackthorn

The fruit of this plant are dark, bitter-tasting sloes

Wildflowers

These plants grow freely in natural places
without being planted by people

Marsh
cinquefoil

Indian
balsam

Bee orchid

Pheasant's eye

Chamomile

Great willow
herb

Meadowsweet

Meadow
crane's bill

Bluebell

Yellow iris

Devil's-bit
scabious

Poppy

Coastal flowers

Flowers that grow near coasts, on sand dunes
and other damp grassy places

Sea pea

Sea aster

Silverweed

Thrift

Sea kale plant

**Scarlet
pimpernel**

Flower heads
have bright
scarlet petals

Evergreen trees

Trees that keep their leaves all year round

Giant
sequoia

Scots
pine

Douglas
fir

Corsican
pine

Norway
spruce

Juniper

Eucalyptus

Holly

Coast
redwood

Conifers

Most coniferous trees, like cedars
and pines, are evergreen and grow
their seeds in woody cones

84

Deciduous trees

Trees that drop their leaves every fall

Alder

Pendunculate oak

Beech

Common lime

Brazil nut tree

Mulberry

Ash

Horse chestnut

Silver birch

Aspen

English elm

Animal groups

Over 90 percent of all animals are invertebrates—
they have no backbone. Animals with a backbone
are called vertebrates

Invertebrates

This group includes creatures such as mollusks,
crustaceans, worms, arachnids, and insects.
Some have a hard shell, others are soft

Vertebrates

This group is very diverse and includes fish,
amphibians, reptiles, birds, and mammals

Fish
live in the waters of oceans, rivers, and lakes.
They breathe through flaps called gills

Amphibians
such as frogs, toads, salamanders, and newts
live partly in water and partly on land. Most
lay eggs in water

Reptiles
such as crocodiles, lizards, snakes, and turtles usually
live on land. Most baby reptiles hatch out of eggs

Birds
have feathers and wings, and most can fly. All birds
lay eggs that have a hard shell

Mammals
are warm-blooded animals usually with hair or fur.
Nearly all mammals give birth to live young, which
feed on their mother's milk

INVERTEBRATES

This animal group includes mollusks, crustaceans, worms, arachnids, and insects

Mollusks

The mollusk group includes gastropods, bivalves, and cephalopods. Most have a strong muscular foot and can live on land or in water

Land gastropods

Giant African land snail

Partula tree snail

Red triangle slug

Garden snail

Garden slug

Slugs have no shell

Marine gastropods

Cone shell

Sea slug

Limpet

Painted topshell

Dog whelk

Periwinkle

Bivalves

Common cockle

Razor clam

Two shells joined by a strong hinge ·······

Mussel

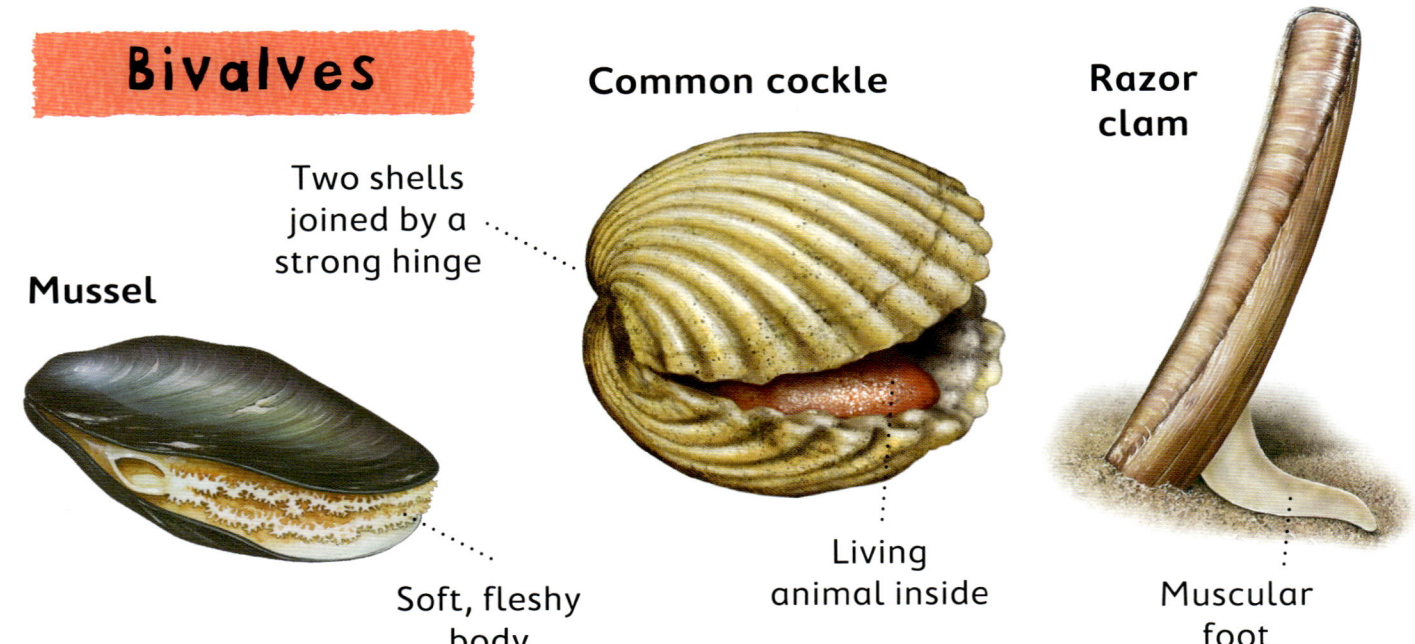

Living animal inside

Soft, fleshy body

Muscular foot

Cephalopods

Bobtail squid

Cuttlefish

Blue-ringed octopus

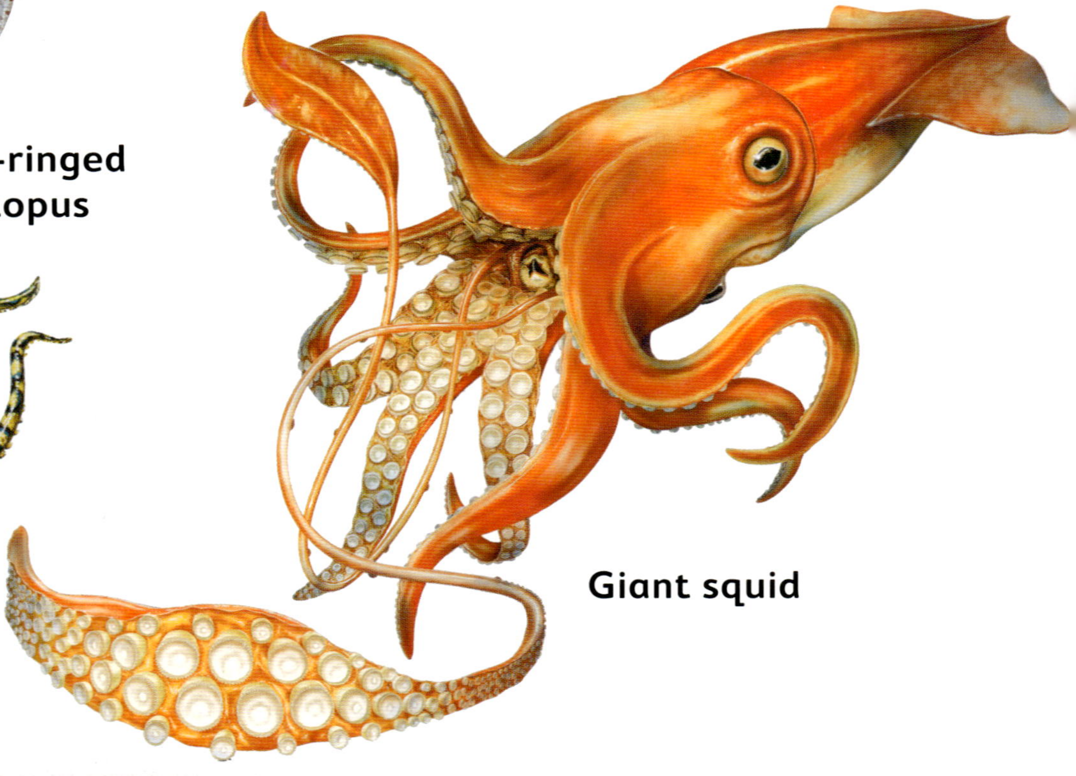

Giant squid

Crustaceans

This group of invertebrates is mostly marine.
All have a hard outer-body casing

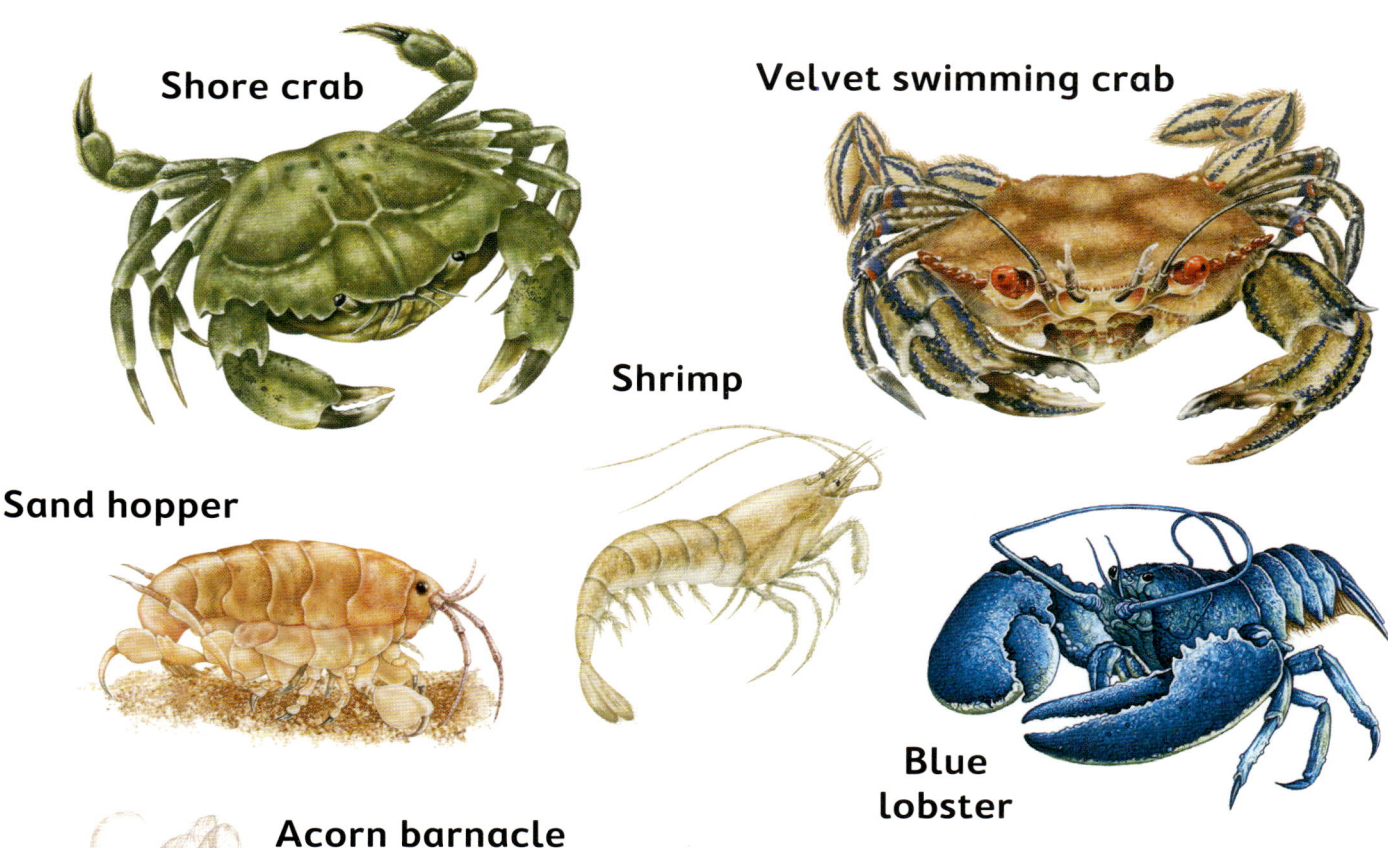

Shore crab

Velvet swimming crab

Shrimp

Sand hopper

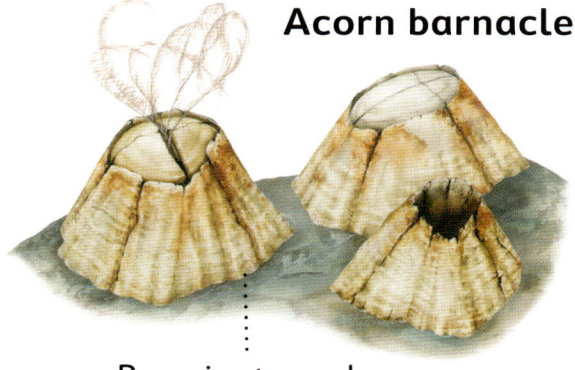

Blue lobster

Acorn barnacle

Base is strongly
attached to rocks

Pill bug

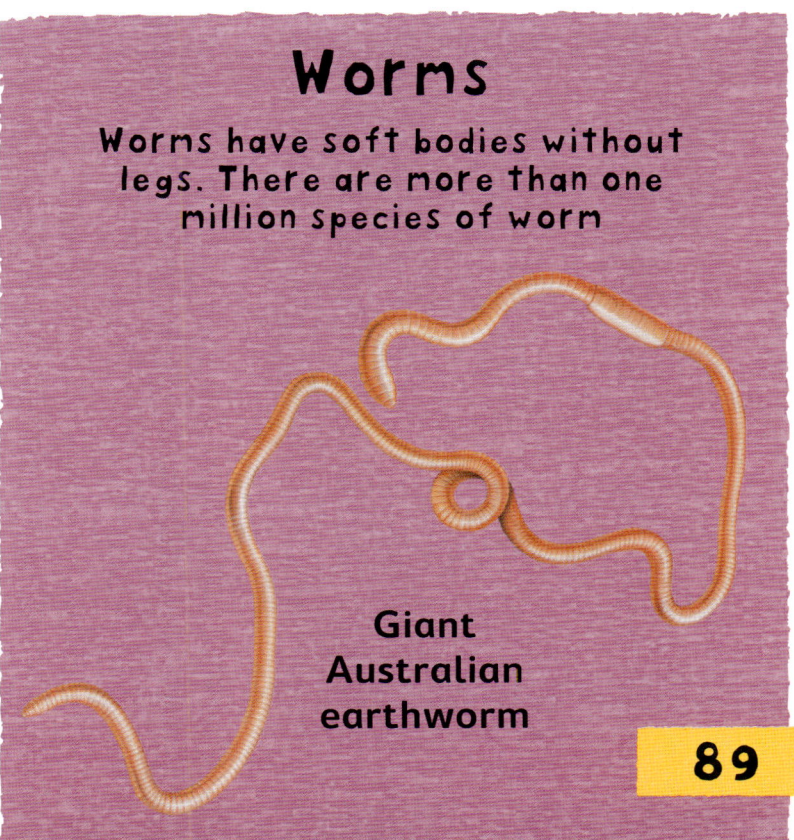

Worms

Worms have soft bodies without
legs. There are more than one
million species of worm

**Giant
Australian
earthworm**

Arachnids

Spiders, scorpions, ticks, and mites belong to a group of animals called arachnids. All members of this invertebrate group have eight legs. Almost all types live on land and hunt other animals to eat

Spiders

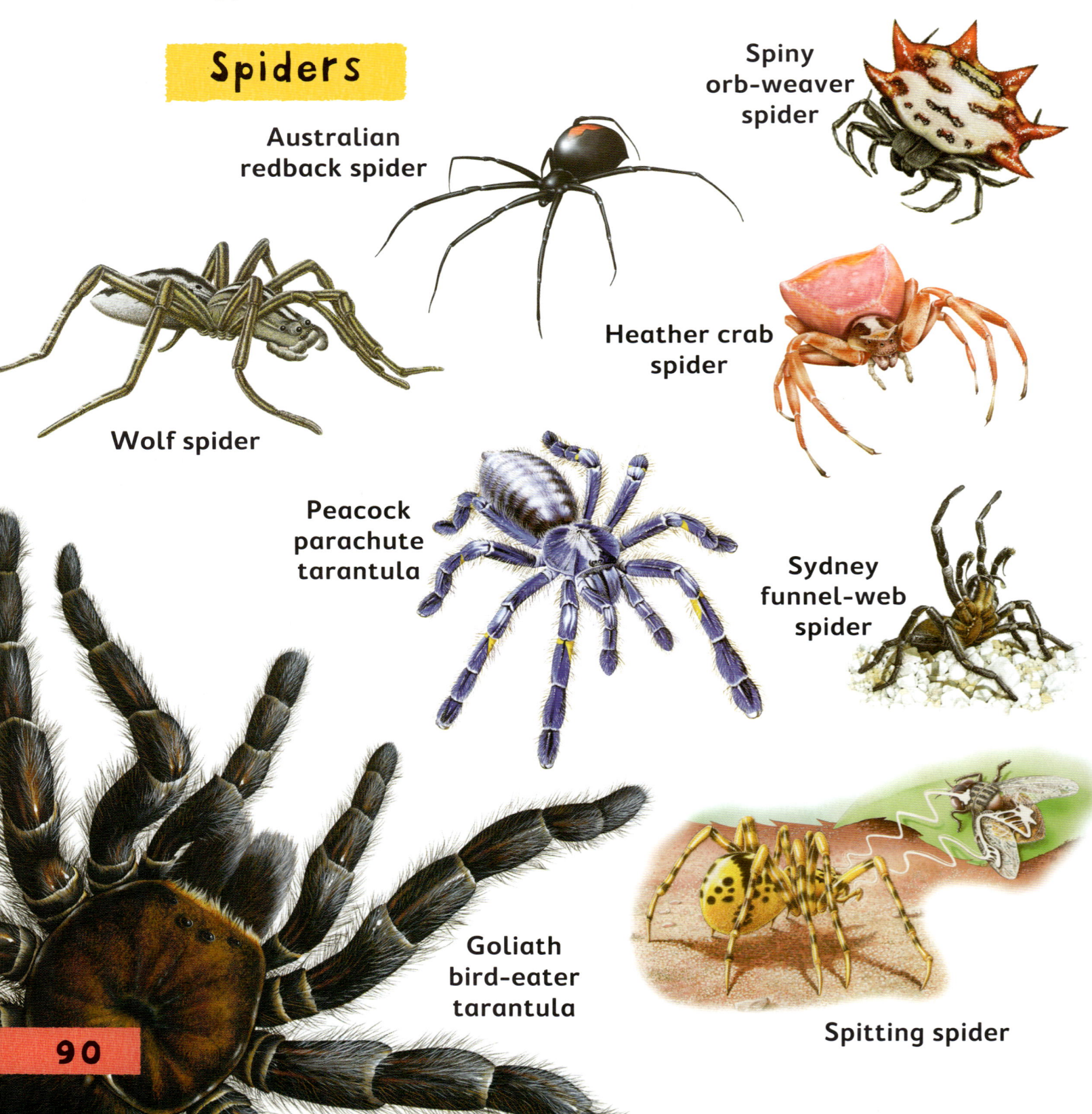

Spiny orb-weaver spider

Australian redback spider

Heather crab spider

Wolf spider

Peacock parachute tarantula

Sydney funnel-web spider

Goliath bird-eater tarantula

Spitting spider

House spider

Ladybug spiders

Female

Male

Mexican red-kneed tarantula

Scorpions and other arachnids

Common yellow scorpion

Death stalker scorpion

Harvestman

Emperor scorpion

Tick

Velvet mite

Body is about the size of a grain of rice

Insects

All insects have six legs and an outer body casing called an exoskeleton. Their bodies are divided into three parts — the head, thorax (middle section), and abdomen (rear section)

True flies

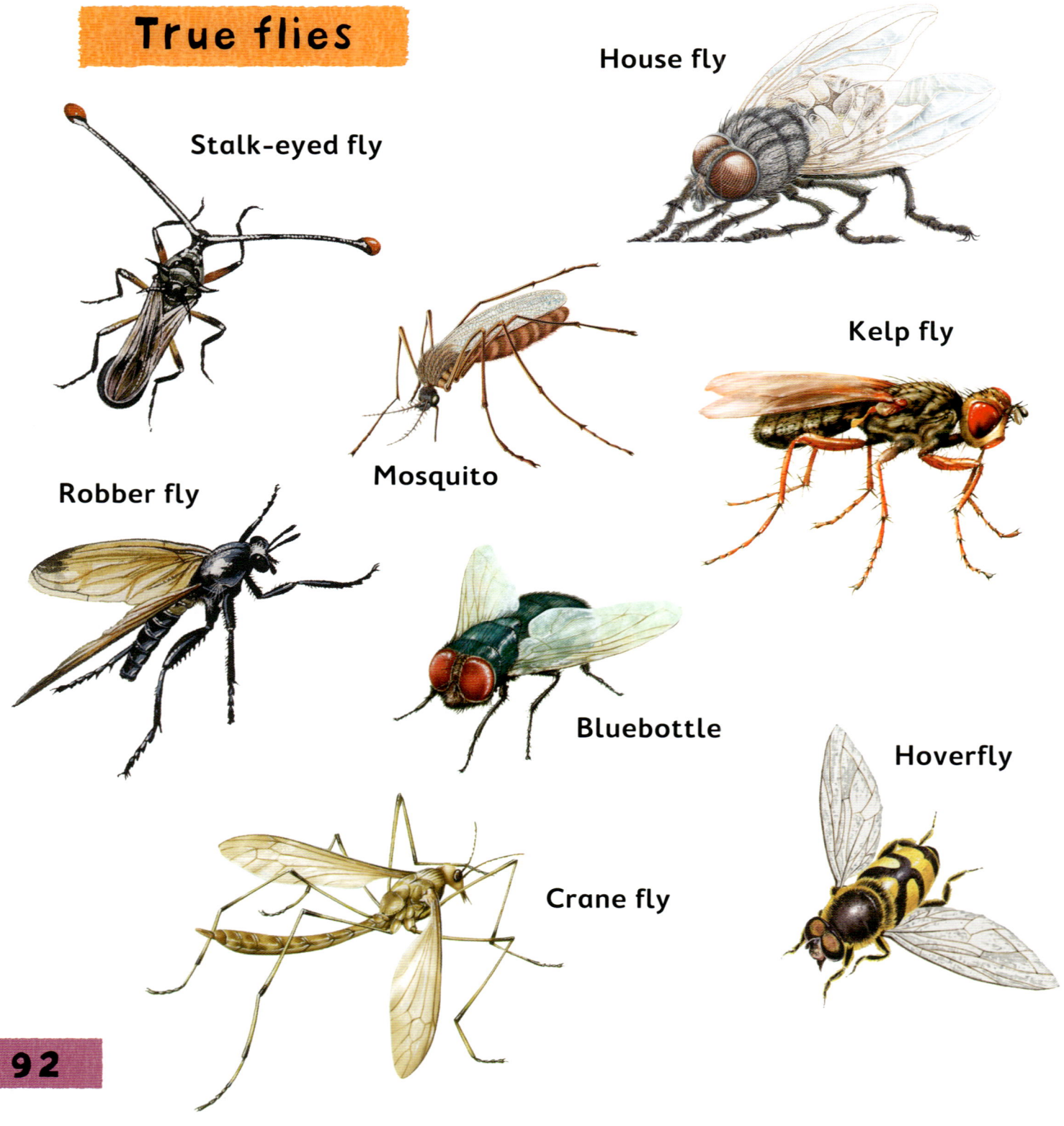

Stalk-eyed fly

House fly

Mosquito

Kelp fly

Robber fly

Bluebottle

Hoverfly

Crane fly

Dragonflies and damselflies

Dragonfly

Wings open at rest

Wings closed at rest

Damselfly

Crickets and grasshoppers

Grasshopper

American grasshopper

Giant green slantface grasshopper

Bush cricket

Cave cricket

Mantids, cockroaches, and termites

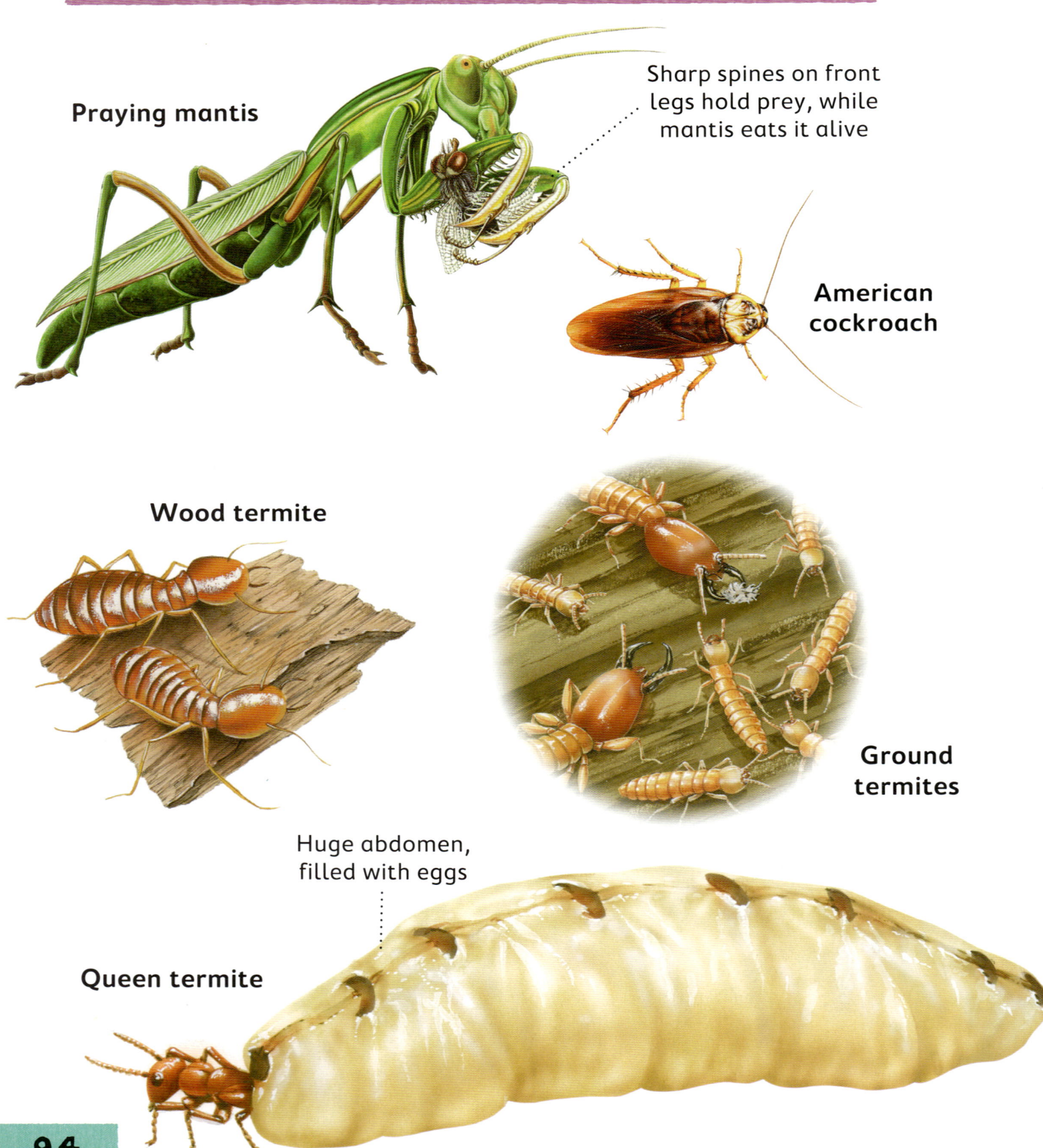

Praying mantis

Sharp spines on front legs hold prey, while mantis eats it alive

American cockroach

Wood termite

Ground termites

Huge abdomen, filled with eggs

Queen termite

Beetles

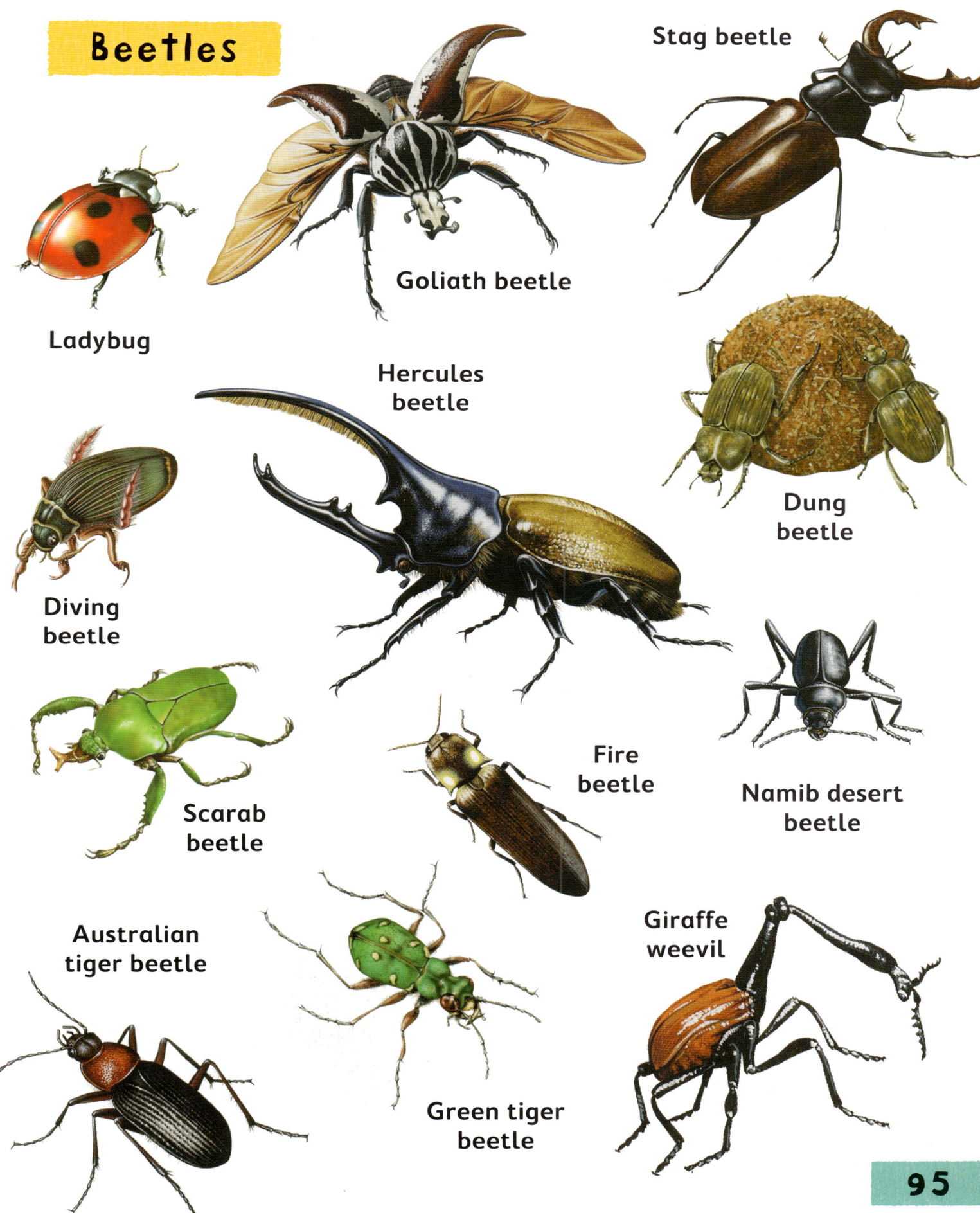

Stag beetle

Ladybug

Goliath beetle

Hercules
beetle

Dung
beetle

Diving
beetle

Scarab
beetle

Fire
beetle

Namib desert
beetle

Australian
tiger beetle

Giraffe
weevil

Green tiger
beetle

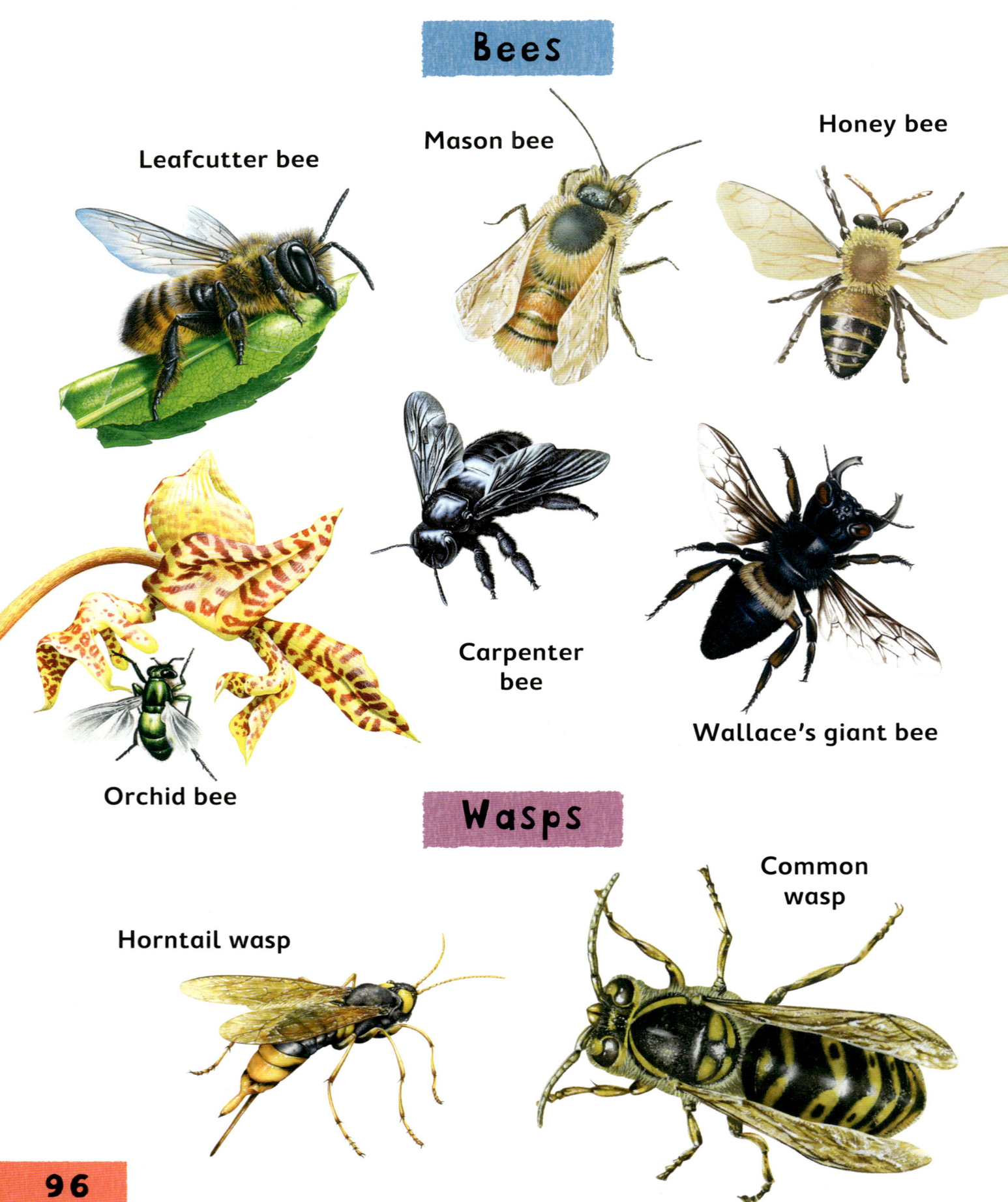

Bees

Leafcutter bee

Mason bee

Honey bee

Carpenter bee

Wallace's giant bee

Orchid bee

Wasps

Common wasp

Horntail wasp

Hornet

Gall wasp

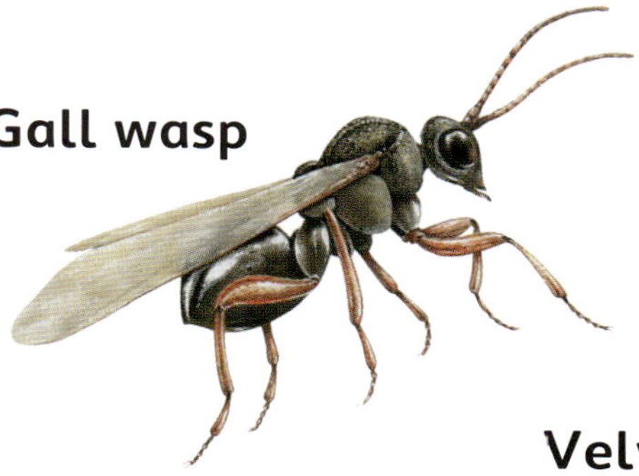

Velvet ant

A type of hairy wasp ....

Fairy wasp

Ichneumon wasp

Wasp nest

A majority of wasps live alone, but some can live in huge colonies

1 Eggs laid by queen

2 Cells made from paper

3 Wasps adding paper around the outside of the nest

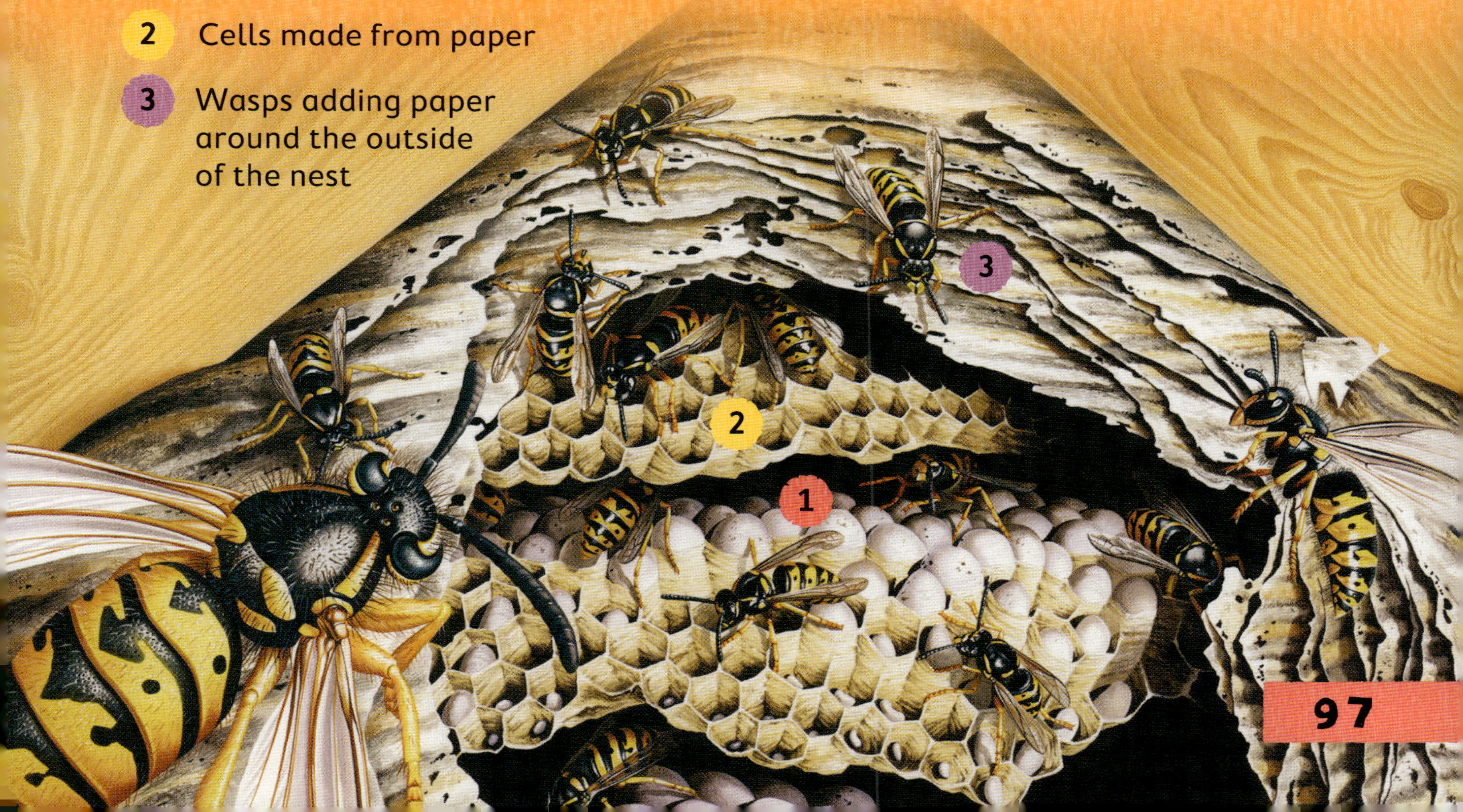

Ants

Harvester ant

Fire ant

Army ant

Carpenter ant

Bullet ant

Leafcutter ant

Weaver ants

Ant's nest

Ants are social insects living in huge colonies, often housing thousands of ants

1. Queen ant
2. Eggs
3. Larvae
4. Winged males and young queens

98

Butterflies

Orange tip butterfly

Adonis blue butterfly

Holly blue butterfly

Comma butterfly

Brimstone butterfly

Brown argus butterfly

Red admiral butterfly

Clouded yellow butterfly

Purple emperor butterfly

Large white butterfly

Green hairstreak butterfly

Small tortoiseshell butterfly

Purple hairstreak butterfly

Large heath butterfly

Moths

Privet
hawk-moth

Six-spot
burnet
moth

Feathered
thorn moth

Elephant
hawk-moth

Moon
moth

Swallow-tailed
moth

Garden carpet
moth

Cinnabar
moth

Common
emerald moth

**Angle
shades moth**

**Lime
hawk-moth**

**Scarlet
tiger moth**

**Scalloped
oak moth**

Butterfly and moth life cycle

Both butterflies and moths change in form during
their life cycle. This is called metamorphosis

(2) The egg hatches
into a tiny larva
(caterpillar), which
eats and eats

(1) Egg laid by a
fertilized adult
female butterfly
or moth

(3) The caterpillar
attaches itself to a
twig and forms a
hard outer shell
(pupa)

**Peacock
butterfly
life cycle**

(4) Inside the
pupa, the
caterpillar
changes into a
butterfly or moth,
and emerges as a
fully grown adult

(5) Adults have a
short life span. They
will fly, mate, and
reproduce before
they die

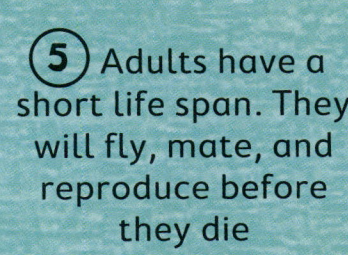

VERTEBRATES

These animals all have a backbone, or spine. The group includes fish, amphibians, reptiles, birds, and mammals

Bony fish

Fish are the largest group of animals with backbones — there are almost 21,000 species of fish

Freshwater fish

Brown trout

Minnow

Roach

Common carp

Marine fish

Salmon
This fish starts out living in freshwater, then lives in salty seawater before returning to freshwater to breed

Flatfish

Flying fish

Cod

Large side fins allow them to glide over the waves

Antarctic icefish

Atlantic wolffish

Coral reef fish

Moray eel

Lionfish

Queen angelfish

Puffer fish
When threatened, the puffer fish swallows large amounts of water, making its body swell up and its spines stand on end

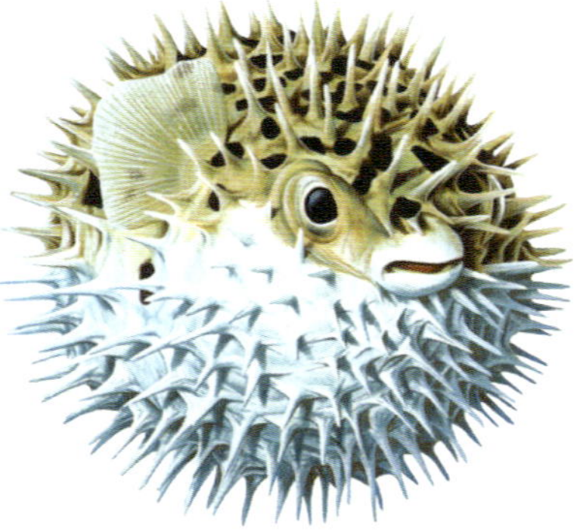

Clown fish

Leafy sea dragon

Deep sea fish

Black swallower

Spookfish

Viperfish

Deep-sea angler

Tassel-chinned angler

Dragonfish

Long rod anglerfish

Light producing spots along its body

Fangtooth

Snailfish

Tripod fish

Cartilaginous fish

Three groups of fish — sharks, skates and rays, and chimeras — have a skeleton made of cartilage, not bone

Sharks

Black-tip reef shark

Cookiecutter shark

Shortfin mako shark

Bramble shark

Bonnethead shark

Greenland shark

Lemon shark

Weasel shark

White-tip reef shark

Goblin shark

Basking shark

Great white shark

Bull shark

Shark camouflage

Many sharks blend into their environment with their colors and patterns. This can be for defense or to help the shark surprise its prey

Zebra shark

Stripes turn to spots as the shark matures

Tassels around the mouth disguise its shape

Mottled pattern

Angel shark

Wobbegong

107

Shark senses
Sharks have extraordinary ways of finding their prey

Crocodile shark

Eyesight
Deepwater sharks have large eyes to allow them to pick up as much light as possible in the murky depths

Smell
Smell is the most important shark sense. About two thirds of a shark's brain deals with smell messages

Paired nostrils

Sand tiger shark

Black-tip reef shark

Lateral line

Lateral line
Sensitive pits along the side of the body contain nerve endings that detect vibrations and changes of pressure in the water

Electric sense
Tiny pores in the skin help sharks sense the electrical signals given off by their prey

Skin pores called ampullae of Lorenzini are mainly on the shark's head and under the snout

Blue shark

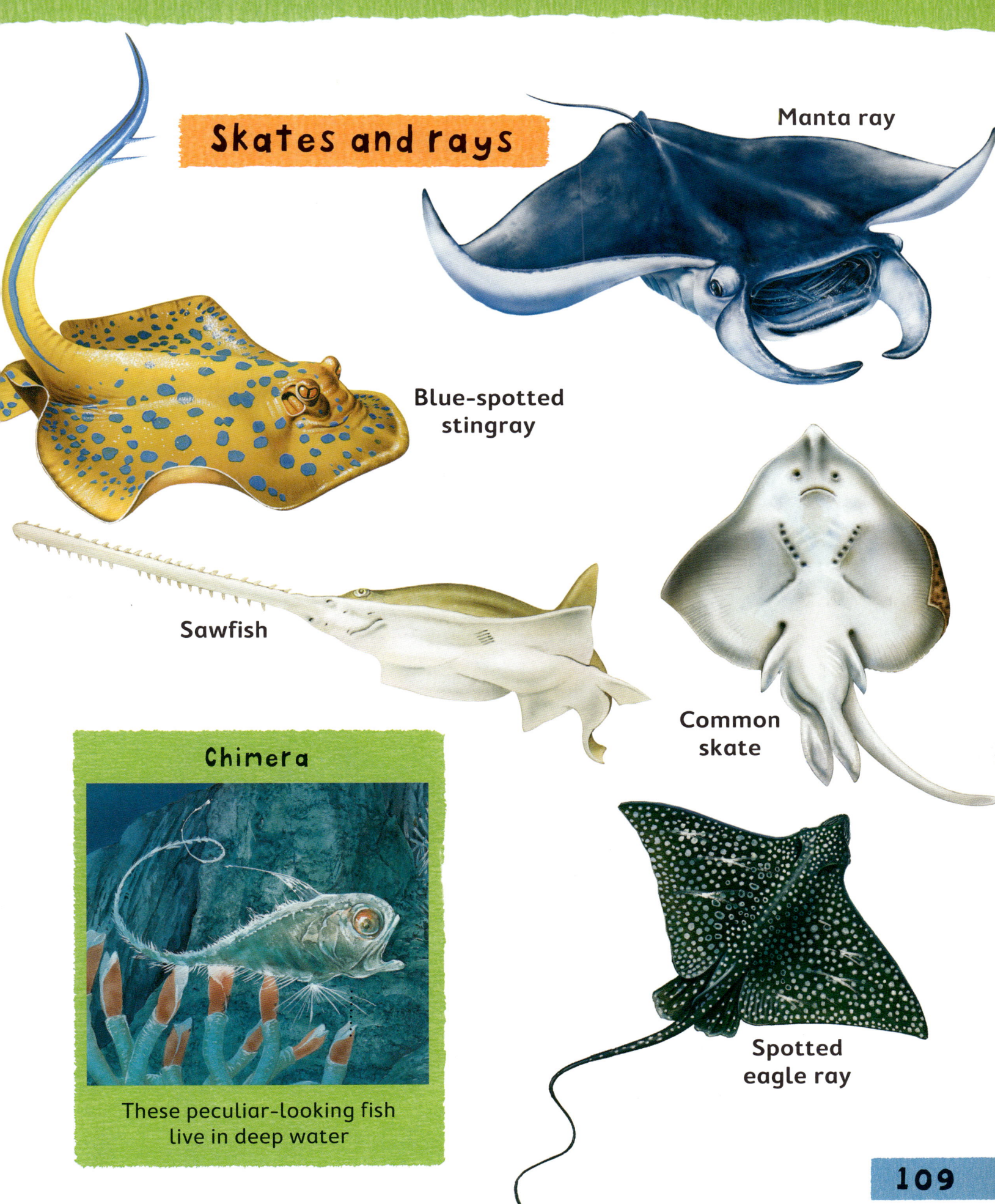

Skates and rays

Manta ray

Blue-spotted stingray

Sawfish

Common skate

Chimera

These peculiar-looking fish live in deep water

Spotted eagle ray

Amphibians

This animal group can live on land and in water,
and includes frogs, toads, newts, and salamanders

Frogs

Green poison dart frog

Common frog
Frogs tend to have webbed feet, long back legs, smooth skin, and live in or near water

American bullfrog

Large eardrum

Malaysian horned frog

Goliath frog

Strawberry poison dart frog

Red-eyed tree frogs

Hamilton's frog

Toads

Common toad

Toads have warty skin and live mainly on land. They have little or no webbing between their toes

Spadefoot toad

Leaflitter toad

Fire-bellied toad

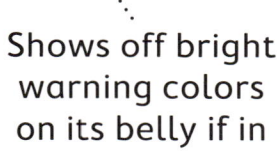

Shows off bright warning colors on its belly if in danger

Cane toad

Natterjack toad

Amphibian reproduction

Most amphibians hatch from eggs and grow up in freshwater habitats such as ponds. They move onto land as adults but return to water to breed

Fertilization
After the female has released her eggs, the male fertilizes them

Life cycle
Most amphibians change from aquatic water larvae that breathe using gills, to land-dwelling adults that use lungs to breathe

Male

Female

Eggs

Adult newt

Adult toad

Toad spawn

Frogspawn

1 Frogspawn (eggs) float on top of fresh water

2 Tadpoles hatch from the eggs

3 Tadpoles grow legs and change into froglets

4 A froglet loses its tail and grows into an adult frog

Salamanders and newts

Axolotl

Mudpuppy salamander

Rough-skinned newt

Californian newt

Hellbender salamander

Tiger salamander

Fire salamander

Great crested newt

Common newt

Eastern newt

Reptiles

These animals are cold-blooded — they have the same body temperature as their surroundings, and most lay eggs. Most reptiles live on land, although some live in water

Crocodiles and gharials

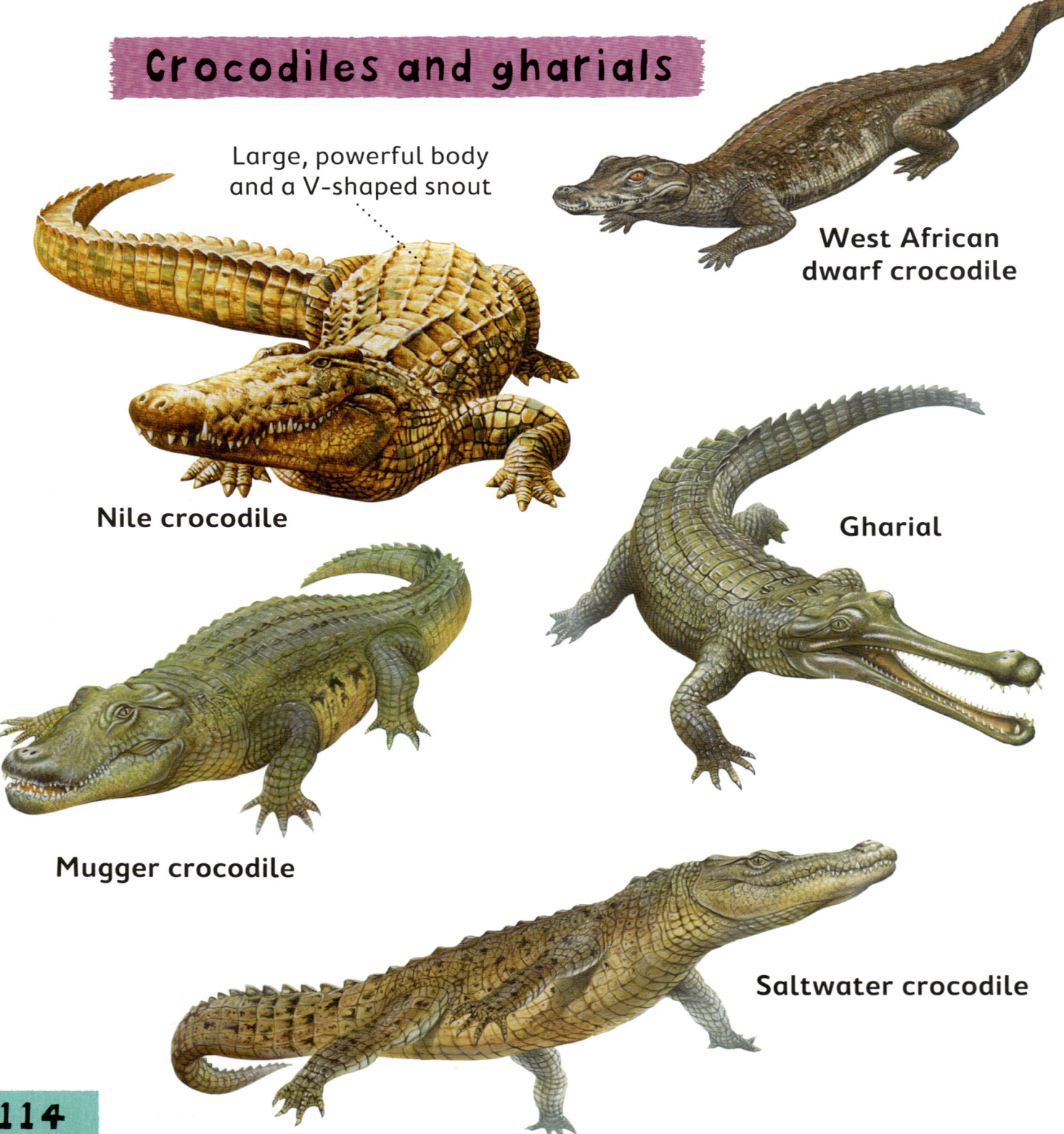

Large, powerful body and a V-shaped snout

West African dwarf crocodile

Nile crocodile

Gharial

Mugger crocodile

Saltwater crocodile

Alligators and caimans

Chinese alligator

American alligator

Wide,
U-shaped
snout

Common caiman

Spectacled caiman

Komodo dragon

Lizards

Gila monster

Anole lizard

This lizard has a
poisonous bite

Continued > 115

Banded iguana

Boyd's forest dragon

Gecko

Chameleon

Crested water dragon

Agama lizard

Common lizard

Frilled lizard

Shingleback lizard

Six-lined racerunner

Chuckwalla lizard

Venomous snakes

Fangs

Some snakes have long, sharp teeth to inject a toxic substance called venom into their prey

Rattlesnake

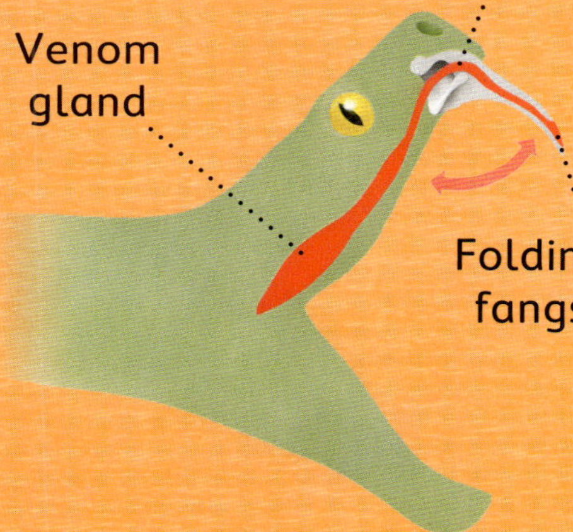

Tube for injecting venom

Venom gland

Folding fangs

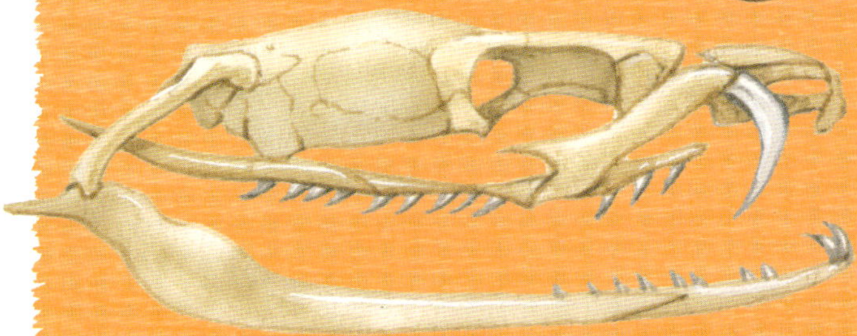

Front-fanged snakes
Fangs are hollow and venom runs down the middle of the teeth

Rear-fanged snakes
Fangs are positioned near the back of the mouth. Venom runs down a groove in the back of the teeth

Taipan

Common krait

Continued >

Leaf-nosed snake

King cobra

Puff adder

Boomslang

Vine snake

Adder

Yellow-bellied sea snake

Constricting snakes

Death by constrictor

These snakes squeeze their prey to death by wrapping their strong coils around it

(1) The snake holds its prey in its teeth and squeezes it to death in its strong coils

(2) When the animal is dead, the snake opens its mouth very wide to swallow its meal

(3) The prey forms a bulge in the snake's body while it is being digested. It may take days, or even weeks, to be fully digested

Reticulated python

Emerald tree boa

Anaconda

Indian python

Land chelonians

Leopard tortoise

Desert tortoise

Galapagos giant tortoise

Marine and freshwater chelonians

Green turtle

Flat, streamlined shell

Alligator snapping turtle

Waits for prey at the bottom of muddy rivers

Matamata turtle

Indian soft shell turtle

Olive Ridley turtle

Leatherback turtle

Hawksbill turtle

Southern river terrapin

Birds

These animals are warm-blooded, have backbones, and lay eggs. Their feathers keep them warm and help most birds to fly

Perching birds

Blue bird of paradise

Goldfinch

Australian king parrot

Chiffchaff

Feet grip a perch tightly

Fieldfare

Wren

Bullfinch

Brambling

Pied wagtail

Carrion crow

Nuthatch

Blackbird

Splendid fairy wren

Treecreeper

American robin

Mistle thrush

Magpie

Manakin

Goldcrest

Jay

Types of feather

Feathers are made of keratin—the same material as our hair and nails

Tail feather
Used to control flight

Down feather
Traps warm air next to the body

Contour
Covers the body, making it streamlined

Flight feather
Shape helps to lift the bird in the air as well as twist and turn in flight

Rain forest and woodland birds

Great tit

Crimson topaz
hummingbird

Song
thrush

Lyrebird

Garden
warbler

Hornbill

Potoo

Trogon

Cuckoo

Quetzal

Hoatzin

Nightjar

Jacamar

Lesser spotted woodpecker

Toco toucan

Feet and talons

Birds have different feet and claws, depending on where they live and what they eat

Claws for clinging to tree trunks

Woodpecker

Two big, strong toes for running fast

Ostrich

Strong feet with long claws to scratch for food

Pheasant

Sharp, curved talons to catch prey

Osprey

Webs between toes to help with swimming

Duck

125

Game birds

Sandgrouse

Ptarmigan

Partridge

Pheasant

Peacock

"Eye" pattern can be seen when the bird fans out its tail

Flightless birds

Kakapo

Emu

Cassowary

Rhea

Bennet's cassowary

Kiwi

Ostrich

Extinct flightless birds
These birds have died out forever

Great auk

Dodo

Waders

Dunlin

Avocet

Turnstone

Purple
sandpiper

African
jacana

Curlew

Redshank

Bar-tailed
godwit

Ringed
plover

Lapwing

Oystercatcher

Water birds

Gannet

Tufted
duck

Common
gull

Puffin

Common
tern

Guillemot

Shelduck

Canada
goose

Moorhen

Whooper
swan

Mallard

Razorbill

Teal

Albatross

Penguins that live in icy conditions

Macaroni

Emperor

Adélie

Largest penguin species, reaching up to 4 feet in height

Rockhopper

King

Gentoo

Chinstrap

Royal

Penguins that live in warm conditions

Humboldt

Yellow-eyed

Galapagos

Little

Magellanic

Snares
Island

Smallest penguin
species, reaching just
14 inches in height

African

Fjordland

Erect-crested

Birds of prey

Gyrfalcon

Peregrine
falcon

Common
black hawk

Kestrel

Red-tailed
hawk

Eurasian
sparrow hawk

Golden eagle

Harpy eagle

Swallow-tailed
kite

White-tailed
eagle

Philippine
eagle

Boobook
owl

Brown
fish owl

Scops owl

Eagle owl

Tawny owl

Great horned owl

Snowy
owl

134

Little owl

Barn owl

Elf owl

Vultures

Not all birds of prey hunt live prey— some eat dead or rotting meat, and are called scavengers

Lappet-faced vulture

American black vulture

King vulture

Egyptian vulture

Long-billed vulture

135

Nests, eggs, and chicks

Most birds make nests in which to lay their eggs and keep them safe, but not all nests are the same

Cave swiftlet

Weaver bird

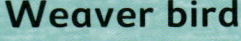

(1) The male weaver bird twists strips of leaves around a twig

(2) Then he makes the roof and the entrance

(3) When finished, the long entrance helps to provide a safe shelter for the eggs

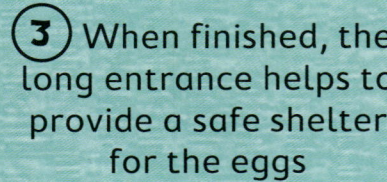

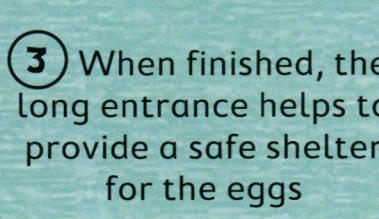

Nest made of the bird's saliva, or spit, which sets hard, like cement

Bald eagle
Makes the biggest nest of any bird

Mallee fowl
This bird makes a mound of rotting leaves and twigs, covered with sand, to keep its eggs warm

Egg colors and patterns

Jacana

Hedge sparrow

Cetti's warbler

Quail

Blue jay

Common snipe

Auk

Scarlet tanager

Catbird

House wren

Peregrine falcon chick

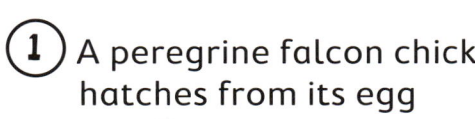

① A peregrine falcon chick hatches from its egg

② At two days old, the chick is fluffy and cheeps for food

③ At 28 days old, the young bird is growing its plumage (adult feathers) and the old, fluffy down feathers are falling out

④ Juvenile (young) peregrines have brown feathers, and the face markings are paler than in older birds

Mammals

A group of warm-blooded animals with a bony skeleton. There are three main groups of mammals: marsupials (pouched mammals), monotremes (egg-laying mammals), and placental mammals, which give birth to well-developed young. Most mammals are placental mammals, including humans

Marsupials

Wallaby

Lesser bilby
This marsupial is now extinct

Kangaroo

Joey (young kangaroo) develops inside mother's pouch

Opossum

Tree kangaroo

Koala

138

Monotremes

This is the only group of egg-laying mammals

Duck-billed platypus

Echidna
The egg is kept in a pouch in the stomach

Mongooses

Kusimanse mongoose

Meerkat

Mustelids

Otter

Polecat

Skunk

Stoat

Weasel

Badger

Bats

Brown long-eared bat

Bats are the only mammals that can fly

False vampire bat

Fruit bat
Also called flying fox

Noctule bat

Horseshoe bat

Vampire bat

Flying fox

Pipistrelle bat

Echolocation

Some bats use this special sense to find their way in the darkness and to catch prey

① Bat produces high-pitched squeaks

② When the sound waves hit the moth, they bounce back to the bat

Moth

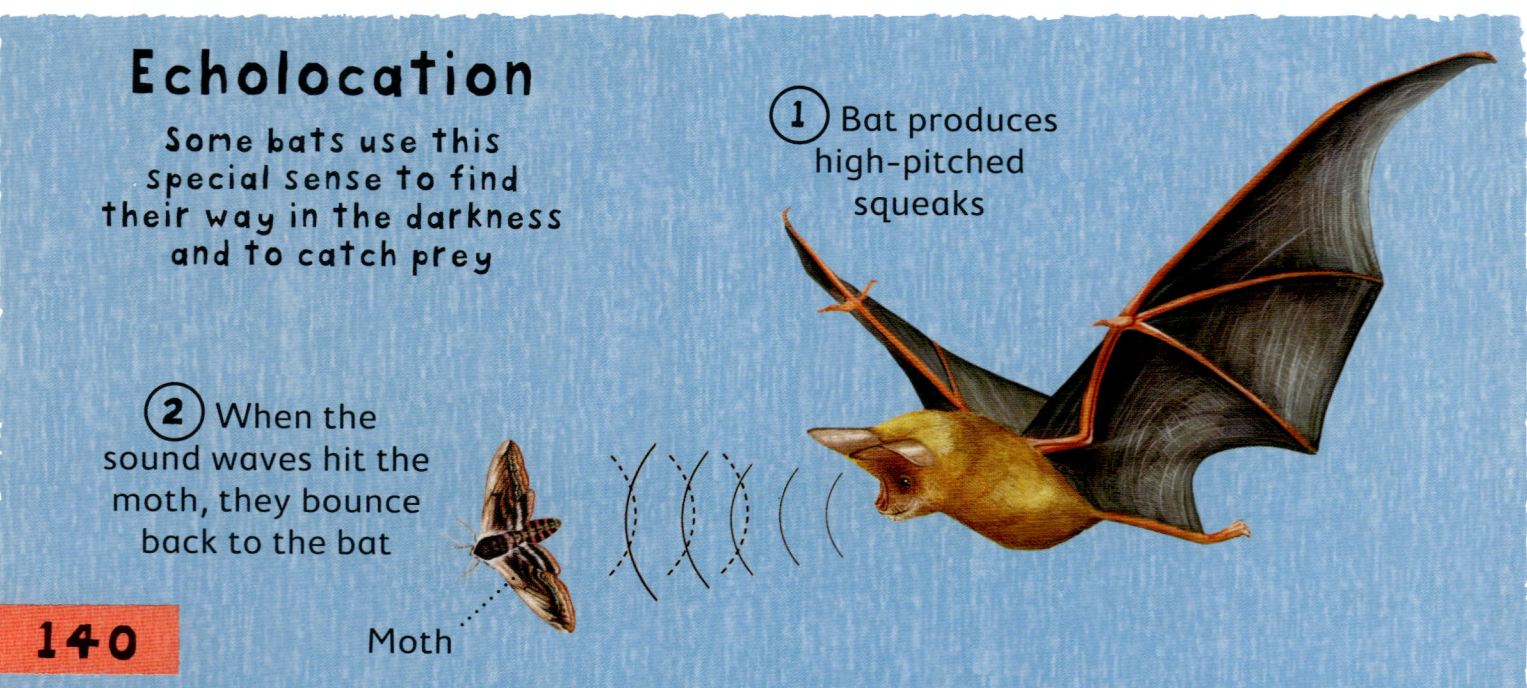

Moles, hedgehogs, and shrews

Hedgehog

Mole

Water shrew

These mammals are also known as insectivores, meaning insect-eaters

Cuban solenodon

Pygmy shrew

Rabbits and hares

Mountain hare

Coat is brown in summer, white in winter

Brown hare

Ears are similar length to head

Warrens
Rabbits dig these homes underground

Baby rabbits are called kits. They are born in a nest inside the warren

Long ears with black tips (but shorter than a hare's ears)

Rabbit

Rodents

Yellow-necked mouse

Capybara
The largest rodent
in the world

Harvest mouse

Field vole

Bank vole

Brown rat

Sharp quills

Red squirrel

Porcupine

Dormouse

Gray squirrel

Agouti

Bears

American black bear

Giant panda and cub

Asiatic black bear

Spectacled bear

Sloth bear and cubs

Polar bear

Sun bear
The smallest bear in the world

Brown bear

Prosimians

Slow loris

Lesser bush baby

Most prosimians live in trees and are nocturnal

Tarsier

Slender loris

Long, thin middle finger to find insect grubs under bark

Aye-aye

Ruffed lemur

Ring-tailed lemur

Monkeys

Black-handed spider monkey

Golden lion tamarin

Silvered langur monkey

The baby's bright orange coat changes to gray at about three months old

De Brazza's monkey

All types of monkey have tails

Baboon

Proboscis monkey

Red (or bald) uakari

Crab-eating macaque

Mandrill (male)

Apes

Apes are intelligent mammals, and our closest living relatives

Eastern gorilla

Gibbon

Bonobo

Apes do not have tails

Like chimps, bonobos lean on their knuckles when they walk

Orangutan

Chimpanzees

Using grass stems as tools

Wild cats

Jaguar

Siberian tiger

Lion

Lynx

Puma

Snow leopard

Clouded leopard

Caracal

Cheetah

Leopard

Wild dogs

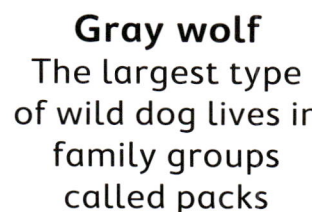

Coyote

Gray wolf
The largest type of wild dog lives in family groups called packs

Dingo

Jackal

Gray fox

Red fox

Horses

Suffolk Punch

Camargue

Lipizzaner

Shire

Przewalski's horse
A true wild horse that has never been tamed

Appaloosa

Arab

150

Ponies

Fell pony

Welsh cob pony

Connemara pony

Shetland mare and foal

Rhinoceroses

Indian rhino

Sumatran rhino

White rhino

Javan rhino

Black rhino

Deer, zebra, giraffes, and hippos

Okapi

Red deer

Moose

Reindeer

Fallow
deer

Roe
deer

Zebra

152

Giraffe

Hippopotamus

African elephant

Elephants

Asian elephant

Huge ears—
the Asian
elephant's are
smaller than
the African's

Tusks—the
African elephant's
are longer than
the Asian's

153

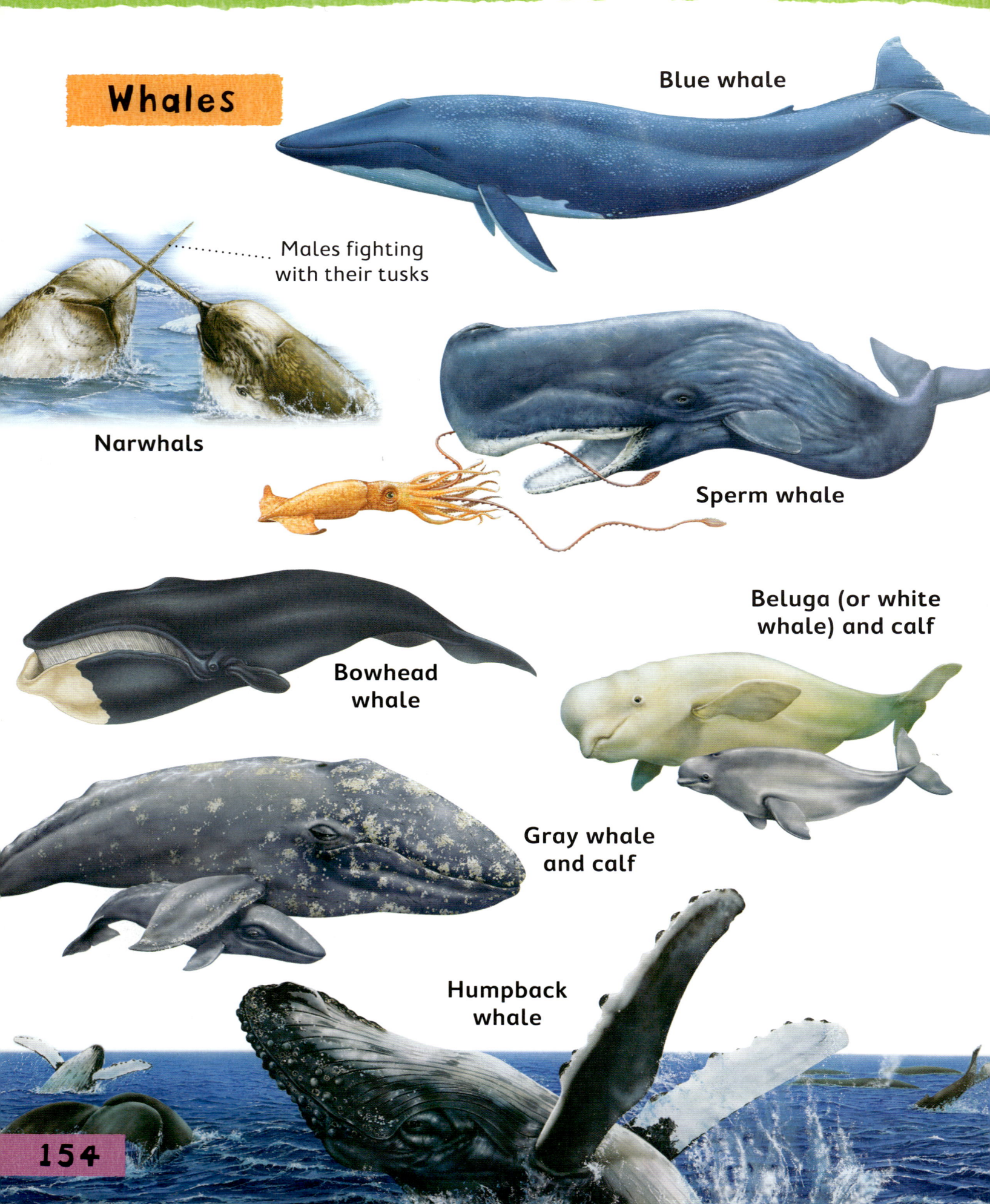

Whales

Blue whale

Males fighting with their tusks

Narwhals

Sperm whale

Beluga (or white whale) and calf

Bowhead whale

Gray whale and calf

Humpback whale

Dolphins and porpoises

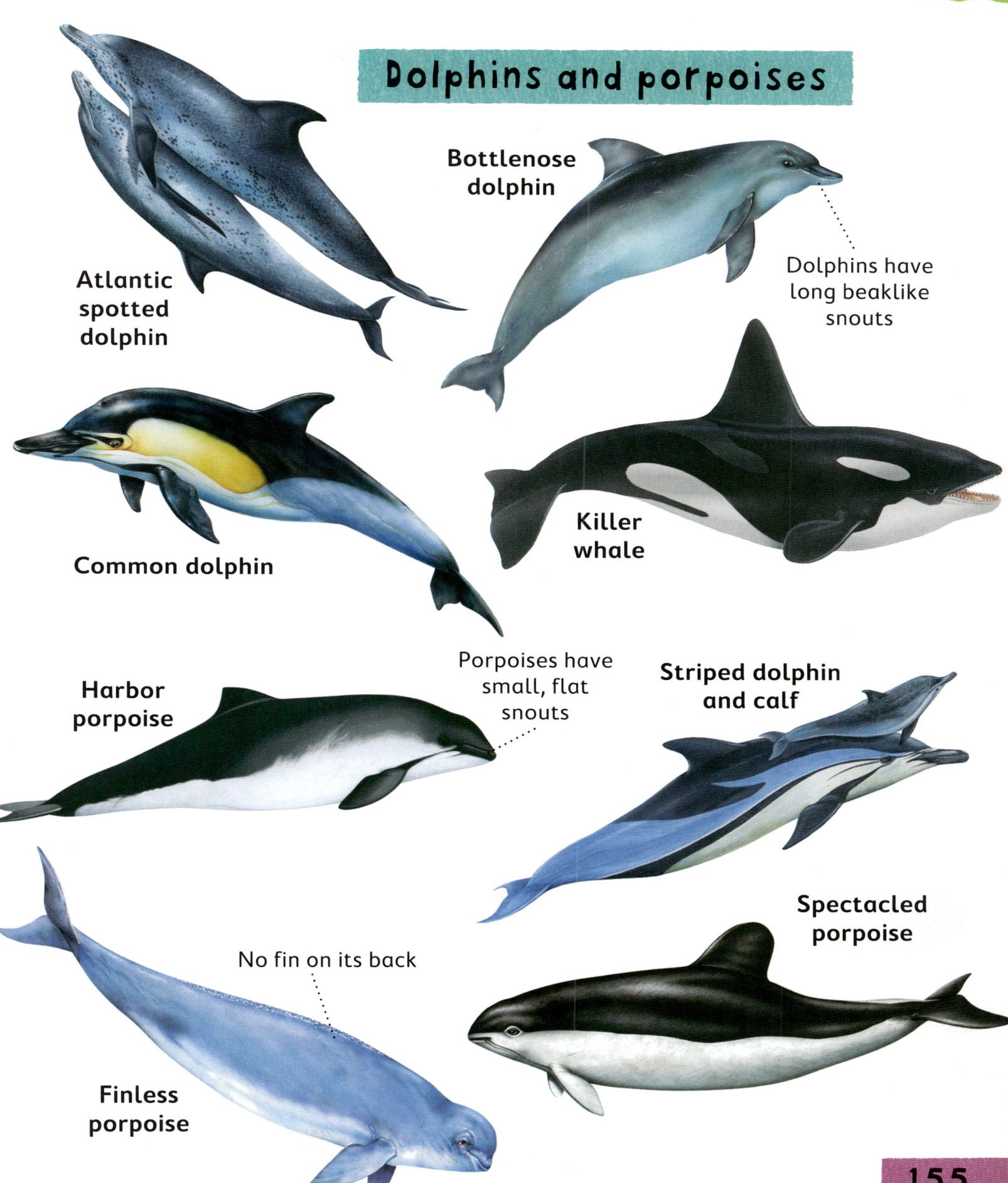

Atlantic spotted dolphin

Bottlenose dolphin

Dolphins have long beaklike snouts

Common dolphin

Killer whale

Harbor porpoise

Porpoises have small, flat snouts

Striped dolphin and calf

Spectacled porpoise

No fin on its back

Finless porpoise

Cells

Cells are the tiny, basic building blocks of your body. In your body there are many different kinds of cell, including bone cells, blood cells, and muscle cells

Inside a single cell

1 Cell membrane
A thin layer of protein and fat surrounds the cell

2 Mitochondria
These release energy by breaking down sugars in the blood

3 Nucleus
The cell's control center

4 Golgi bodies
These send chemicals to parts of the body where they are needed

5 Cytoplasm
A jellylike liquid that fills the cell

6 Lysosomes
These are the cell's trash cans. They digest any unwanted material

DNA

Inside every cell there is a substance called DNA (deoxyribonucleic acid) which carries all your genetic information

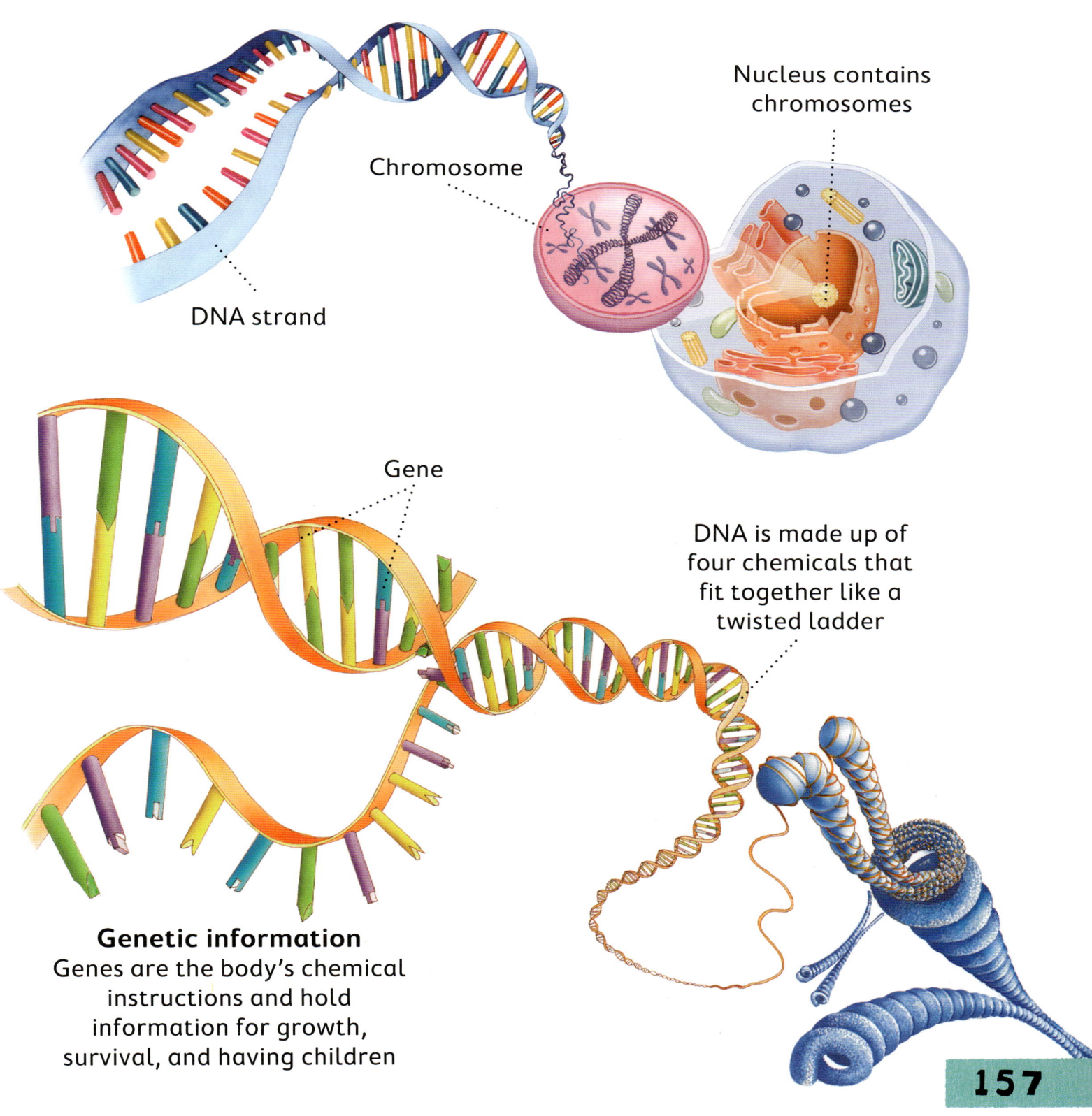

Nucleus contains chromosomes

Chromosome

DNA strand

Gene

DNA is made up of four chemicals that fit together like a twisted ladder

Genetic information
Genes are the body's chemical instructions and hold information for growth, survival, and having children

157

Heart

A pump made almost entirely of muscle.
The stronger left ventricle (chamber) pumps blood
around the body, and the smaller right ventricle
pumps blood to the lungs

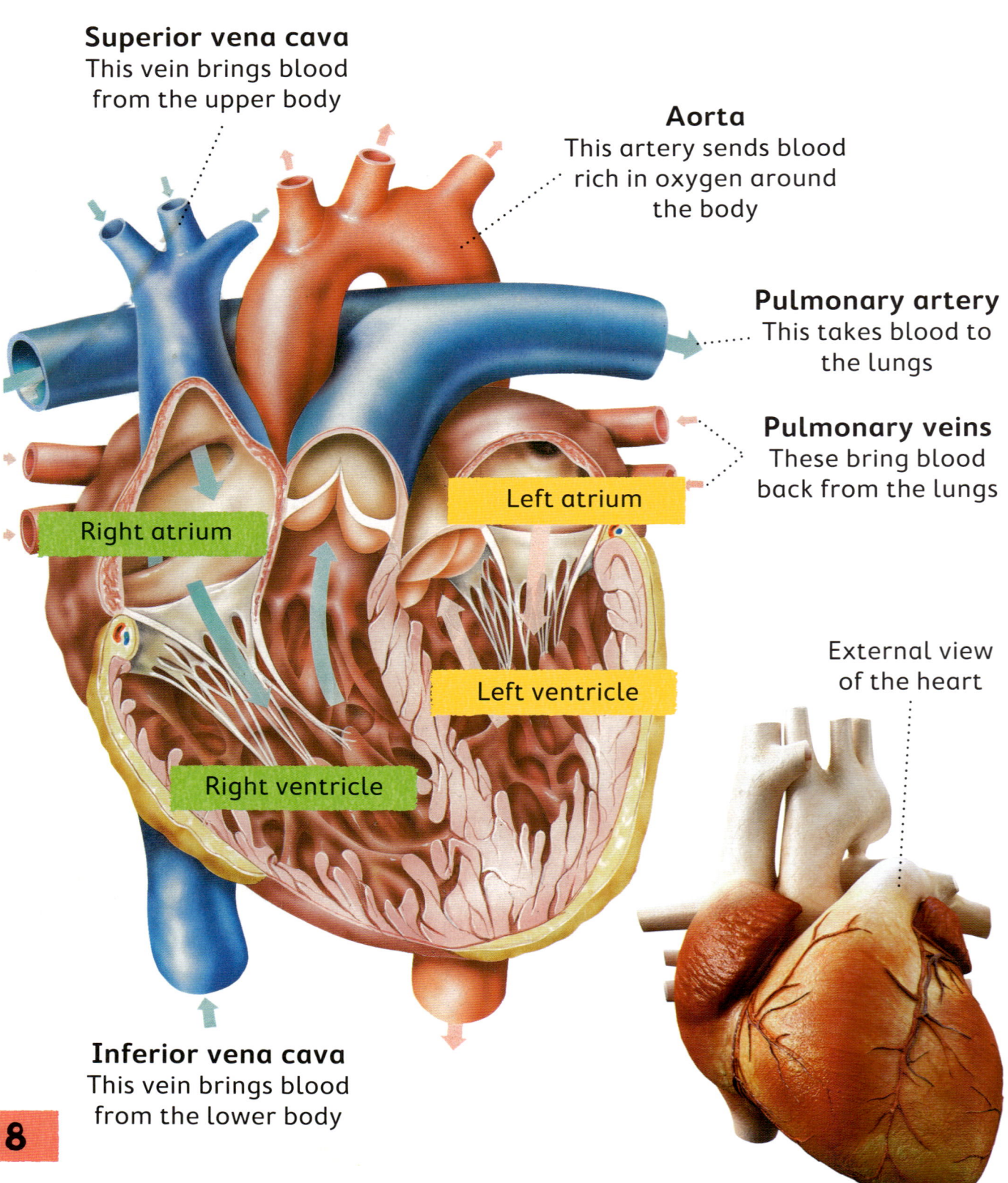

Superior vena cava
This vein brings blood
from the upper body

Aorta
This artery sends blood
rich in oxygen around
the body

Pulmonary artery
This takes blood to
the lungs

Pulmonary veins
These bring blood
back from the lungs

Left atrium

Right atrium

Left ventricle

Right ventricle

Inferior vena cava
This vein brings blood
from the lower body

External view
of the heart

Circulatory system

Blood is transported around the body by a network of vessels

Blood transportation

Blood vessels allow the blood to flow around the body

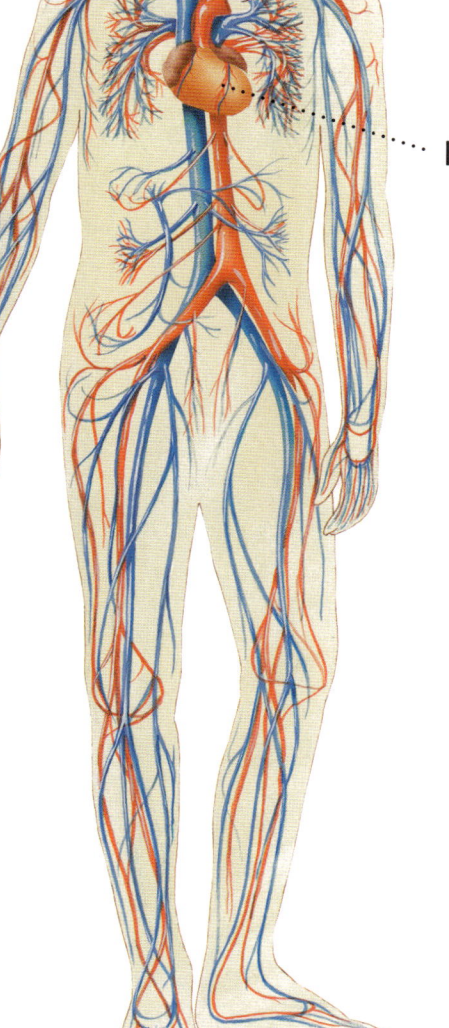

The brain receives more blood than any other part of the body

Heart

Blood vessels

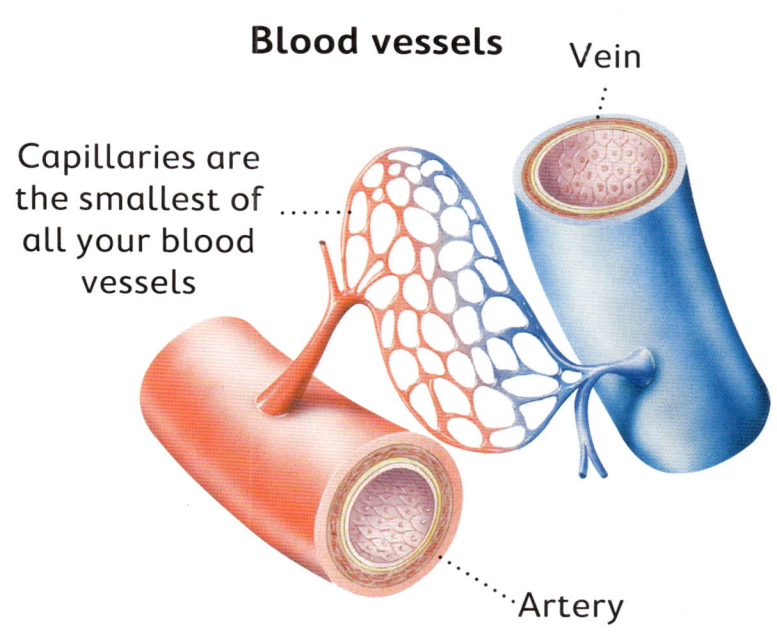

Capillaries are the smallest of all your blood vessels

Vein

Artery

Inside a blood vessel

The blood is made up of lots of different cells

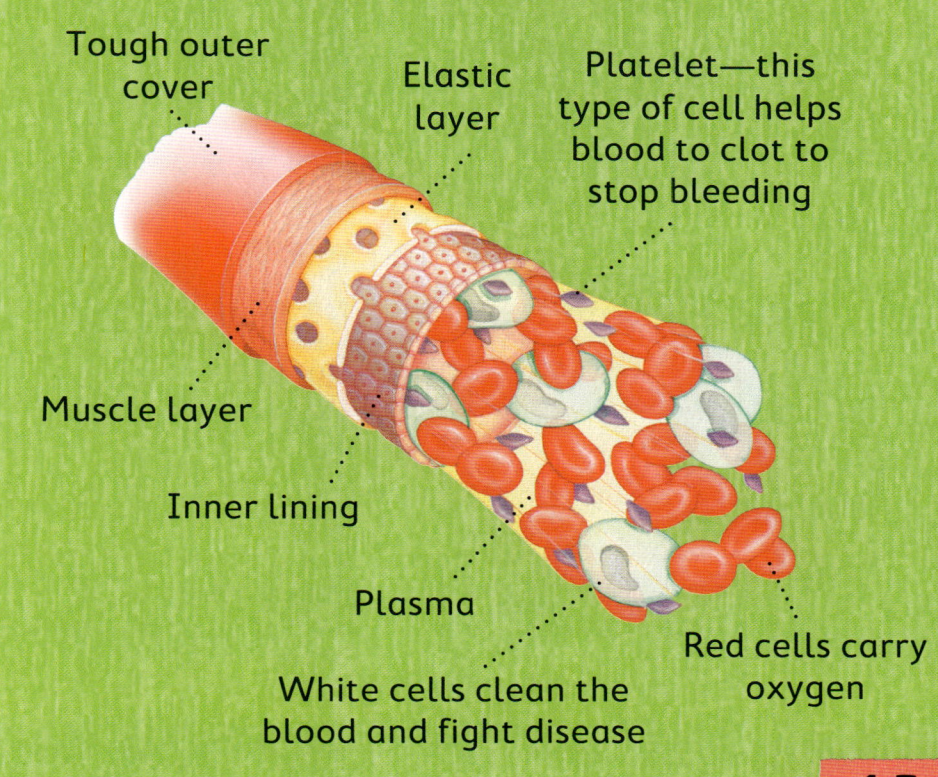

Tough outer cover

Elastic layer

Platelet—this type of cell helps blood to clot to stop bleeding

Muscle layer

Inner lining

Plasma

White cells clean the blood and fight disease

Red cells carry oxygen

Lungs

These are a pair of spongy, air-filled organs on either side of the chest (thorax)

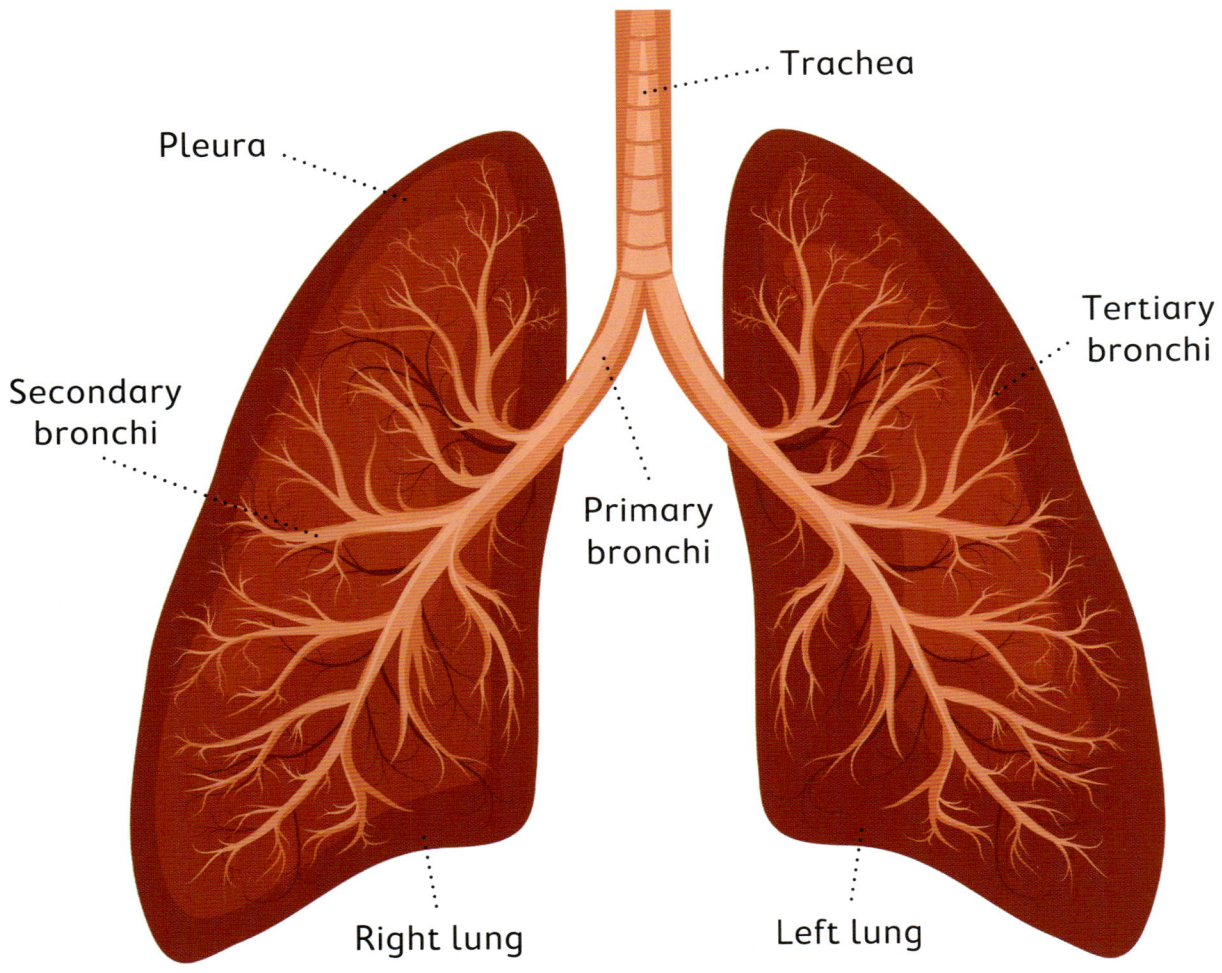

Trachea

Pleura

Tertiary bronchi

Secondary bronchi

Primary bronchi

Right lung

Left lung

Alveoli

The lungs consist of bunches of tiny air sacs called alveoli, which transfer oxygen to the blood and pick up carbon dioxide from the blood

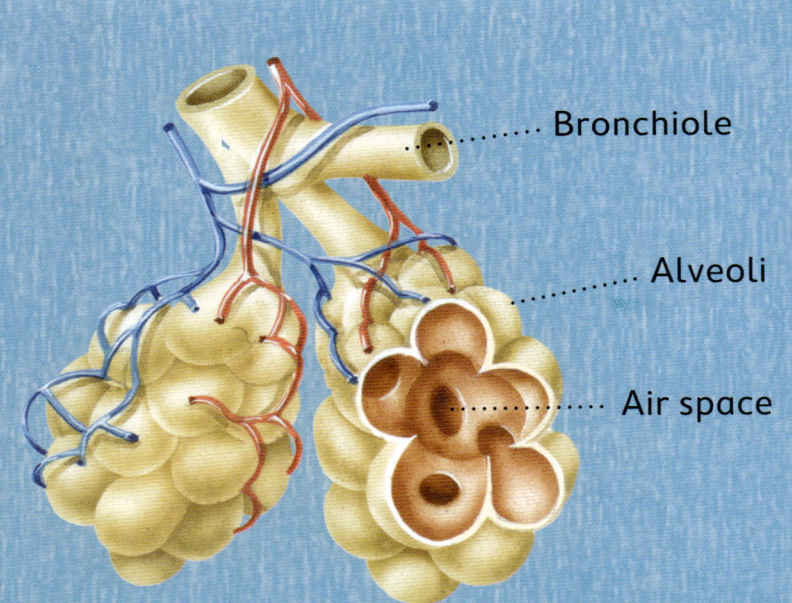

Bronchiole

Alveoli

Air space

Respiratory system

The lungs, airways, and diaphragm make up this breathing system

Oxygen transportation

Oxygen is taken into the body and carbon dioxide is breathed out. Red blood cells are responsible for transporting oxygen around the body

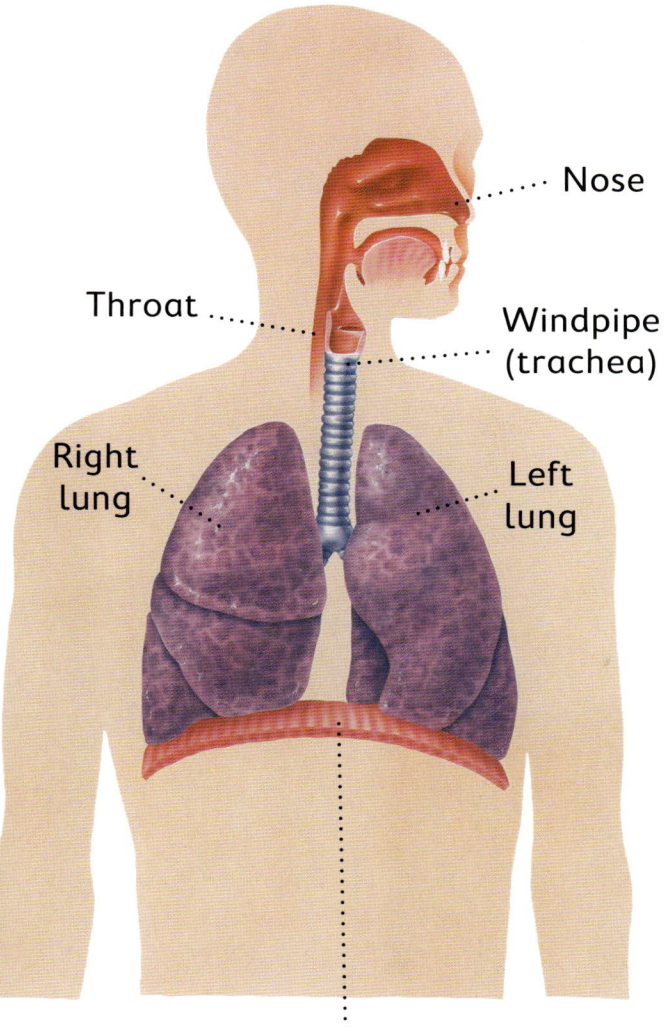

Nose

Throat

Windpipe (trachea)

Right lung

Left lung

Diaphragm
A large muscle under the lungs

How we breathe

Our diaphragm helps us to inhale and exhale

Inhale (breathing in)

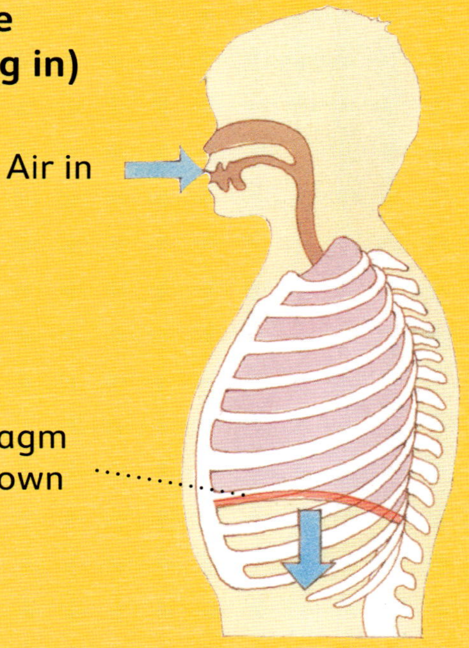

Air in

Diaphragm pulls down

Exhale (breathing out)

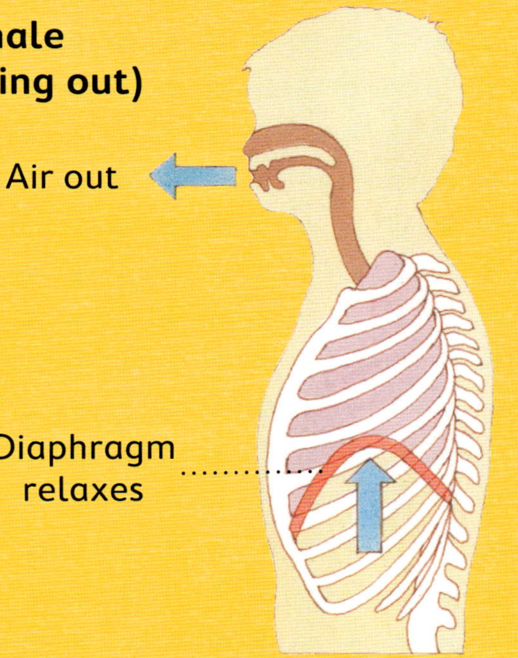

Air out

Diaphragm relaxes

Digestive system

Breaks down food so it can be absorbed by the body

Liver
The body's main processing center. It stores nutrients and substances for when they are needed

Gullet
Also known as the esophagus, it helps to push food down into the stomach

Stomach
A muscular walled bag that mashes food into a pulp

Gall bladder
Stores bile which digests fats

Pancreas
Helps digest food by releasing enzymes to break down food

Large intestine
Undigested food is made into solid waste

Appendix
Has no function in humans

Rectum
Waste collects here before you are ready to go to the toilet

Small intestine
Food enters this long tube and the nutrients and useful substances are absorbed into the body

Villi

The lining of the small intestine has thousands of tiny, fingerlike folds called villi, which absorb nutrients from food

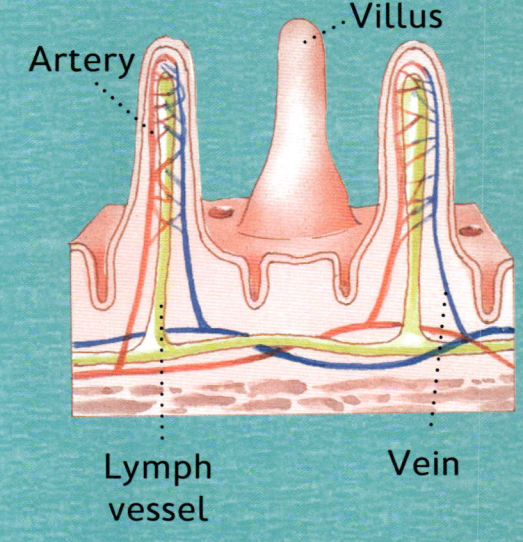

Artery

Villus

Lymph vessel

Vein

Urinary System

Removes waste products from the blood and the body

Inferior vena cava (vein)

Abdominal aorta (artery)

Renal vein

Renal artery

Kidney
Filters the blood to produce urine

Ureter
Connects the kidney to the bladder

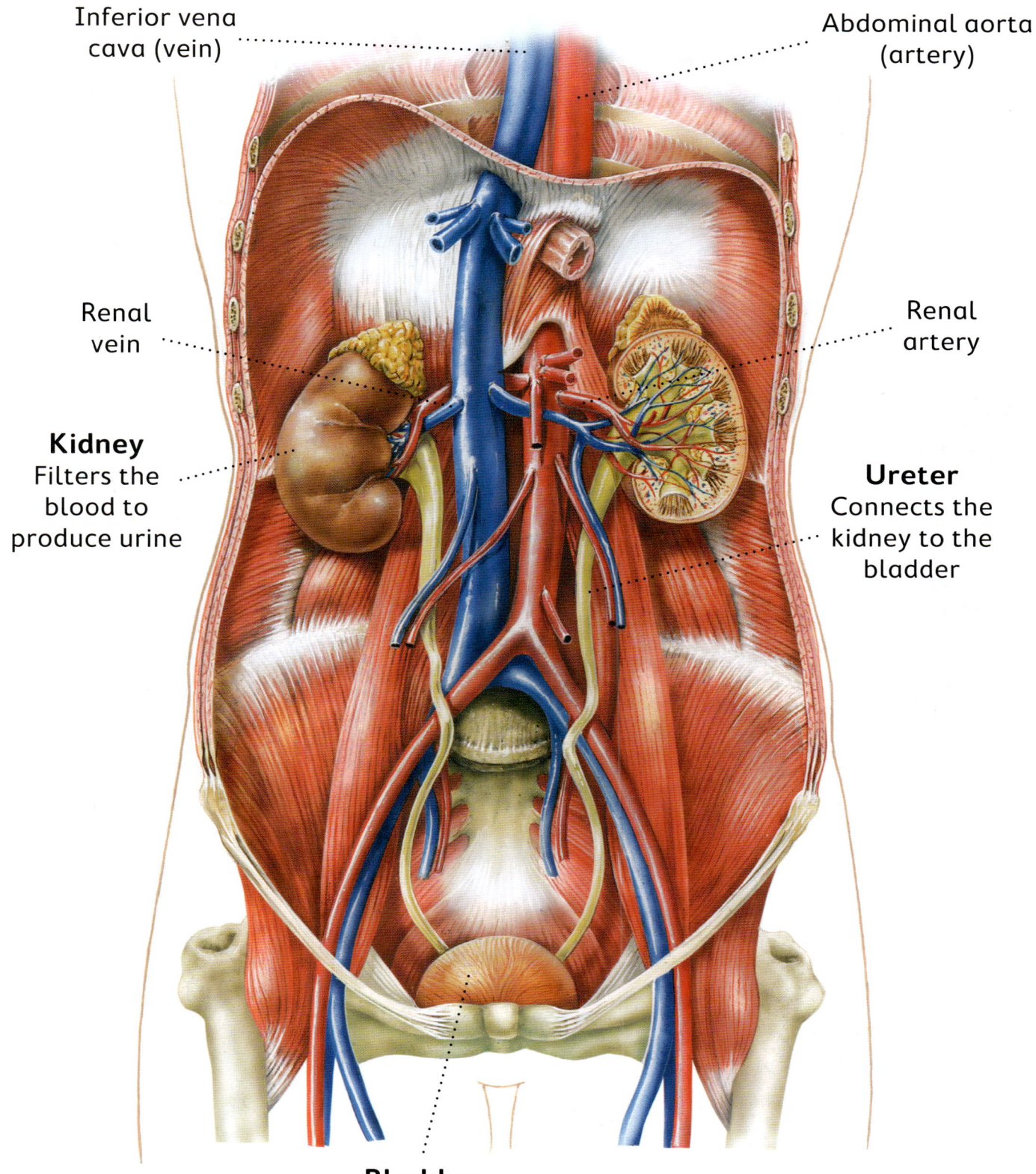

Bladder
Collects the urine

163

Brain

Controls your actions and responses, as well as allowing you to think, learn, understand, and create

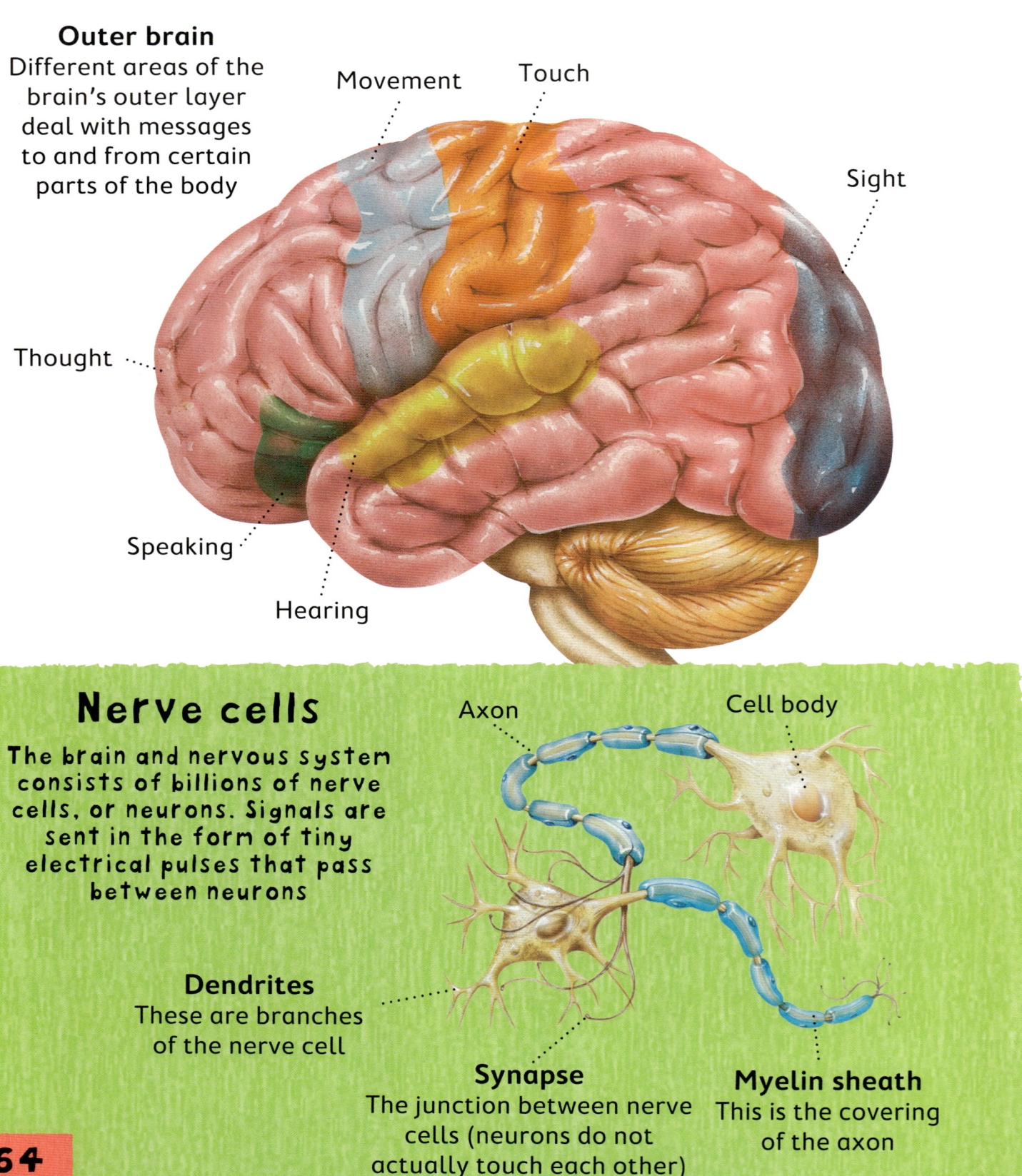

Outer brain
Different areas of the brain's outer layer deal with messages to and from certain parts of the body

Movement

Touch

Sight

Thought

Speaking

Hearing

Nerve cells

The brain and nervous system consists of billions of nerve cells, or neurons. Signals are sent in the form of tiny electrical pulses that pass between neurons

Axon

Cell body

Dendrites
These are branches of the nerve cell

Synapse
The junction between nerve cells (neurons do not actually touch each other)

Myelin sheath
This is the covering of the axon

164

Inner brain
Inside the brain each area is
responsible for different functions

Cerebrum
Where you think and
decide what to say

Thalamus
Affects
awareness and
alertness

Limbic system
Affects emotions
and smell

Hypothalamus
Controls body heat,
water, and hunger,
and also wakes you up

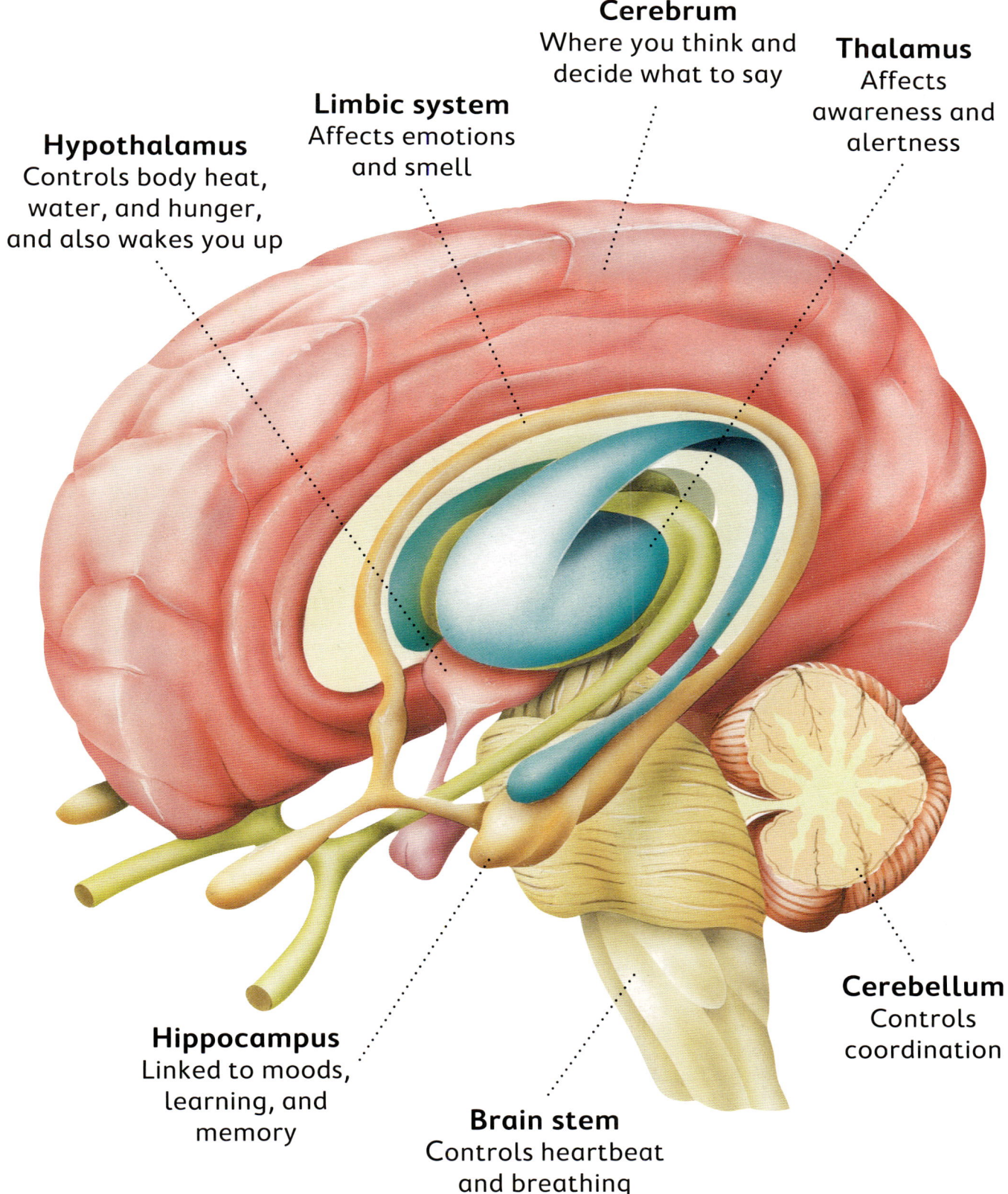

Hippocampus
Linked to moods,
learning, and
memory

Brain stem
Controls heartbeat
and breathing

Cerebellum
Controls
coordination

Nervous system

The body's control and communication system, made up of nerves and the brain

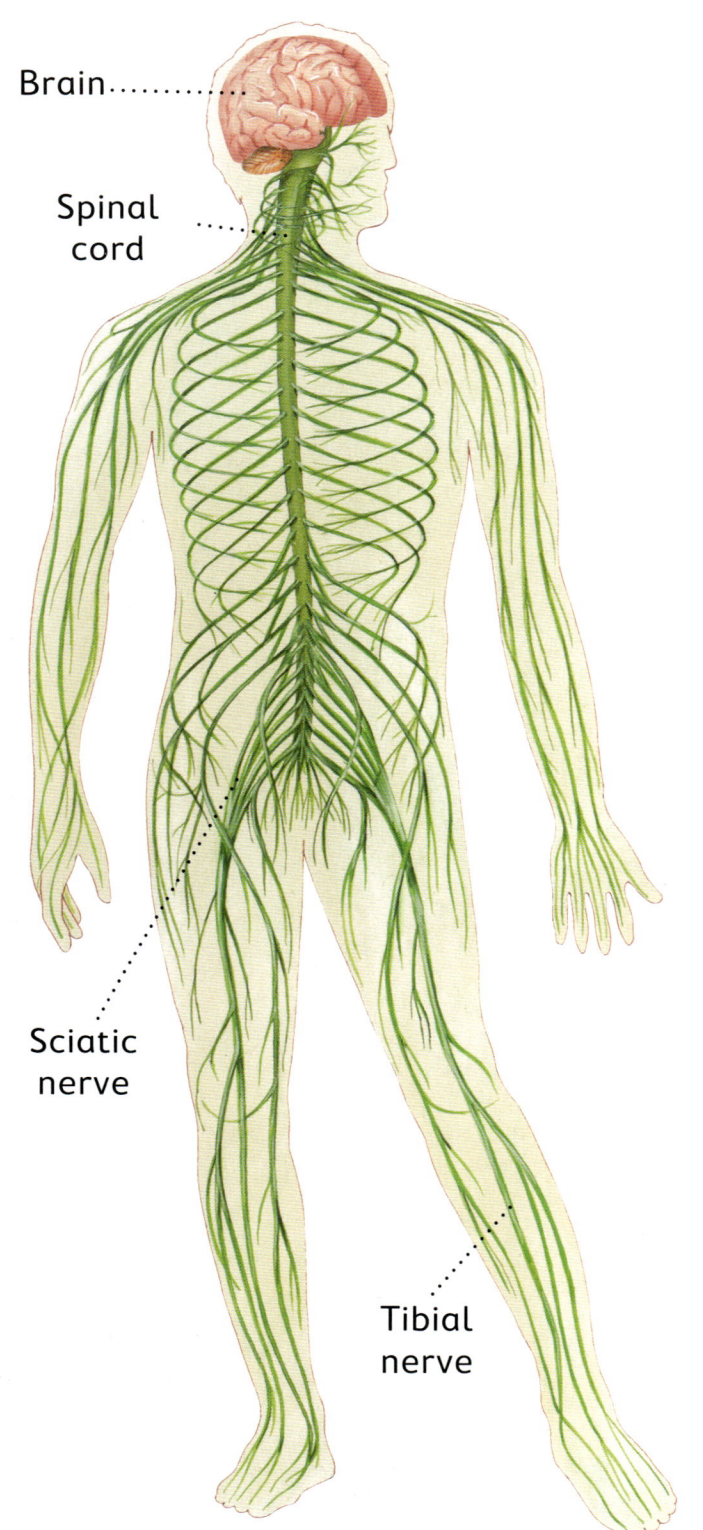

Brain

Spinal cord

Sciatic nerve

Tibial nerve

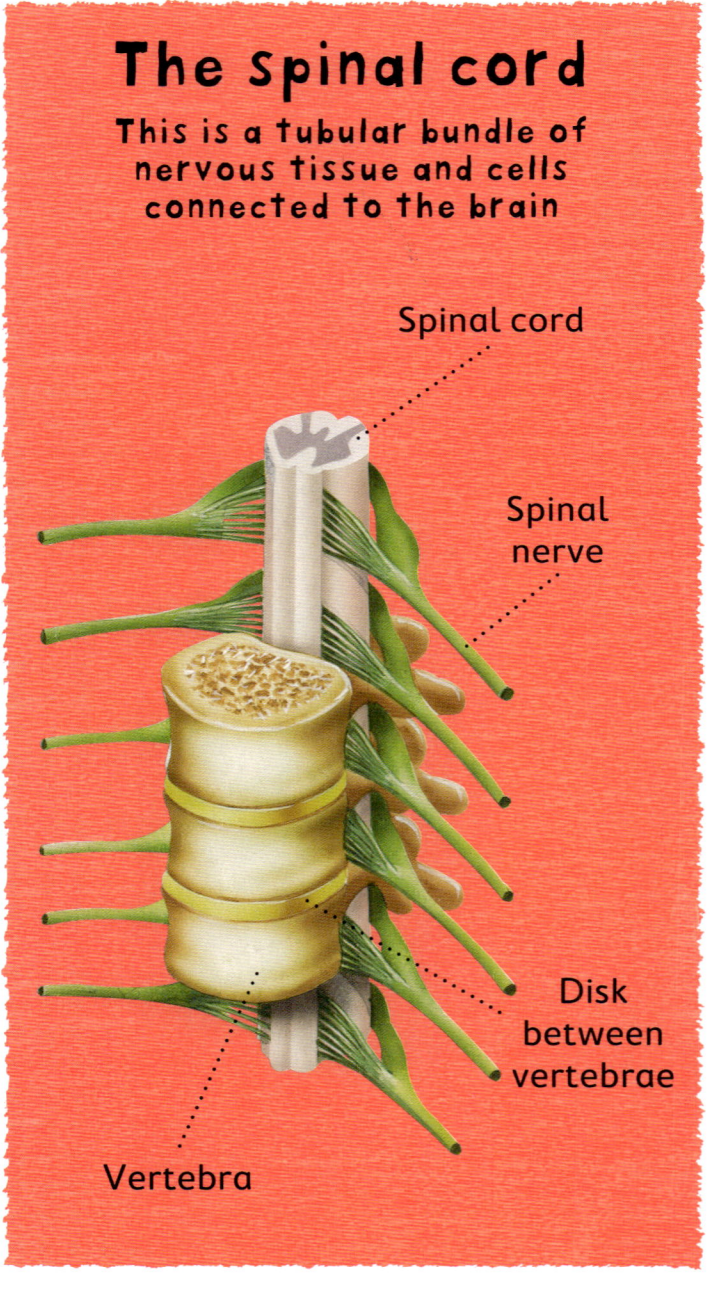

The spinal cord

This is a tubular bundle of nervous tissue and cells connected to the brain

Spinal cord

Spinal nerve

Disk between vertebrae

Vertebra

Immune system

The system of defenses that your body uses to prevent or fight off germs

Adenoids
Release cells to fight infection

Tonsils
Release cells to fight throat infections

Thymus
Changes white blood cells into T cells, which fight harmful bacteria

Spleen
Destroys worn-out red blood cells

Lymph glands
Make white blood cells. Glands in the groin often swell up as the body fights an infection

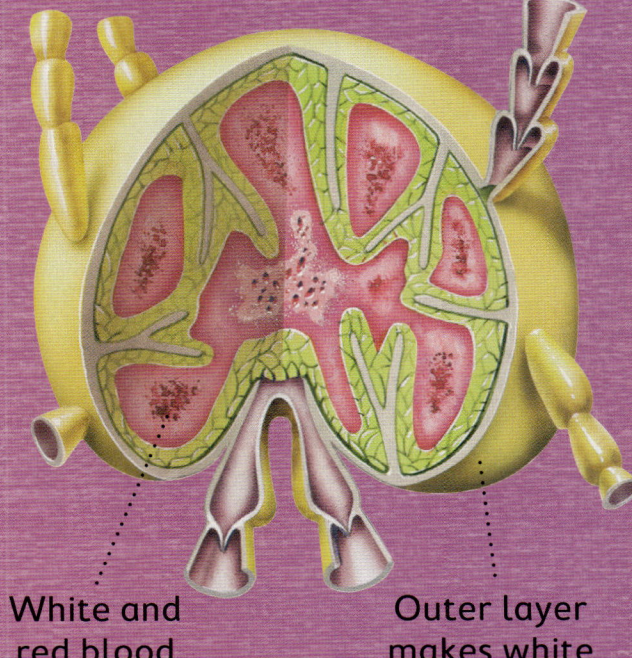

Lymph node

During an infection, these nodes may swell up as the white blood cells fight the infection

White and red blood cells

Outer layer makes white blood cells

167

Sight

Your body finds out about the world around it by its senses. One of your five main senses is eyesight

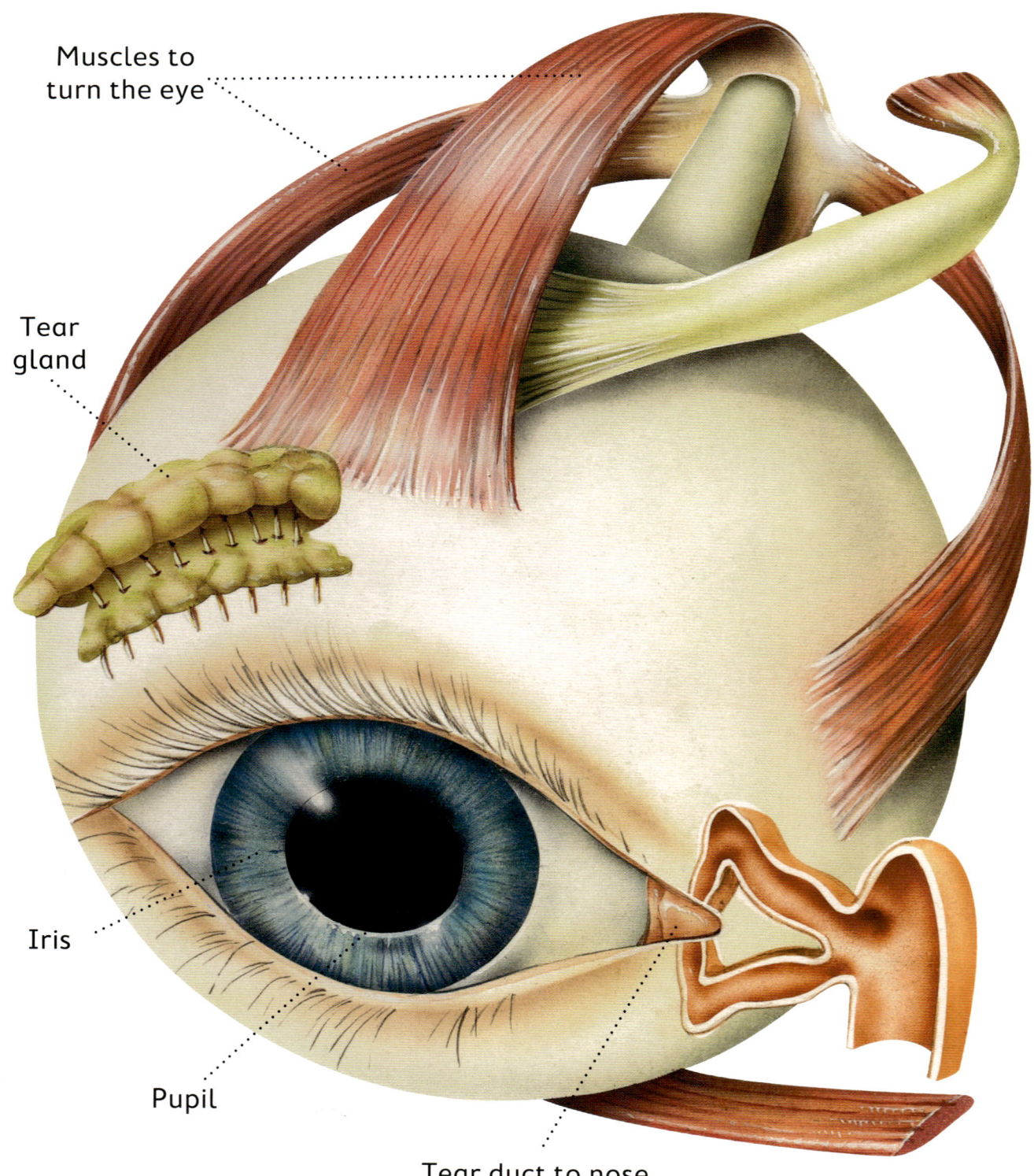

Muscles to turn the eye

Tear gland

Iris

Pupil

Tear duct to nose

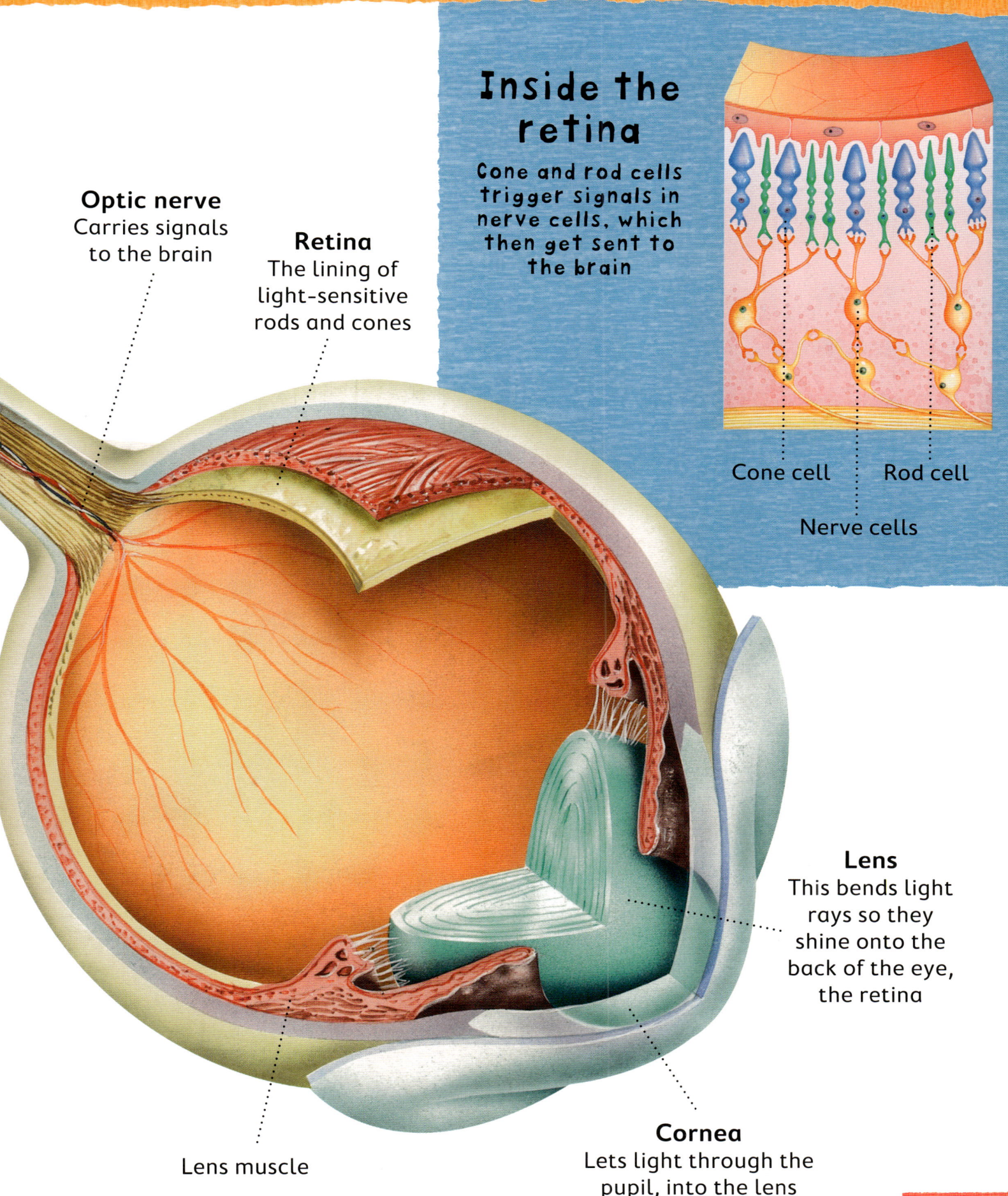

Inside the retina
Cone and rod cells trigger signals in nerve cells, which then get sent to the brain

Cone cell

Rod cell

Nerve cells

Optic nerve
Carries signals to the brain

Retina
The lining of light-sensitive rods and cones

Lens
This bends light rays so they shine onto the back of the eye, the retina

Lens muscle

Cornea
Lets light through the pupil, into the lens

Hearing and speaking

Ears allow you to hear and you use
your vocal cords to speak

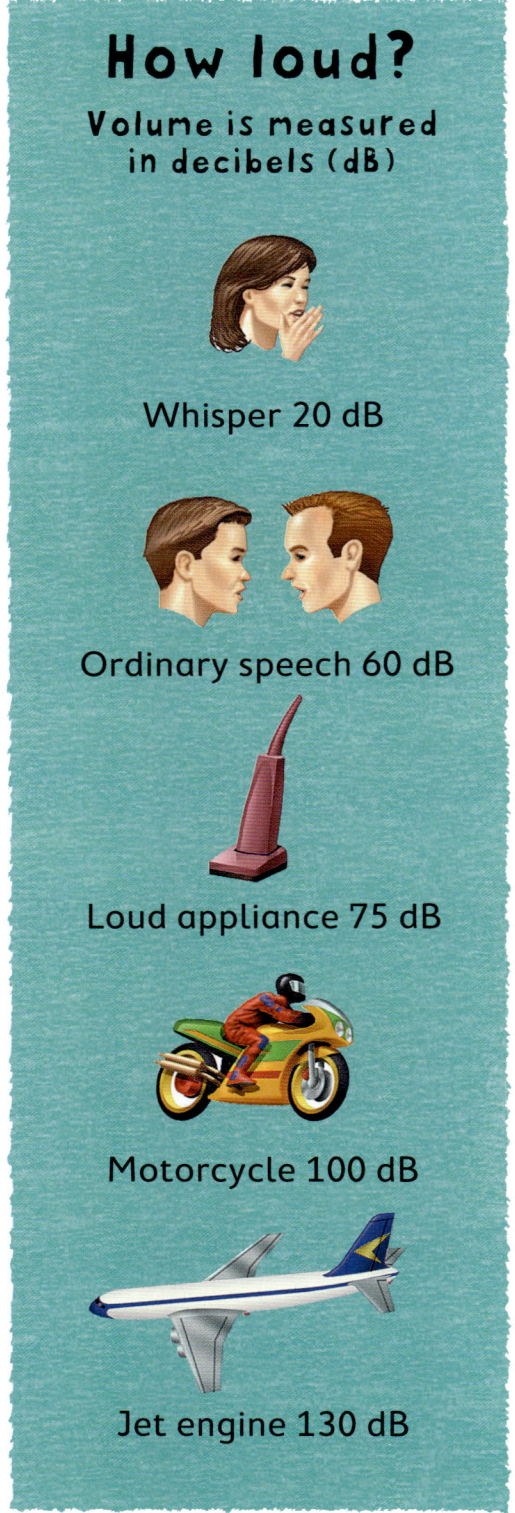

How loud?

Volume is measured
in decibels (dB)

Whisper 20 dB

Ordinary speech 60 dB

Loud appliance 75 dB

Motorcycle 100 dB

Jet engine 130 dB

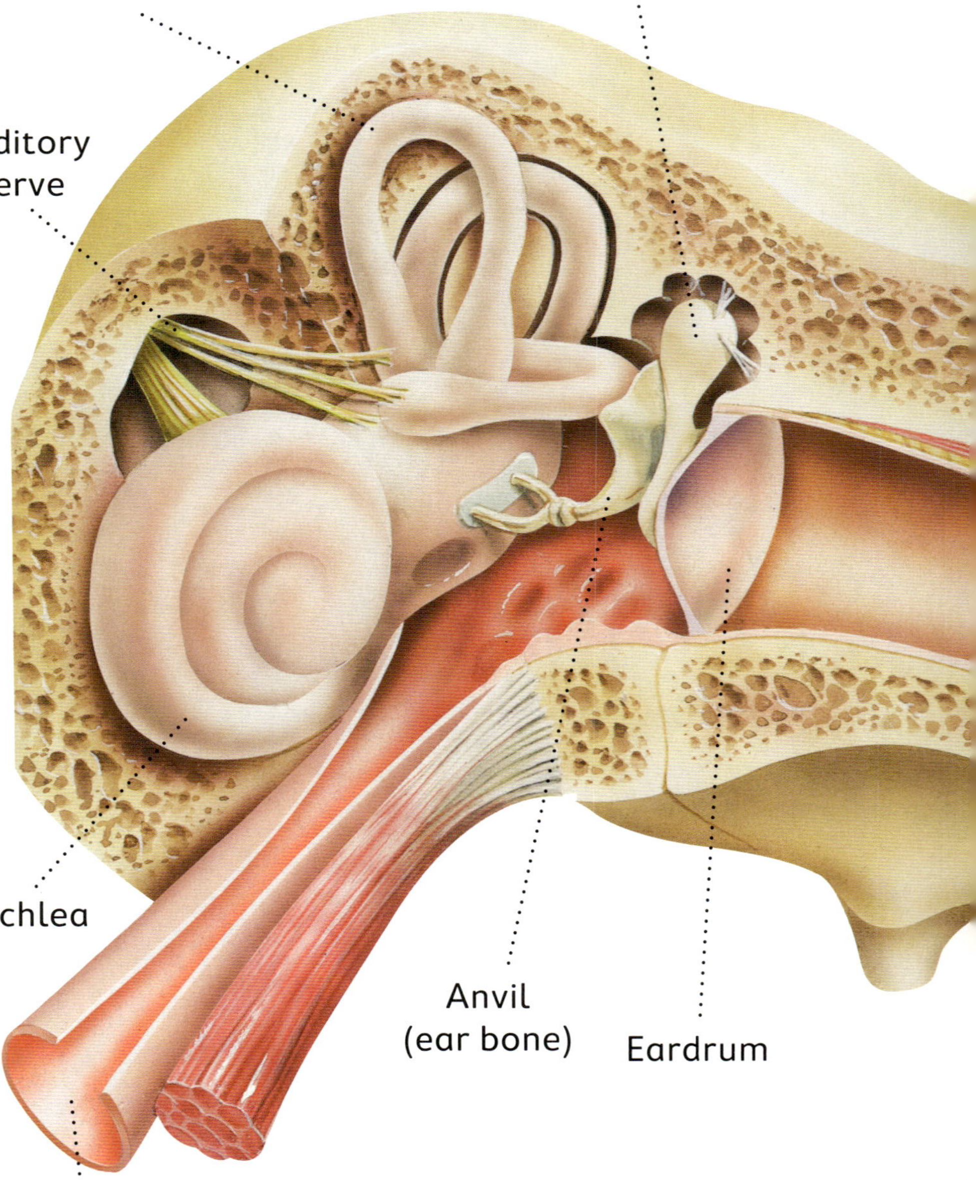

Semicircular
canal helps you
to balance

Hammer
(ear bone)

Auditory
nerve

Cochlea

Anvil
(ear bone)

Eardrum

Air tube
to throat

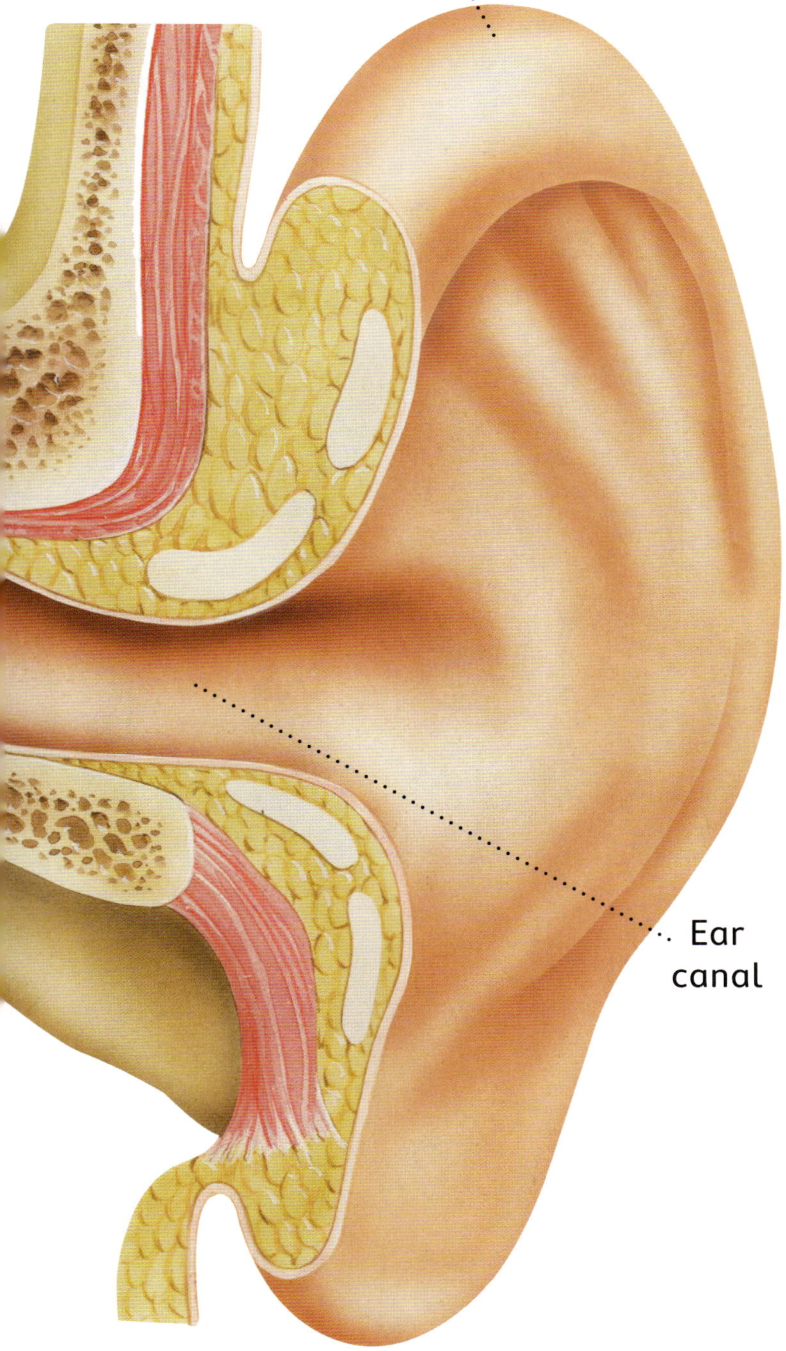

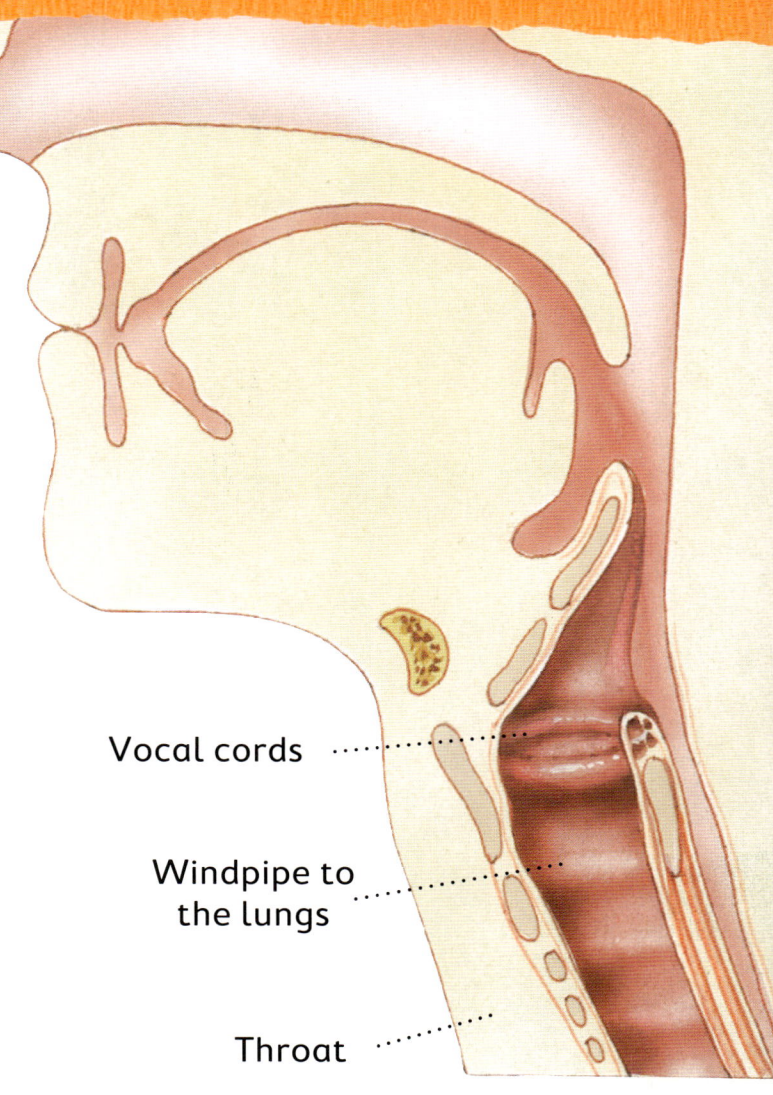

Outer ear

Ear canal

Vocal cords

Windpipe to the lungs

Throat

Vocal cords
The vocal cords are held apart for breathing and pulled together for speaking

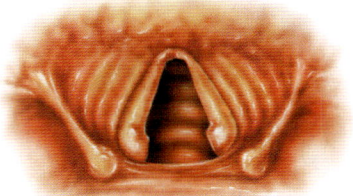

Breathing

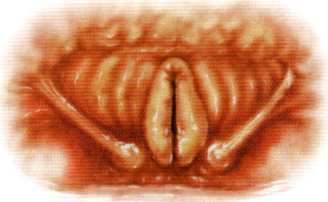

Speaking

Taste

The tongue is a flexible muscle used to help us eat, as well as detect the flavor, texture, and temperature of food

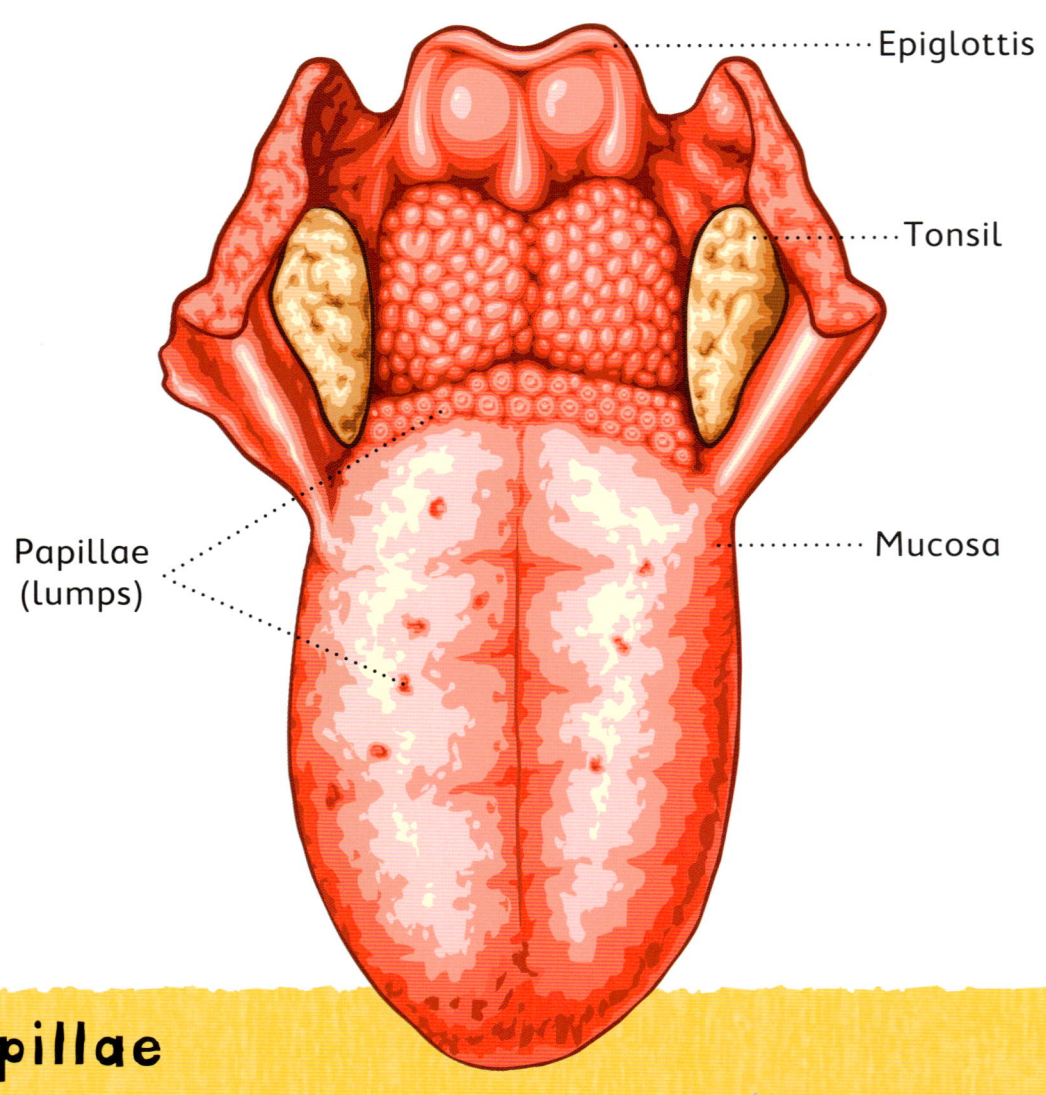

Epiglottis

Tonsil

Mucosa

Papillae (lumps)

Papillae

These tiny bumps give the tongue its rough texture. There are thousands of taste buds (nervelike cells) covering the papillae

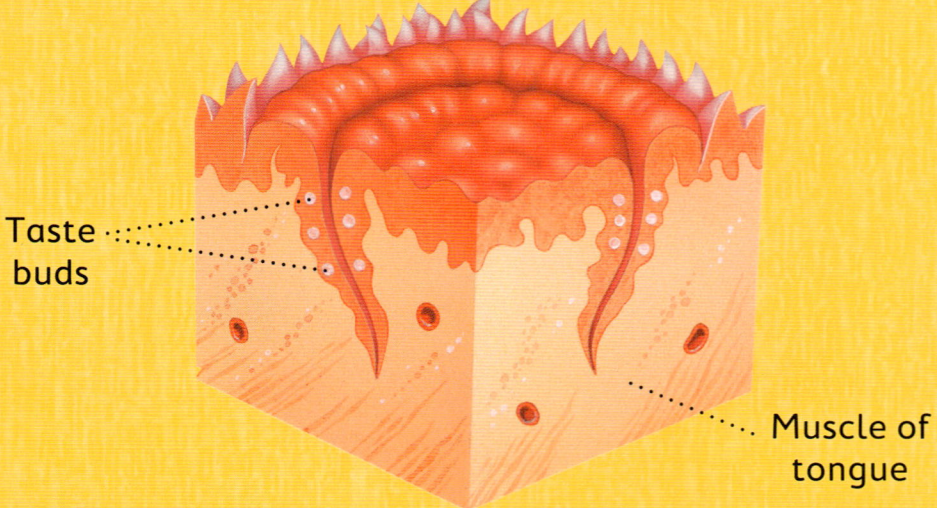

Taste buds

Muscle of tongue

Smell

You cannot see smells because they are tiny particles floating in the air, but your nose can detect them

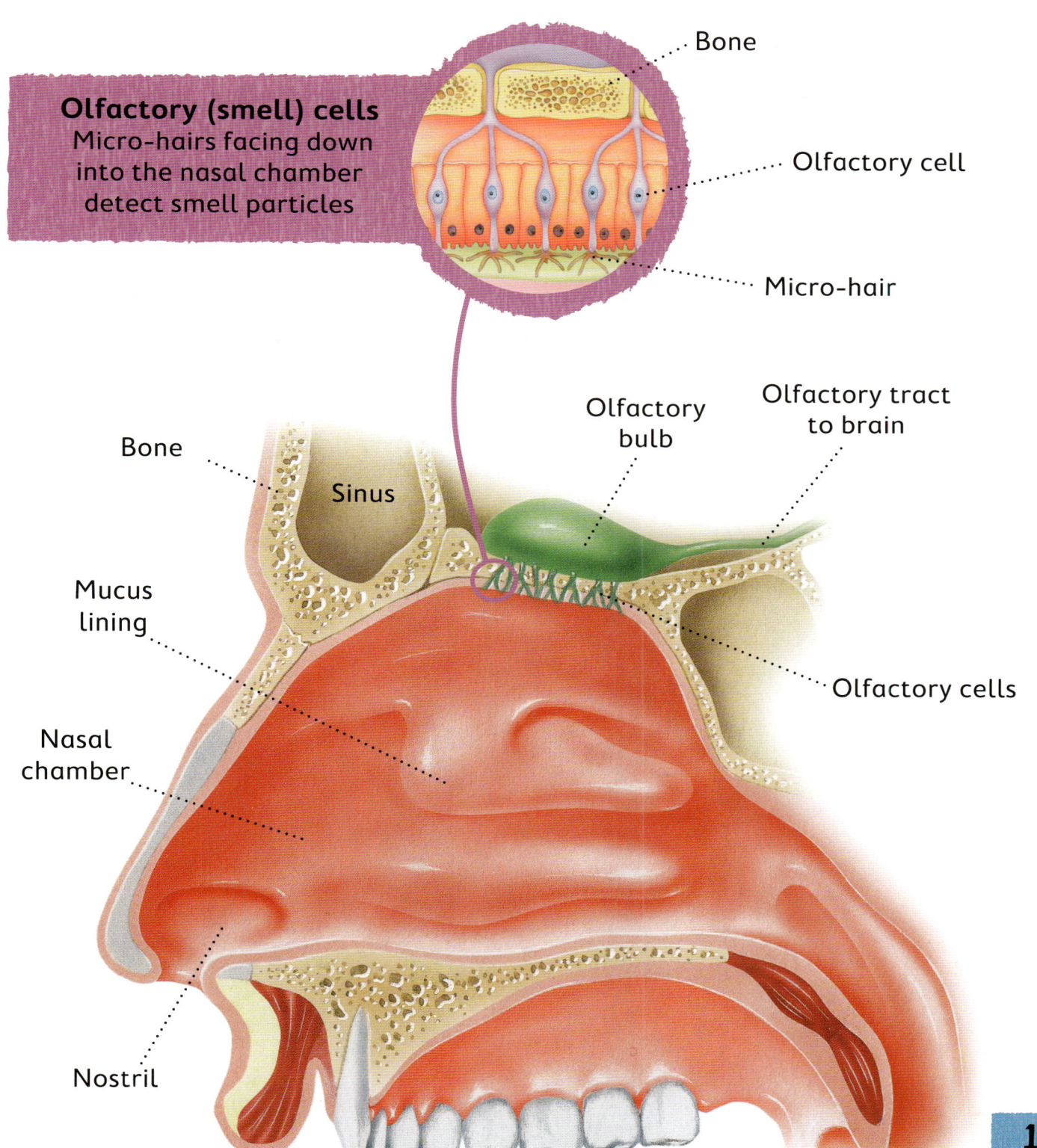

Olfactory (smell) cells
Micro-hairs facing down into the nasal chamber detect smell particles

Bone

Olfactory cell

Micro-hair

Olfactory bulb

Olfactory tract to brain

Bone

Sinus

Mucus lining

Olfactory cells

Nasal chamber

Nostril

173

Cranium (skull)

Mandible (jaw)

Clavicle (collarbone)

Sternum (breastbone)

Humerus

Rib

Vertebra (backbone)

Radius

Ulna

Pelvis (hip bone)

Phalanges (fingers)

Femur (thigh bone)

Patella (kneecap)

Tibia

Fibula

Tarsals

Metatarsals (foot bones)

Skeleton

Supports the body, protects major organs, and provides an anchor for the muscles

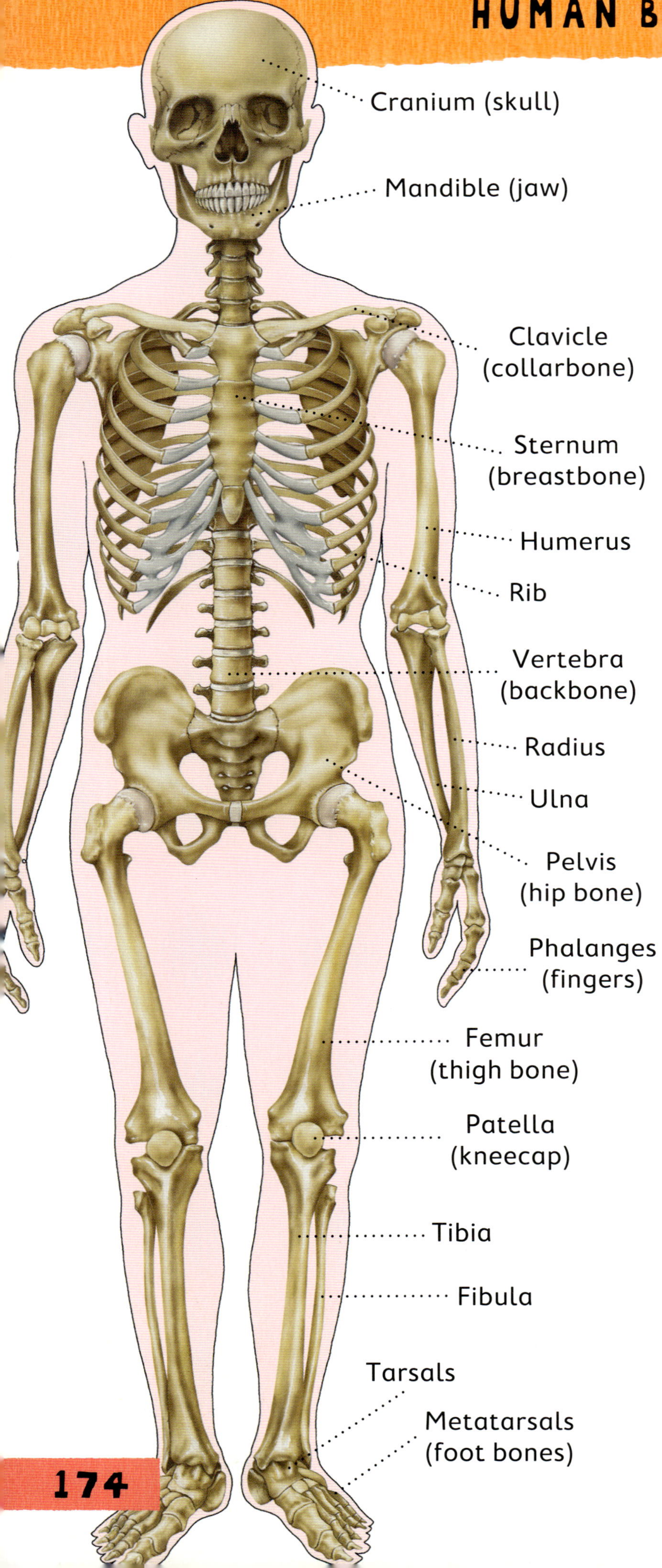

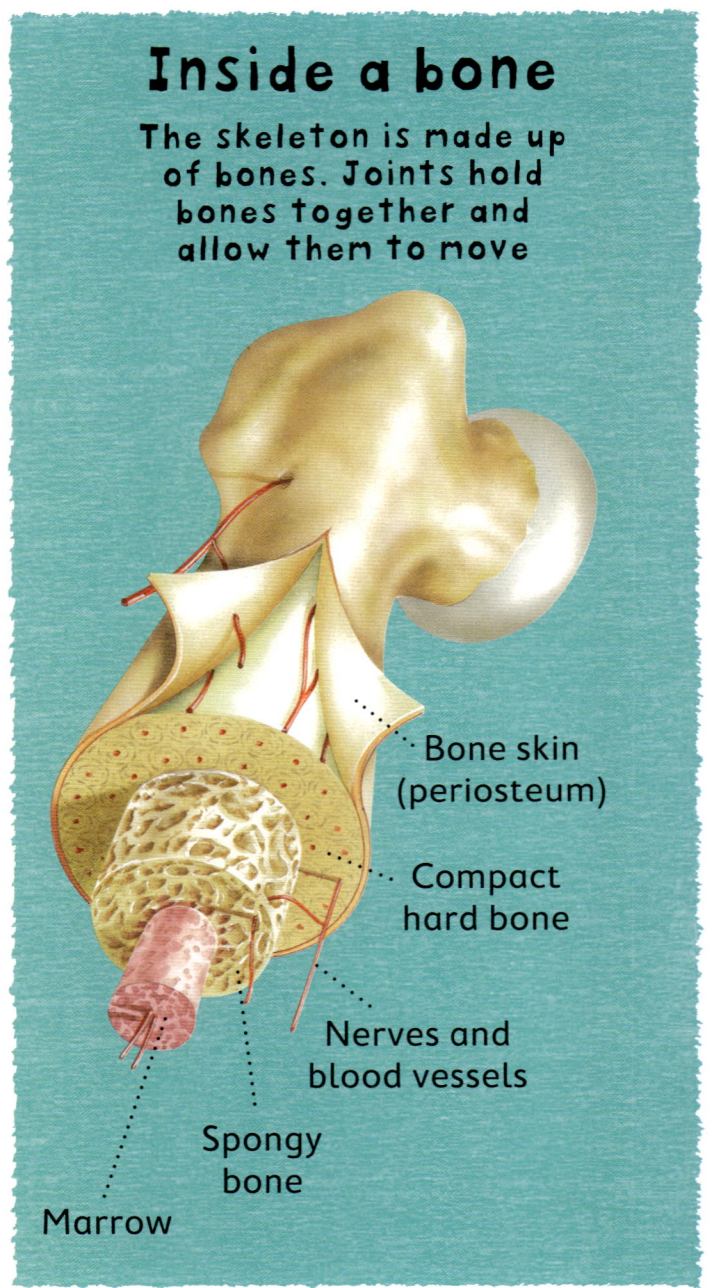

Inside a bone

The skeleton is made up of bones. Joints hold bones together and allow them to move

Bone skin (periosteum)

Compact hard bone

Nerves and blood vessels

Spongy bone

Marrow

Muscles

Made of special fibers, muscles contract (tighten) and relax to move parts of the body

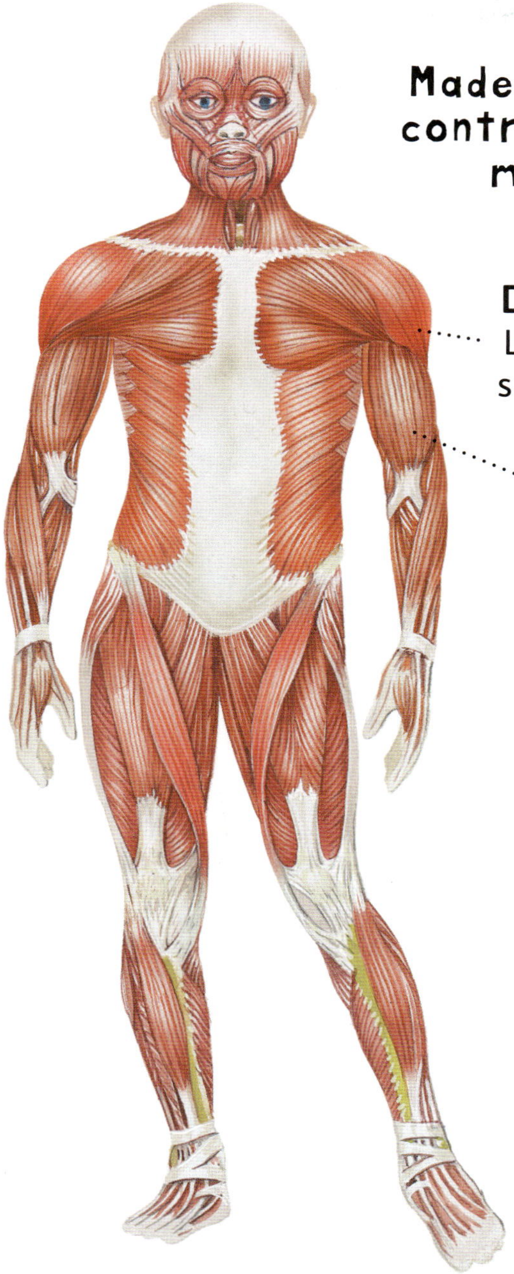

Trapezius
Turns the head

Deltoid
Lifts the shoulder

Biceps
Raises the arm

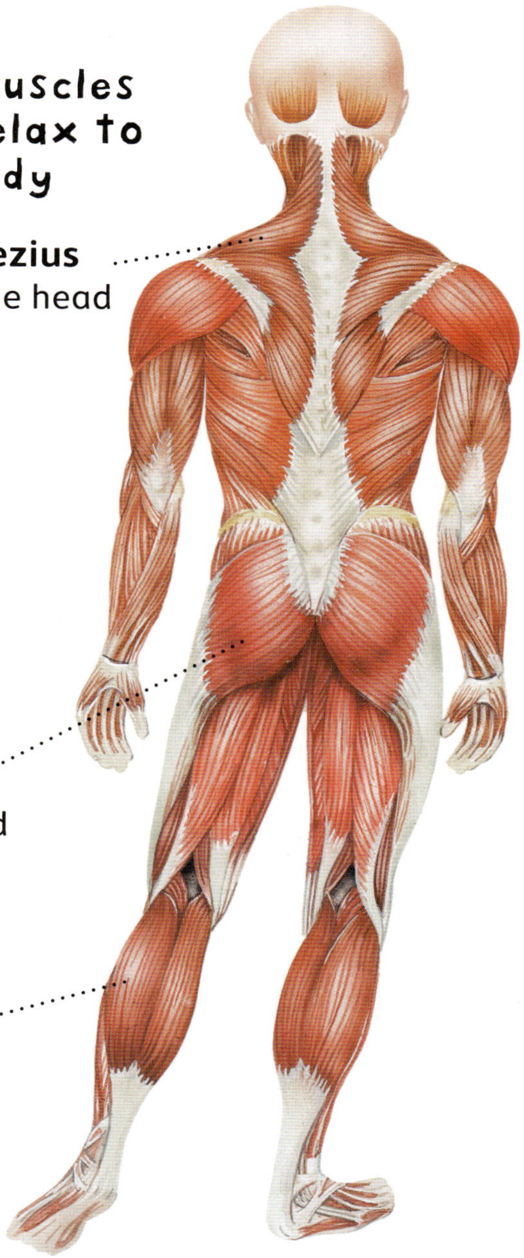

Gluteus maximus
Helps you stand

Gastrocnemius
Bends the knee and foot

Inside a muscle

Each muscle contains nerves, blood vessels, and fibers packed into bundles

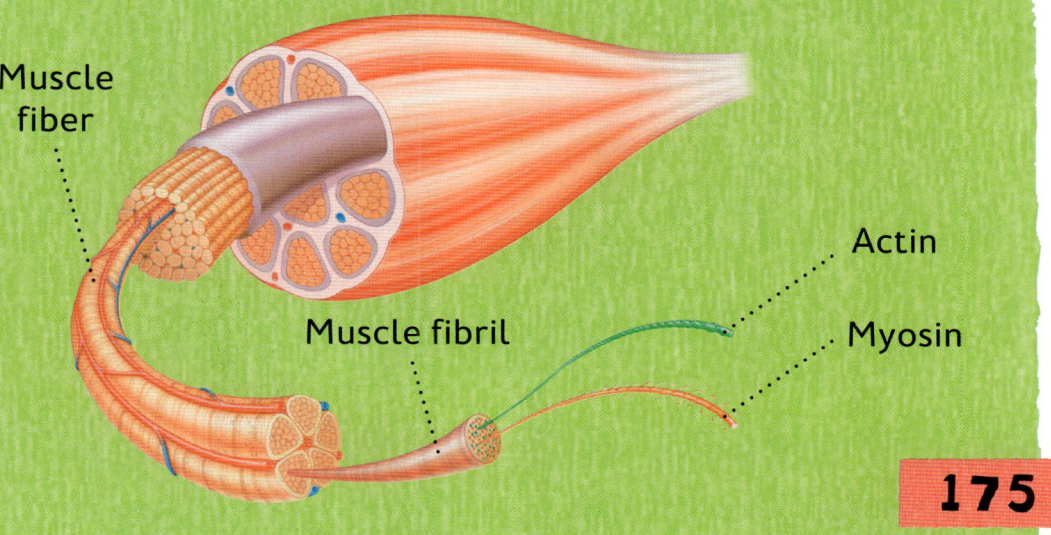

Muscle fiber

Actin

Muscle fibril

Myosin

175

Skin, hair, teeth, and nails

Skin cross section
Your body is protected by your skin

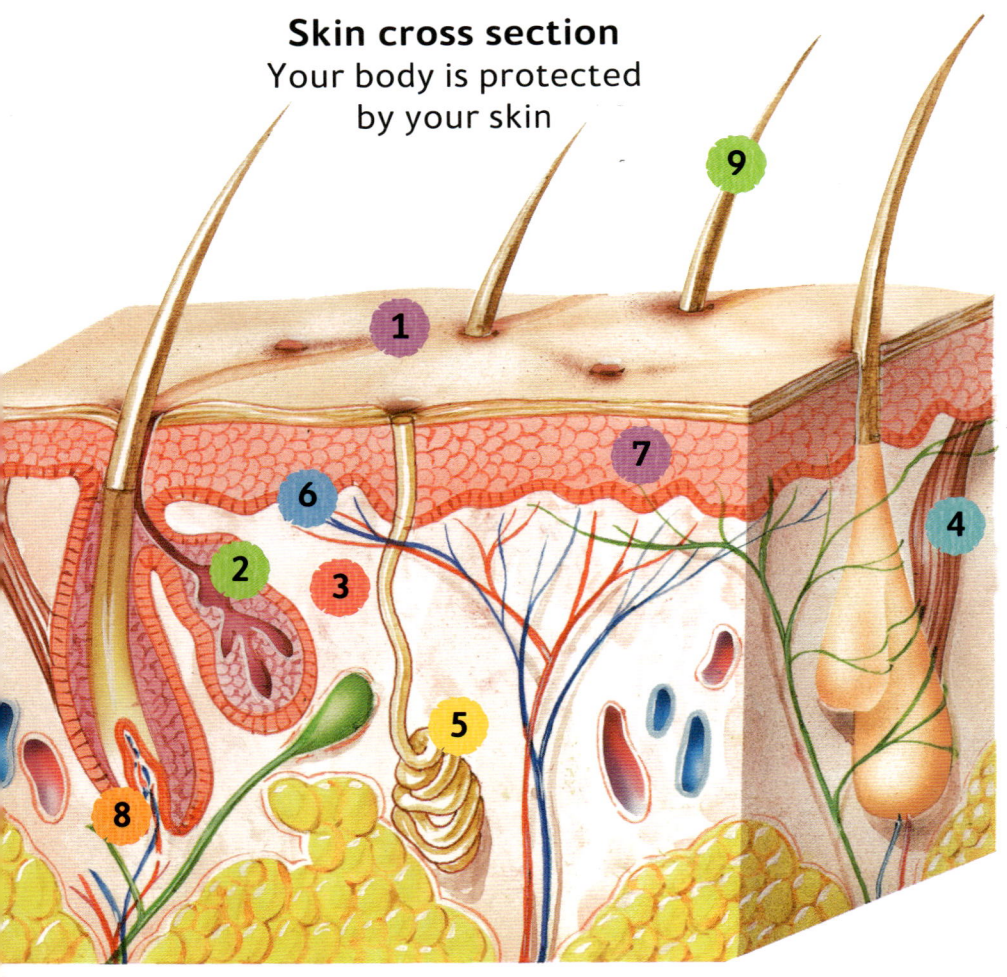

1. Keratin layer
2. Gland making oily sebum to waterproof hair
3. Dermis
4. Hair erector muscle
5. Sweat gland
6. Basal layer, where new cells grow
7. Epidermis
8. Hair follicle (root)
9. Hair

Hair color
Different amounts of pigments (colored substances) called melanin and carotene cause different hair colors

Blond wavy hair

Black curly hair

Straight red hair

Straight black hair

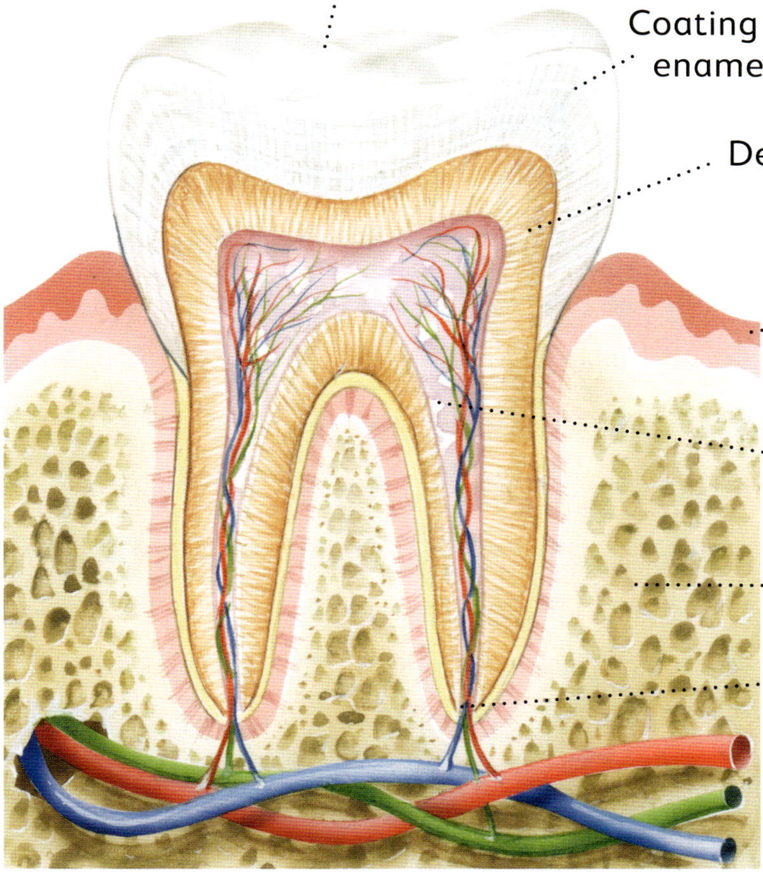

Molar surface

Coating of enamel

Dentine layer

Gum

Soft core or pulp

Jawbone

Root canal

Teeth and gums
This molar tooth sits at the back of the mouth. It is shaped for grinding food

Nail root

Cuticle (skin edge)

Inside the finger
Nails protect the ends of your fingers (and toes)

Nail

Nail bed

Bone

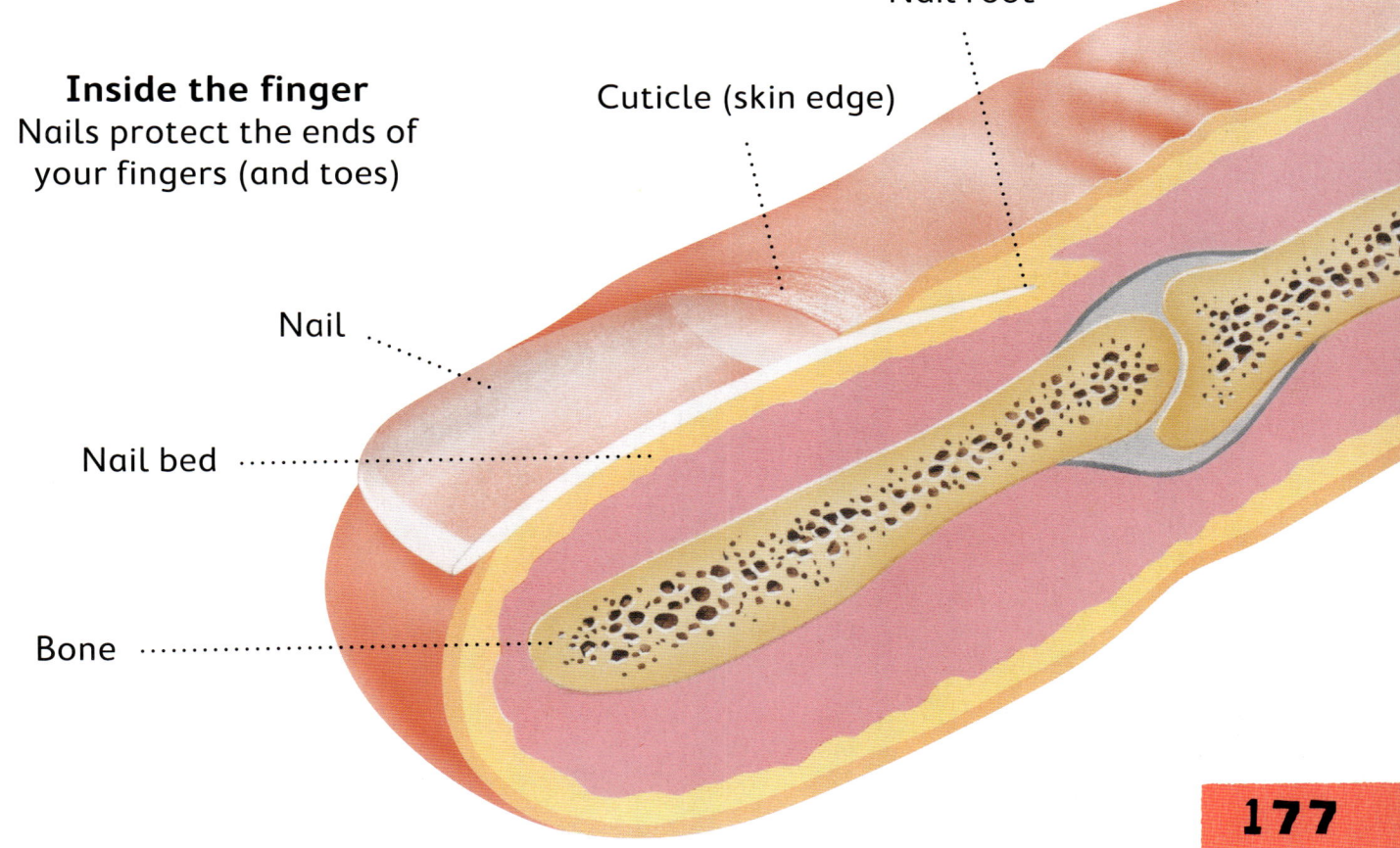

Reproductive system

The organs that enable people to reproduce (have babies)

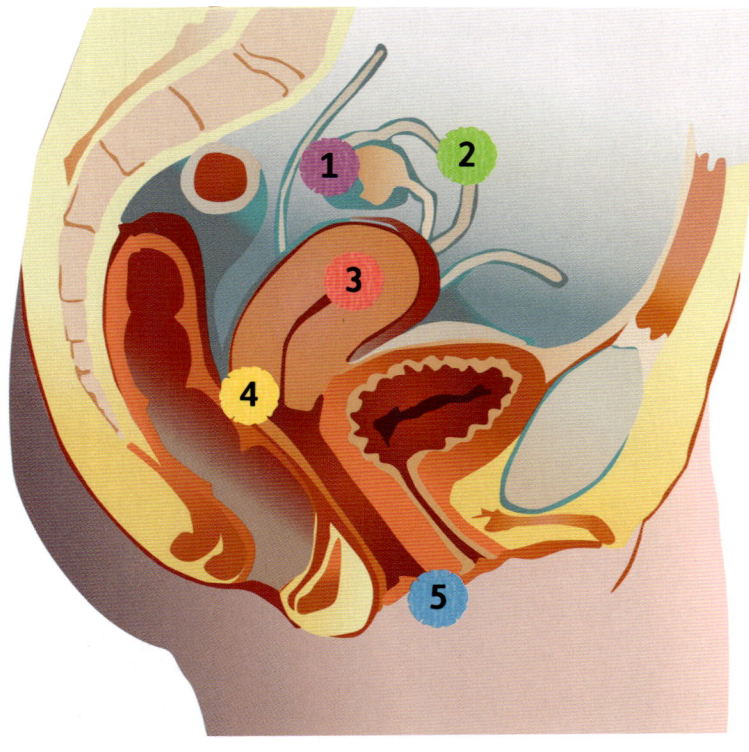

Female reproductive system

1 Ovary—where egg cells are stored

2 Fallopian tube—egg cells travel along this tube and into the uterus

3 Uterus—can stretch to fit a baby as it grows in the womb

4 Cervix—entrance to the womb

5 Vagina—the canal from the uterus to the outside of the body

Male reproductive system

1 Urethra

2 Penis

3 Testes—where sperm cells are made

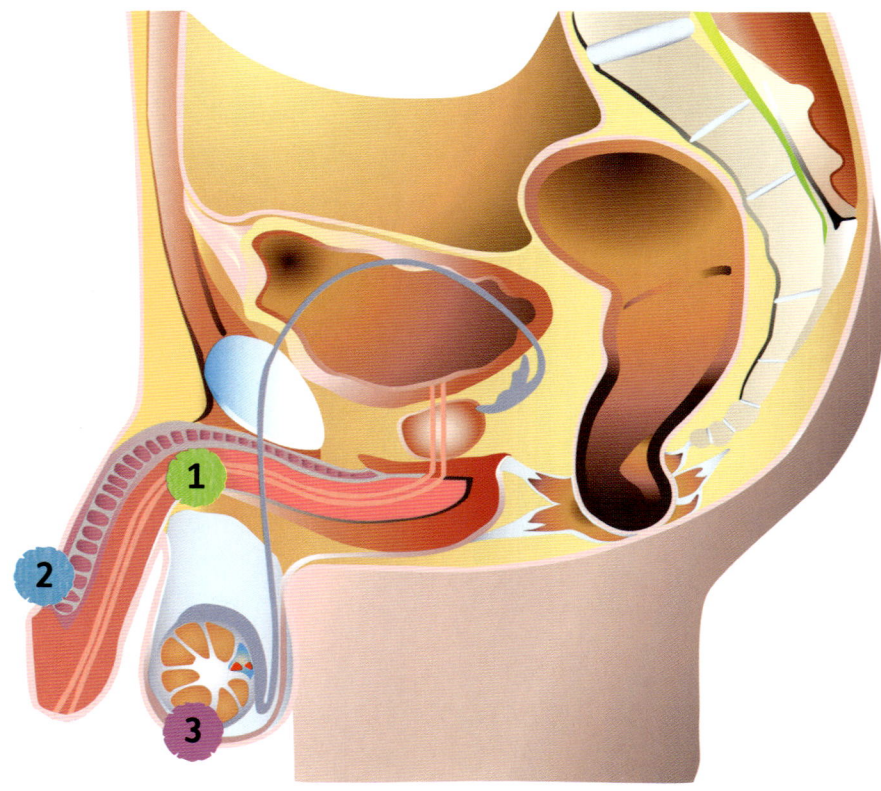

Sperm cell

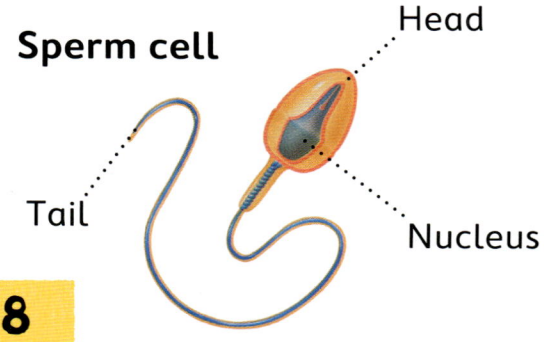

Head

Tail

Nucleus

Baby development

The growth of a baby inside its mother's womb

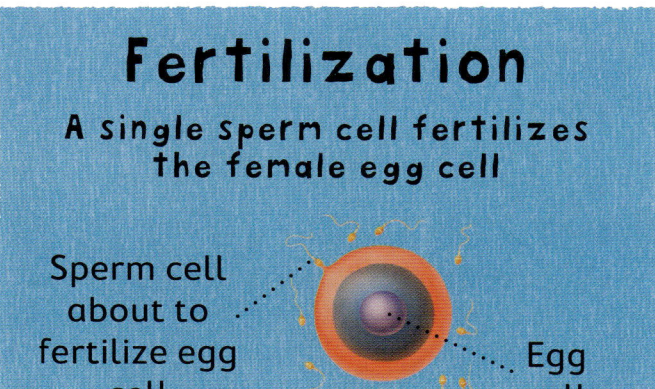

Fertilization

A single sperm cell fertilizes the female egg cell

Sperm cell about to fertilize egg cell

Egg cell

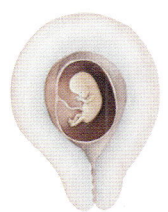

8 weeks
Main organs are formed

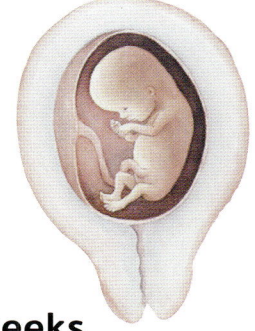

12 weeks
Heart beats, and kicking movements begin

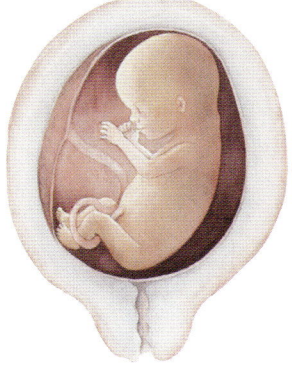

16 weeks
Face has taken shape and bones of skeleton start to form

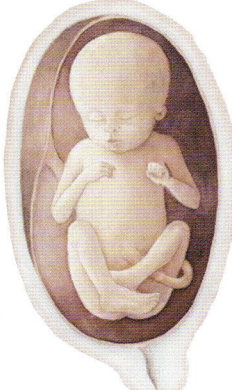

20 weeks
Hair begins to grow

Placenta (food and oxygen are passed to the baby via the placenta)

32 weeks
Fat collects under skin

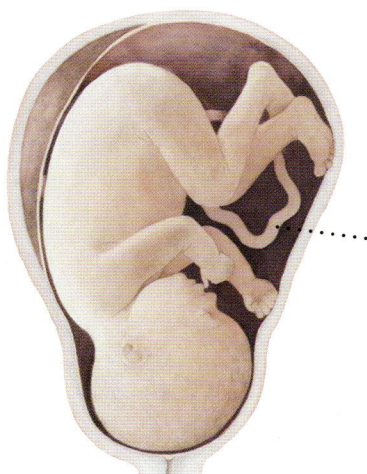

Umbilical cord (runs between the baby and the placenta)

36 weeks
Baby usually turns head down

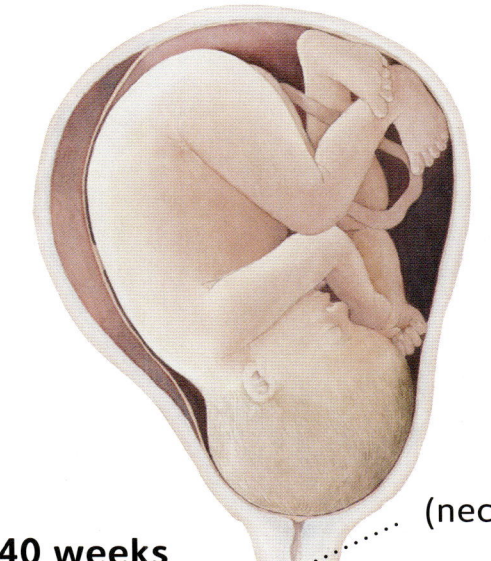

40 weeks
Ready for birth

Cervix (neck of womb)

Bicycles

Modern bicycles still have the same basic design as old ones. People ride them for fun and exercise

Early pedal bikes

Hobby
(1818)

Velocipede
(Boneshaker)
(1861)

Penny Farthing
(early 1870s)

Modern bicycles

Mountain bike

Aerodynamic bicycle

Tandem bicycle

Road race bicycle

Motorcycle

Motorcycles have been around for over
100 years. Superbikes are very lightweight and fast

Honda CBR

Harley
Davidson

Early motorcycles

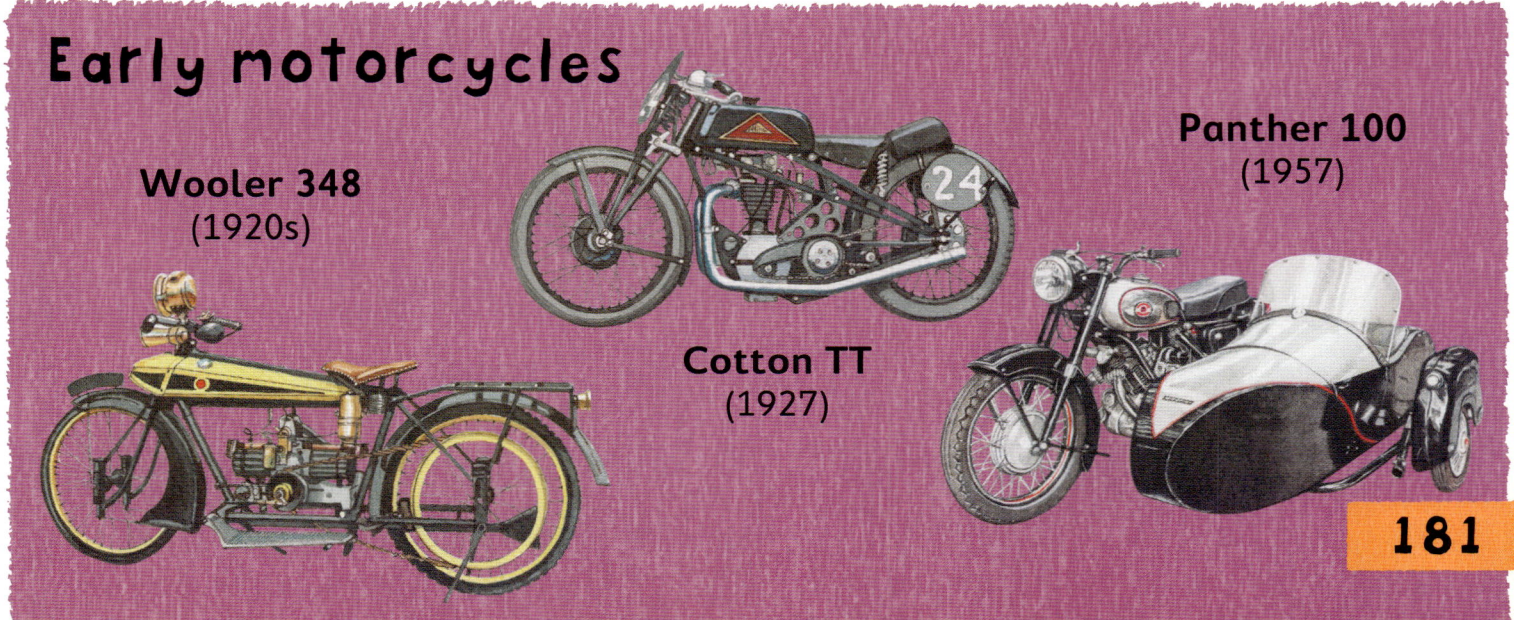

Wooler 348
(1920s)

Cotton TT
(1927)

Panther 100
(1957)

181

Cars

The first car was designed in 1807 and was powered by an engine fueled by hydrogen

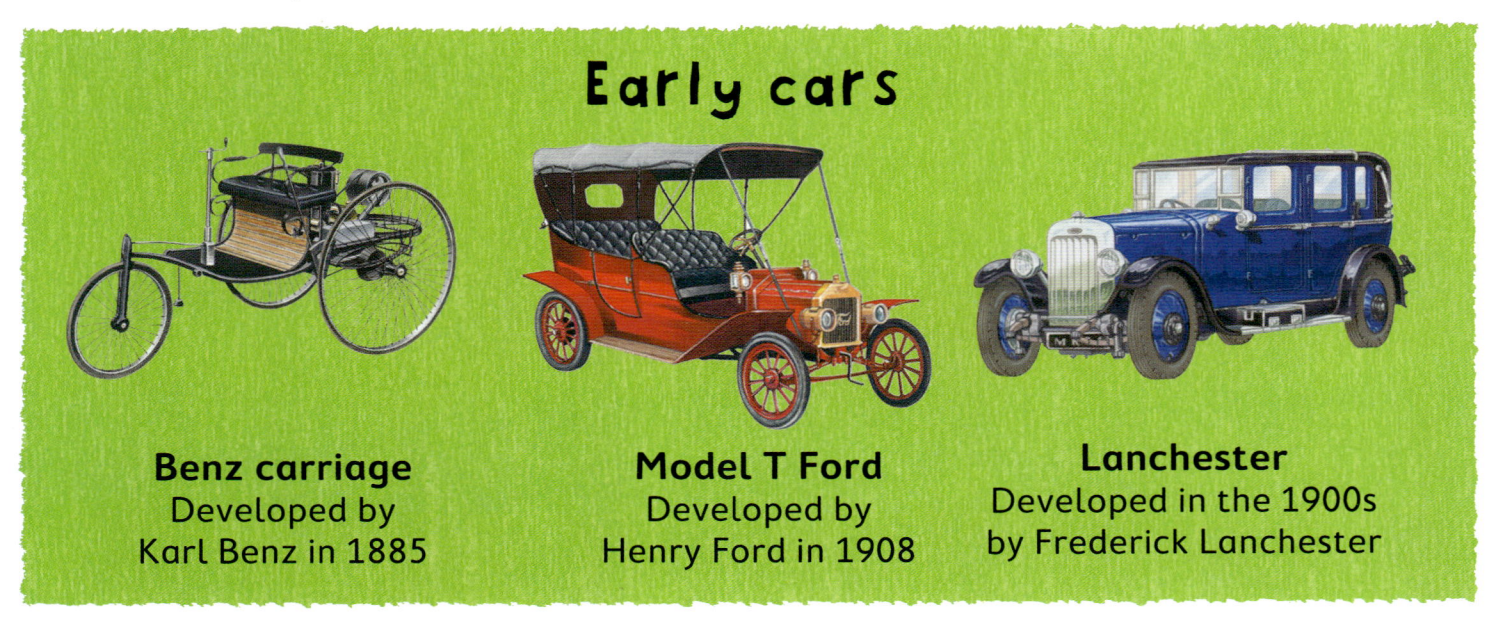

Early cars

Benz carriage
Developed by
Karl Benz in 1885

Model T Ford
Developed by
Henry Ford in 1908

Lanchester
Developed in the 1900s
by Frederick Lanchester

Super sports car

Saloon car

F1 racing car

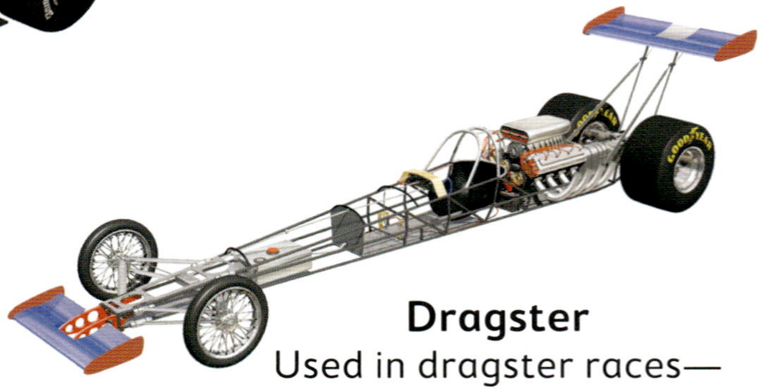

Dragster
Used in dragster races—
the fastest, loudest form
of motor racing

Rally car
A car with a tuned-up
engine and stronger
mechanical parts

182

Trains

Since the invention of the first steam engine more than 200 years ago, trains have been a popular way to travel and transport goods

Freight train
Carries goods such as coal, oil, steel, and timber

Funicular
This train can travel easily up and down steep slopes

Subway

Early trains

The Rocket
Designed by George Stephenson in 1829, this was an early steam locomotive

The Flying Scotsman
This train has carried passengers since 1862

Maglev train
Uses magnets to glide along tracks

Pendolino

Ships and boats

Long before cars and aircraft, people transported cargo,
went into battle, or explored new lands by boat or ship

Early ships and boats

Viking longship
(Viking Age
AD 793–1066)

Coracle
(Bronze Age
c.2500–800 BC)

**Ancient Greek
cargo ship**
(300–400 BC)

Aircraft carrier

Oil supertanker

**Racing
catamaran**

Cruise liner

Hydrofoil
These watercraft "fly"
above the surface on
winglike foils

**Passenger
hovercraft**

Submarines and submersibles

Submarines are normally used for warfare
and submersibles for exploration

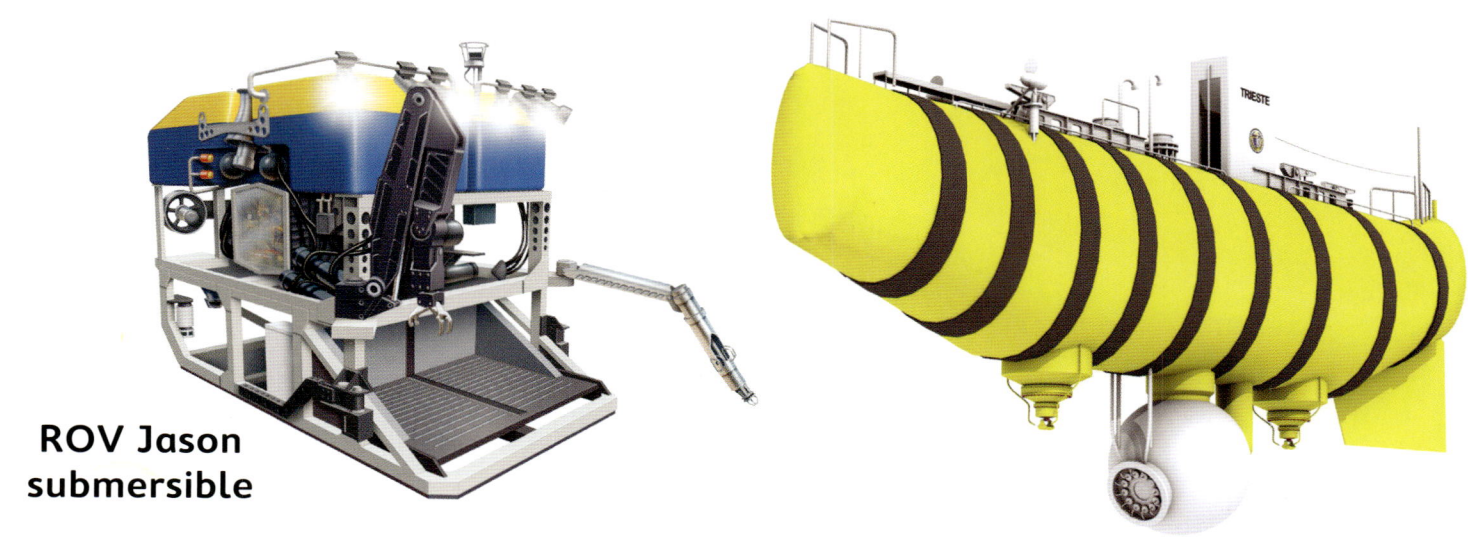

**ROV Jason
submersible**

Trieste submersible
This submersible successfully
ventured to the Mariana Trench
—the deepest part of any ocean

Rescue submersible

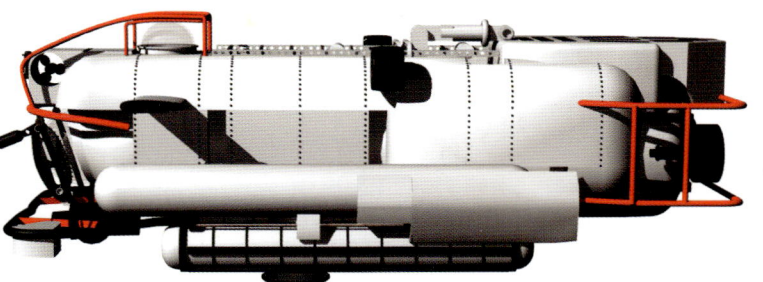

**Polaris
submarine**

Early submarine

The **Turtle** was the first
combat submarine. It made
its first test dive in 1776

**Russian Typhoon
submarine**

Aircraft

Over 200 years ago in France, the Montgolfier brothers made a large balloon and were the first people to take to the skies

Early aircraft

Spirit of St. Louis (1927)

1903 Wright Flyer
The Wright Brothers completed the first-ever flight in a controlled aircraft

Concorde

Hang glider

Chinook helicopter

Sailplane

Hot-air balloon

Airbus A380

War planes

During times of war, planes attack the enemy, drop bombs, and carry troops and equipment

Sopwith Camel
One of the best fighter planes of World War I (1914–1918)

German Messerschmitt 262

Supermarine Spitfire

German Junkers 87 dive-bomber

B-2 Spirit

F-35B Lightning fighter-bomber
One of the world's most advanced aircraft

INDEX

INDEX

INDEX

INDEX